Creative Writing and the Critical Commentary

Creative Writing and the Critical Commentary

Reflection, Influence, Process

EDITED BY
KAREN STEVENS AND
JONATHAN TAYLOR

BLOOMSBURY ACADEMIC
LONDON · NEW YORK · OXFORD · NEW DELHI · SYDNEY

BLOOMSBURY ACADEMIC
Bloomsbury Publishing Plc, 50 Bedford Square, London, WC1B 3DP, UK
Bloomsbury Publishing Inc, 1359 Broadway, New York, NY 10018, USA
Bloomsbury Publishing Ireland, 29 Earlsfort Terrace, Dublin 2, D02 AY28, Ireland

BLOOMSBURY, BLOOMSBURY ACADEMIC and the Diana logo are trademarks
of Bloomsbury Publishing Plc

First published in Great Britain 2026

Cover image: Watercolor painting, abstract man and woman illustration © Anna
Ismagilova / Adobe Stock

Bloomsbury Publishing Plc does not have any control over, or responsibility for, any
third-party websites referred to or in this book. All internet addresses given in this
book were correct at the time of going to press. The author and publisher regret
any inconvenience caused if addresses have changed or sites have ceased
to exist, but can accept no responsibility for any such changes.

A catalogue record for this book is available from the British Library.

A catalog record for this book is available from the Library of Congress.

ISBN: HB: 978-1-350-43988-7
         PB: 978-1-350-43989-4
         ePDF: 978-1-350-43990-0
         eBook: 978-1-350-43991-7

Typeset by Integra Software Services Pvt. Ltd.
Printed and bound in Great Britain

For product safety related questions contact productsafety@bloomsbury.com.

To find out more about our authors and books visit www.bloomsbury.com
and sign up for our newsletters.

For all our brilliant Creative Writing students
(past, present and, indeed, future).

Contents

About the Contributors ix

PART ONE Introductory 1

1   Preface 3
        By Karen Stevens and Jonathan Taylor

2   On Reflection in Creative Writing 8
        By Karen Stevens and Jonathan Taylor

3   On Influence in Creative Writing 21
        By Karen Stevens and Jonathan Taylor

PART TWO Sample Critical Commentaries 31

4   The Personal Is Always Political 33
        By Karen Stevens

5   The Art of Persuasion 45
        By Joanna Nadin

6   On the Genealogy of Memoirs: Influence, Revenge and
        Ressentiment 58
        By Jonathan Taylor

7   'The Community of Sorrow': Searching for Harmony in a
        Fragmented Novella 78
        By David Swann

8   The End Is Never Where You Think: How Preclosure Theory
        Turned *Finally* into a Collection of Short Fiction Obsessed with
        Ending and Not Ending 100
        By Dan Powell

9   The Anxiety of Influence in the Age of Authenticity, OR: Salt in
         the Soup 115
         By Jemma Kennedy

10   'Go Outside': Nature and Chance as Poetic Influence 128
         By Shaindel Beers

11   Jesus, Fairy Tales and Flash Fiction 135
         By Kit de Waal

12   Alternate Truths and Fake News 143
         By Anietie Isong

13   Memoir and Main Character Syndrome: A Reflection 149
         By Jenn Ashworth

14   Experimental Poetic Autography: Writing the Languaged Self 163
         By Lila Matsumoto

15   Digital Narratives, Technology and the Domestic Gothic 179
         By Kate Pullinger

PART THREE Postscript 187

16   Further Reading: Selected Bibliography 189

Index 191

Contributors

Jenn Ashworth's first novel, *A Kind of Intimacy*, was published in 2009 and won a Betty Trask Award. On the publication of her second, *Cold Light* (2011), she was featured on the BBC's *The Culture Show* as one of the UK's twelve best new writers. In 2019, she published a memoir-in-essays, *Notes Made While Falling*, which was a New Statesman Book of the Year and was shortlisted for the Gordon Burn Prize. Her latest novel is *Ghosted: A Love Story*, and her new memoir, *The Parallel Path*, was published in 2025. She is a Fellow of the Royal Society of Literature, an Honorary Fellow of Newnham College, Cambridge University, and a Professor of Writing at Lancaster University.

Shaindel Beers is the author of three full-length poetry collections: *A Brief History of Time* (2008), *The Children's War and Other Poems* (2013) and *Secure Your Own Mask* (2018), winner of the White Pine Press Poetry Prize, a Woodrow Hall Top Shelf Award, and finalist for the Oregon Book Award. She teaches at Blue Mountain Community College in Pendleton, Oregon.

Kit de Waal is the author of the novels *My Name Is Leon,* which was shortlisted for the Costa First Novel Award and won the Kerry Group Irish Novel of the Year; *The Trick to Time*, which was longlisted for the Women's Prize for Fiction; a short story collection, *Supporting Cast*; and a memoir, *Without Warning & Only Sometimes*, which was a Radio 4 Book of the Week and was shortlisted for Biography of the Year at the Irish Book Awards. She is also editor of the *Common People* anthology and co-founder of the Big Book Weekend festival. Kit is a Fellow of the Royal Society of Literature and Professor and Jean Humphreys Writer in Residence at Leicester University. Her new novel, *The Best of Everything*, was released in April 2025.

Anietie Isong is a researcher and creative writer. He completed his PhD in New Media and Writing at De Montfort University, Leicester. His thesis explored the influence of new media technologies on African literature. His debut novel, *Radio Sunrise* (2017), won the McKitterick Prize and was listed for other prizes, including the 9mobile Prize for Literature. The book has also been adapted into a movie. Dr Isong's second novel, *News at Noon* (2022), was longlisted for the Diverse Book Awards. His collection of short stories, *Someone Like Me*, won the inaugural Headlight Review Chapbook Prize for Prose Fiction.

Jemma Kennedy is a playwright and screenwriter. She was awarded a Jerwood Arvon Young Playwright's Apprenticeship in 2006 and was Pearson Playwright in Residence at the National Theatre in 2010. Produced plays include stage adaptations of *The Prince and the Pauper, The Summer Book* and *Maggot Moon* (all for the Unicorn Theatre); *The Grand Irrationality* (Lost Theatre Studio, Los Angeles); *Don't Feed the Animals* (National Theatre Connections); *The Gift* (New Vic Theatre, Stoke-on-Trent); *Second Person Narrative* for Tonic Theatre's inaugural Platform play series; and *Genesis Inc.* for Hampstead Theatre's main stage. Film and TV credits include the original screenplay *Captain Webb* (Marathon Films) and ITV's thriller *Secret Service* as co-writer. She has adapted several novels for the screen by authors including Barbara Pym and Iris Murdoch. Jemma's book on playwriting is published by Nick Hern Books, and she has taught playwriting and screenwriting for the National Theatre, Arvon Foundation and many more.

Lila Matsumoto is an Assistant Professor of Creative Writing from the University of Nottingham, UK, where she directs the Centre for Literary Creativity, Community, and Place. Her full-length poetry collections are *Two Twin Pipes Sprout Water* (2021) and *Urn & Drum* (2018). Other publications include a book chapter in *Poetry and Work* (2019), a radio piece for BBC Radio 3's 'The Essay' series (2018) and several pamphlets and poem-objects, including *Your Dangerous Shoe* (2024), *Light Hazzles* (2022) and *Foggy Eyes* (2022). She creates experimental music and poetry in the band Food People.

Joanna Nadin is a former broadcast journalist, special adviser to the prime minister, and government speechwriter. Since leaving politics, she's written more than a hundred books for children, teenagers and adults, including the *Sunday Times*-bestselling *Worst Class in the World* series and the Carnegie-nominated *Joe All Alone*, which is now a BAFTA-winning and Emmy-nominated BBC drama. She is an Associate Professor of Creative Writing at the University of Bristol, with research focusing on the formation and reflection of self and identity during adolescence and class. She still freelances as a speechwriter and ghostwriter.

Dan Powell is a prize-winning author of short fiction currently based in the East Midlands. He holds a PhD in Creative Writing at the University of Leicester, and his stories have appeared in *New Short Stories*, *Unthology*, *The Lonely Crowd*, *The London Magazine*, *Carve*, *Being Dad*, and *Best British Short Stories*. His debut collection, *Looking Out of Broken Windows*, was shortlisted for the Scott Prize and longlisted for the Frank O'Connor International Short Story Award and the Edge Hill Prize. When not writing, he facilitates writing workshops in festivals, schools and universities and is a First Story writer-in-residence.

Kate Pullinger writes novels as well as works of digital media. Her most recent works include the novel *Forest Green* (2020) and a ghost story for the smartphone, *Breathe*. Kate has won many prizes, including Canada's Governor General's Award for Fiction in 2009 with *The Mistress of Nothing*. She is Professor of Creative Writing and Digital Media at Bath Spa University, where she is co-director of the Centre for Cultural and Creative Industries. In 2024, she was elected as a Fellow of the Royal Society of Literature. A Canadian, she lives in London, England.

Karen Stevens writes short fiction and has been published in a variety of anthologies and journals, including *The Big Issue*, Fish Publishing, Salt Publishing and Valley Press. She was runner-up for the prestigious ALCS Tom-Gallon Trust Award in 2023. Her edited collection of essays, *Writing a First Novel: Reflections on the Journey*, was published in 2014. Her co-edited collection of short stories, *High Spirits*, won a Saboteur Award for Best Anthology in 2019. Karen is a senior lecturer in Creative Writing at the University of Chichester. Her debut short story collection *Brilliant Blue* (2025) was published with Barbican Press.

David Swann is a former journalist and university lecturer, who is now a Royal Literary Fund Fellow at the University of Cumbria, where he helps nurses and paramedics with their academic work. His novella, *Season of Bright Sorrow* (2021), illustrated by Sam Hubbard, was named 2023 Rubery Book of the Year. Dave's other five books include *The Privilege of Rain* (2010), which was shortlisted for the Ted Hughes Award for its evocation of a prison residency. In 2025, Dave worked as club poet at Blackburn Rovers Football Club, the team he's supported since he was six.

Jonathan Taylor is an author, editor, lecturer and critic. His books include the memoirs *Take Me Home* (2007) and *A Physical Education* (2024), the novel *Melissa* (2015) and the short story collection *Scablands and Other Stories*

(2023). He directs the MA in Creative Writing at the University of Leicester and has taught in higher education for over twenty-five years. Originally from Stoke-on-Trent, he now lives in Leicestershire with his wife, the poet Maria Taylor, and their twin daughters, Miranda and Rosalind.

PART ONE

Introductory

1

Preface

By Karen Stevens and Jonathan Taylor

Welcome to the mirror world: the world of Creative Writing in higher education, where the assumption is that learning is, in part, reflective. You learn to write – or learn to write better – by reflecting on your own work and the work of others. The mirror-world reflects both yourself and your (literary) surroundings, and you learn by studying those reflections, by staring into the mirror. In that sense, a reflective practitioner is a split self: you are both a writer and someone who stands outside yourself, reflecting on your own practice, reading and critically evaluating your work as if you were someone else. You are both a writer and a writer who writes about their own writing.

To put this more simply, almost all Creative Writing courses in formal education – whether at undergraduate, postgraduate or PhD level – include some kind of reflective element, and this manifests itself most obviously in the form of a written text which accompanies your creative work. That is, when you are asked to submit a piece of Creative Writing as part of your course, it is (as you may already know) customary for that work to be accompanied by some kind of 'supplementary discourse' – a 'reflective commentary' or 'critical commentary' or 'critical exegesis'. (The names vary from institution to institution, but for the purposes of this book we'll stick with 'critical commentary', for the most part). As Maria Taylor suggests, the 'critical commentary' allows the writer to see their

'other' self … the twin … in the mirror …. Reflective writing allows for engaging with that mysterious mirror-image figure, and gives the writer fresh insights into the practice of their own writing …. Students must be encouraged to take that brave first step through the looking glass into themselves in order to understand their motives and processes as writers.

(2021: 130–1)

This book aims to help you to take that 'step through the looking glass'. It is about the process of reflection generally and its written incarnation, the 'critical commentary', more specifically. Most academic courses which concern the creative arts include some element of self-evaluation or meta-textual commentary: Fine Arts, Creative Computing, Dance, Music, Music Technology, and so on, all ask students to reflect on the artworks they produce. Creative Writing in higher education grows out of this tradition. It is, in fact, one of the main things that differentiates Creative Writing as an academic subject from writing creatively *per se*. As Steve May writes,

> A university creative writing course must do more than 'just' teach you to write well. It is primarily in the non-creative assessment items that you can demonstrate what you have learned outside of the finished writing product .... Common to all these items is reflection on your own work and the work of others, and the contextualisation of your writing .... The untaught intuitive genius, who simply writes what inspiration dictates, ... may feel at a disadvantage here. However, the counter-arguments are, first, that you won't know what you've learned, or be able to consolidate it, until you reflect on what you've done; and secondly, a university creative writing course isn't usually just a writing course – there are other places to go 'just' to learn to write.
>
> (2007: 20, 76–7)

Having said all that, we would argue that reflection is also useful (maybe vital) for writers beyond the academy. We believe that the kinds of reflective practice discussed and exemplified in this book are relevant not only to undergraduates and postgraduates studying Creative Writing in formal academic contexts but also to aspiring writers interested in gaining further insight into their own processes and those of published writers – and, for that matter, readers in general who want to understand more about the influences behind creativity. Reflection and the critical commentary are – we believe – important both within *and* beyond the immediate academic context.

As an evaluation of 'what you've done', the written commentary, as May suggests, generally consists of two main elements: reflection on process and reflection on reading and research ('reflection on your work and the work of others, and the contextualization of your writing'). Of course, there are wide variations between courses and institutions, but by and large you will probably be asked to write about subjects such as:

- How and why your creative work changed during the editing and redrafting process.

- How and why you changed your creative work in response to feedback.

- How your creative work was informed or influenced by comparable literary texts.

- How your creative work was informed and shaped by wider reading and research.

- How your creative work relates to other (professional, vocational, literary, creative, disciplinary) contexts.

This book aims to demonstrate how you might best address these questions in a critical commentary. It aims to model varied ways of tackling the critical commentary, showcasing the different approaches you might take. In the first part of the book, Chapter 1 is an introduction to the mechanics – the whats, whys and hows – of the critical commentary: i.e. what is it, why do it and how to do it. Its aim is to help you understand the point of the commentary, and what, on a fundamental level, it should consist of 'in order to help you *think* like a writer'.

Chapter 2 broadens out the discussion to consider reflection-in-context. Students, and authors in general, are frequently asked to reflect on their 'influences' – to contextualize their creative work in relation to others'. It's certainly a key aspect of critical commentaries: as Taylor writes, 'through reflective writing', you are 'participating in a form of dialogue with other writers', meditating on 'influences that informed [your] ... ideas' (2021: 132, 139). Chapter 2 aims to demonstrate the wide range of influences and contexts which might inform your writing, and, on a more theoretical level, it also encourages you to reflect on how 'influence' might function in Creative Writing. We often take the idea of literary 'influence' for granted and use the term casually – but what actually is it? What does it do? How do we both absorb and reshape our influences and inspirations? How do we move from initial influences and inspirations towards a final 'product'?

Part Two puts all of these ideas into practice. It consists of a series of sample critical commentaries in which professional author-academics reflect on their own writing: their processes, creative decisions, reading, research and influences. The authors chosen all have experience as both published authors and educators in higher education. They encompass, in both spheres, all the major forms of writing (prose fiction, creative non-fiction, script-writing, poetry and new media), and there are commentaries included here about a wide range of forms and genres.

Despite the prevalence of critical commentaries in higher education, there are very few examples of good practice in this area. There are many texts in which authors reflect on their own writing (see the Sample Bibliography at the end of this book), but no published anthologies of critical commentaries, as they are understood in formal educational contexts. This book aims to address that strange pedagogical gap.

Each of the sample commentaries includes the following elements in relation to one of the author's own pieces of writing:

- reflection on process

- reflection on research

- reflection on the ways in which research and process have informed each other

- reflection on textual influences (and, indeed, on the author's own conception of influence).

Above and beyond these basic elements, the sample commentaries demonstrate a huge variety of different approaches, ranging from the philosophical to the autobiographical-confessional to the experimental. They variously engage with theory, rhetoric, craft, politics, linguistics, literary history, journalism, technology, and so on. The book, we hope, demonstrates the flexibility of the critical commentary – that, within its pedagogical parameters, it is a protean, malleable and potentially heterogeneous form. At best, the commentary can be as individualistic and surprising as creative work.

Above all, we believe that the sample commentaries herein show that the sometimes-maligned 'critical commentary' can itself be a fascinating, entertaining and aesthetically satisfying piece of writing in itself. Of course, students first and foremost want to write creatively. Of course, it's common to think of the commentary element of an assignment as a kind of afterthought, an add-on or even an irritating distraction. But what these sample commentaries demonstrate – we think – is that, if approached with the same thoughtfulness as the creative work, they are not only profoundly helpful to an author, they might also stand as works of art in themselves. 'A finished piece of reflection', claim Graham and Leach, 'is arguably creative writing in its own right' (2005: 83). We agree: we believe that, if they are worth doing, they are worth doing well – and should be approached in the same spirit, and with the same aesthetic sense, as the creative work on which they are based. In the words of Roland Barthes: 'let the commentary itself be a text' (1981: 44).

Works Cited

Barthes, R. (1981), 'Theory of the Text', in R. Young (ed.), *Untying the Text: A Post-Structuralist Reader*, Boston: Routledge and Kegan Paul, pp. 31–7.

Graham, R. and Leach, H. (2005), 'Reflection', in R. Graham, H. Leach, H. Newall and J. Singleton (eds), *The Road to Somewhere: A Creative Writing Companion*, Basingstoke: Palgrave Macmillan, pp. 80–6.

May, S. (2007), *Doing Creative Writing*, Abingdon: Routledge.

Morley, D. (2007), *The Cambridge Introduction to Creative Writing*, Cambridge: Cambridge University Press.

Taylor, M. (2021), 'Through the Looking Glass and Back Again: Writing Reflectively in Creative Writing', in M. Moore and S. Meekings (eds), *The Place and the Writer: International Intersections of Teacher Lore and Creative Writing Pedagogy*, London: Bloomsbury Academic, pp. 129–42.

2

On Reflection in Creative Writing

By Karen Stevens and Jonathan Taylor

Writing creatively, as with all art forms, is a combination of intuition and craft. We associate 'craft' with an occupation or trade that consciously utilizes knowledge and skills derived from careful study and practical application. In writing, these skills relate to the conscious technical decisions we make about such things as word choice, sentence and text structure. 'Intuition', on the other hand, defies easy articulation, yoked as it is to the imagination – that shady, fertile place where 'impulse, free association, instinct and error reign' (Ford 1998: 16).

No wonder writers can go blank, feel resistant or even fearful when asked to reflect on their writing process in any kind of rational way. Fay Weldon, when analysing the first page of a first draft, commented, 'But how do I know what my real motives were? If you're me you write first, think later' (1993: 182). Elena Ferrante says, 'I can't give an honest account. I'm afraid that it's the same thing as with dreams. Even as you're recounting them, you know that you're betraying them' (2015). Richard Ford talks of the 'pinchy feel' he experiences when asked to 'nail down the connections *linking* the story to some supposed "source"', revealing his fear of 'diminishing an act of creation to some problem of industrial design' (1998: 17).

Such statements suggest that the early stage of germination and imagining is at odds with the realm of straightforward logic. Some authors in the sample commentaries in this book express a similar 'pinchy feel' to Ford about imposing logic, order and 'truth' on their writing process. After discussing the crafting process involved in shaping her work, Kit de Waal says: 'But all this seems to suggest that there is a methodical, step by step process to writing flash fiction or to creative writing in general. This is not my experience'. And Jenn Ashworth queries the ability to get at some sort of 'truth' through the commentary: 'The recollections of the writer about their own writing process are subject to much of the same slipperiness around truthfulness and evasion as more obvious forms of memoir are'.

This slipperiness is sometimes couched in near-mystical terms. In the nineteenth century, George Eliot referred to the exhilaration of the inspirational self as the 'not-self' (Allott 1965: 119), and writers often draw on other-worldly language to express the mysteries of creation. E. M. Forster talks of the creative artist as someone 'taken out of himself', who will look back on the completed work in a state of wonder, marvelling at 'how on earth he did it. And indeed he did not do it on earth' ([1948] 1965: 158).

References to heightened emotional states and mystery suggest that writing is a dynamic, unpredictable practice. Can Creative Writing really be taught and learned when certain aspects of the process defy articulation, are contradictory and unpredictable? David Lodge concluded that 'even the most sophisticated literary criticism only scratches the surface of the mysterious process of creativity; and so, by the same token, does even the best course in Creative Writing' (Morley 2007: 7). Teachers of Creative Writing are all too aware that it contains 'an element of ineluctable mystery along with its elements of craft' (Cunningham 2014), and writers often refer to this mystery as fundamental to the creative process. Hanif Kureishi believes that 'there is a sense – there has to be a sense – in which most writers do not entirely understand what they are doing' (2014: 17).

Andrew Cowan feels this emphasis on the 'unknown' reflects the continuing Romantic legacy that 'assumes literary achievement to be the expression of natural talent, the outcome of a God-given faculty superior to reason and therefore to pedagogy' (2025). But as Joyce Carol Oates points out:

> Despite Romantic notions of divine inspiration, no story writes itself; whatever the original inspiration, the story before us, whether a classic like Chekhov's 'The Lady With the Dog' or Ernest Hemingway's 'Hills Like White Elephants', ... has been consciously, in some cases painstakingly *written*.
>
> (2004: 111)

Oates asserts that writing is an art, and as such 'we can "learn" something about it; though fuelled by the unconscious, we can make ourselves "conscious" and even rather canny – to a degree' (2004: xii). Dorothea Brande similarly explores the dual nature of writing in Freudian terms when she talks of the unconscious mind (the artist) and the conscious mind (craftsman and critic). These two sides are hostile towards each other, but, she says, 'it is possible to train both sides of the character to work in harmony, and the first step in that education is to consider that you must teach yourself not as though you were one person, but two' ([1934] 1996: 41).

To be both artist and critic requires us to be unthinking and spontaneous *and* self-aware and self-critical. This duality doesn't have to be seen in negative terms, as conflict or contradiction. It can also be a dynamic paradox, which is part and parcel of the creative process. Both spontaneity *and* self-criticism are (usually) necessary to generate good writing. As Steve May points out: 'Self-criticism does not mean negativity, but having a willingness to look carefully at your writing with an open and honest frame of mind: to learn to see what the writing says to you' (2007: 71).

The QAA Creative Writing Subject Benchmark Statement (2019) defines Creative Writing 'as a practice-based discipline in which the student is an active participant in their own learning' (2019: 10). This learning process is 'grounded both in the practice of writing and the understanding of creative process' (2019), hence fostering the dual nature of writing that Brande speaks of. The process encourages an exploratory attitude to making and learning, which necessarily involves a process of spontaneity and reflective thinking as a piece of work develops from the first idea to early drafts through to the final finished piece. A key focus underpinning all Creative Writing study is for students to view themselves as practitioners, achieving agency by developing the necessary reflective skills to critically assess their own creative process:

Reflective thinking means stopping and considering what you're doing. It's an opportunity to compare where you are now with where you have come from, a way of discovering how you are changing as a writer and of deciding where you want to go next.

(Graham and Leach [2005] 2014: 67)

All the sample commentaries included in this book demonstrate such self-critical and reflective thinking – about the imagining and reimagining, the experimentation and insights that were crucial in developing the initial spark of inspiration. Shaindel Beers reflects on how her observations of the natural world brought insight into her process as a poet: 'What I learned quickly in writing this series of poems was that I needed the pelicans, something outside of myself to write hard truths. I couldn't have faced my truths directly'. Jonathan Taylor discusses the problematics of recording memory in his memoir: 'I couldn't use irony to "triumph" over past events *too* much, in case the adult perspective drowned out the child's'. Jemma Kennedy discusses the benefit of experimenting with restructuring her play *Genesis Inc.*:

> At some point I elongated the structure from three acts into five .... Judging from my notes from the time, this choice helped me create a clearer timeline for the action of the play, which takes place over about eight months and tracks Serena's preparation for fertility treatment, egg extraction and fertilization, embryo implantation, and subsequent miscarriage. This extended structure helped me clarify major turning points and escalations in the drama.

And Jenn Ashworth reflects on the effect of reimagining an event shared with her daughter and what she learnt about the genre of memoir and her writerly self:

> As I larded up the scene and wrote my new versions, inhabiting my daughter's point of view by deploying a close third person while making it clear I was only imagining what she might have thought, the memoir became speculative and my daughter became a fictional creation, her body merely a hollow container for me to pour more of myself into. The problem is partly ordinary human narcissism and partly one of memoir's built-in fissures. My tinkering taught me that in memoir, all attempts to inhabit the point-of-view of someone else inevitably lead back to you, the attempt revealing nothing but your own assumptions.

*

To foster this core skill in reflective thinking, most Creative Writing programmes are comprised of three key components:

- practical engagement with writing
- reading as a writer
- workshopping

These three essential components are designed to intersect. This 'intersection' creates an intangible reflective 'space' where an exciting synergy takes place, in which students can reflect on their practice, both in terms of the writing itself and in the knowledge generated around this practice. As all the sample commentaries in this book demonstrate, the idea is for students to interrogate and consolidate their learning in a range of roles – 'as thinker, artist, "maker" and apprentice' (QAA Creative Writing Subject Benchmark Statement 2019: 4).

'Reading as a writer' demands an approach that is thorough and careful, attentive to the nuances of meaning that arise in a text, particularly within different historical and cultural contexts. Though it is acknowledged that there are processes in writing that are beyond straightforward analysis, 'reading as a writer' involves reflecting on the techniques and crafting decisions taken by the writer of a text. This, in turn, goes on to inform the reader's own writing process. As the commentaries in this book reveal, all the writers are acutely aware of how the writing techniques of others create an intended effect on the reader, and how this, in turn, feeds into their own creative work, as, for example, in the use of satire to expose political corruption and injustice (Anietie Isong); the persuasive power of rhetorical language (Joanna Nadin); and the effect of poetic repetitions on the reader (Kit de Waal).

'Reading as a writer' also encompasses workshopping, a process whereby students share and read their work in small workshop groups, offering and receiving sensitive critique on work in progress. Virtually all writers operate with some kind of feedback, and likewise a key goal of all Creative Writing programmes is to offer the writer a trusted audience. This is illustrated in Anietie Isong's commentary:

I wrote the novel long after I had left journalism. Therefore, upon completion of my first draft, I wondered if my efforts were adequate. Were my characters fully developed? Were they funny enough? Was I being 'authentic'? Fortunately, I knew practising journalists who were happy to critique the draft. These objective eyes helped uncover ways to strengthen the storytelling, including finding satirical angles on some of the most challenging issues.

'Workshops are places of cultural symbiosis' (Morley 2007: 117). The principle at the heart of a useful workshop is that groups are respectfully attentive to the content of each other's work (thematically, culturally and stylistically) and will offer helpful suggestions for moving forward with a draft (*What was successful? What needed attention? What changes might be made to redraft those areas that did not work?*). This process 'makes the writer alert to other possible interpretations of their work while also developing each participant's critical awareness of technical and aesthetic possibilities' (QAA Subject Benchmark Statement for Creative Writing 2019: 11). Eventually, students learn to reflect upon and 'internalize' the workshop as they redraft and shape their work to their own vision.

*

Steve May states that 'in all undergraduate Creative Writing courses there must be some element of *level* and some element of *progression*' (2007: 20).

These criteria are a key distinction between undergraduate university study and other Creative Writing courses. As a way of demonstrating 'level' and 'progression', almost all undergraduate university courses in the UK include, as a mode of assessment, a critical commentary – also known as 'supplementary discourse', 'reflective commentary', 'critical component', 'critical exegesis'. As the sample commentaries here attest, this is a complementary, semi-formal assessment piece that is submitted alongside the students' finished creative work. In terms of presentation, a commentary usually

- is written in the first person and uses fairly formal academic language;
- draws on technical terms relevant to form and genre (i.e. prose, poetry, screenwriting);
- incorporates quotations from primary and secondary sources as evidence to back up points;
- references works cited in a bibliography;
- is professionally presented, using correct layout, syntax, grammar, spelling and punctuation.

This non-creative assessment turns reflective thinking into *reflective writing*, consolidating students' learning and helping tutors to understand the ideas and thinking behind the development of the creative work. It enables the latter to gauge the level of critical awareness and understanding of theories and crafting in relation to genre. Emma Darwin details three key terms that underpin Creative Writing study, and these are also essential components in the critical commentary. A commentary should be:

- **reflective:** looking back with hindsight, to put what happened in a wider context of both your writing, and writing in general as a creative act that takes place in a particular culture;
- **analytical:** reflecting, but then also digging into the simple account of 'what happened' to understand more: *how* things came about as they did, and *why* they happened that way;
- **critical:** reflecting and analysing, but then also showing that you don't take any one experience, or any one statement (your own, or anyone else's) as the only possible way things might be, the only possible truth (2014).

Key aims in writing the critical commentary are that students will understand and enhance their research and creative processes, developing self-consciousness and self-criticism in order to improve as writers. In doing so, they will understand their intentions, style and voice, evolving a growing awareness of the effect(s) of their writing on others, thus placing themselves in the position of reader. Andrew Cowan says:

> In the act of writing we are also, constantly, engaged in the act of reading – that is, reading ourselves – and of adjusting our writing in the light of reading, and it is this continuous alertness to how we are sounding and what we are saying that allows us to gauge the likely effect our words will have on our eventual readers.
>
> (2024: 188)

Two main ingredients in a commentary are reflection on **process** (i.e. inspiration, selection, editing, redrafting, etc.) and reflection on **reading and research** (which fed into the creative work). In the best reflective commentaries, these two elements are combined: the commentary demonstrates how process is informed by research, and research by process, in a kind of creative feedback loop.

*

As part of professional practice, students are often urged to keep a writer's notebook or journal in which they can reflect on their process, recording inspirations, thoughts, observations and ideas. In his commentary, Dan Powell conveys how useful the notebook is in nurturing emergent creative work:

> My ideas for a story or collection of stories typically grow from some inciting idea or image or phrase that nestles in my thoughts. Once there the idea gathers other often disconnected ideas or images or phrases together in that strange liminal space between brain and notebook, until the vague shape of what it is I am aiming to write about emerges.

'The only kind of writing is rewriting' (Hemingway 2020), Hemingway noted in his memoir *A Moveable Feast*, and the writer's notebook is a good place to record challenges, breakthroughs and key decisions taken in 'rewriting'. Such decisions might be taken in light of reading as a writer, the workshopping process and self-editing. It helps to keep track of them, given that 'all of us think most of the time about what we are doing – thoughts come and go, some deliberate, some spontaneous. The problem with thought is that it is ephemeral and easily forgotten' (Graham and Leach 2014: 67). This is often the case in the somewhat 'dumbfounding tussle between the unconscious and the conscious' (Stevens 2014: 6). As such, the writer's notebook is an excellent resource to prevent the commentary from lapsing into the pitfall of describing, or retelling, the creative work. As Emma Darwin says, 'There's no point in saying what's in the piece unless you're saying something about the whys and hows of how it got like that' (2014).

The writer's notebook is also a good place to jot down thoughts and notes taken from reading and research. It's logical to assume that someone who embarks on Creative Writing study in higher education will be keenly interested in the writing of others, both for enjoyment and for the purposes of learning. As Stephen King famously puts it:

> If you want to be a writer, you must do two things above all others: read a lot and write a lot. There's no way around these two things that I'm aware of, no shortcut .... You cannot hope to sweep someone else away by the force of your writing until it has been done to you.
>
> (King 2021)

The sample commentaries often refer to the force of seminal works that gripped and thrilled the authors, making a lasting impression (interestingly, often in childhood). In his commentary, David Swann beautifully sums up his careful analysis of Mary Robison's work of flash fiction, 'Yours':

> It's thirty years since Robison's story floated like a leaf into my life – and the memory of that first encounter burns just as bright, even now. Most of the qualities I continue to treasure in very short stories were revealed to me right there, right then.

All serious writers agree that one must read widely and deeply. In Creative Writing study, students are expected to read exemplary classic and contemporary texts in a range of different genres (i.e. prose, poetry, drama and new media) and to engage with textbooks on genre and craft. As Steve May points out: 'To write a book in a certain genre without having read other books in [and around] that genre is as impossible as building a dagoba without knowing what a dagoba is' (2007: 95). All the commentaries in this book show the writers' immersion in other writers' work alongside their critical awareness of form and genre, and 'the contexts in which writing is produced and how individual practices relate to that of predecessors and contemporaries' (QAA Subject Benchmark Statement for Creative Writing 2019: 6). Kate Pullinger, for example, examines the theme of technology in Bram Stoker's classic novel *Dracula* (1897), and the connections with both her fiction and digital fiction; Lila Matsumoto explores the genre of 'autography' and how it enables her to comment on material from her life in order to work through issues about the (writing) self; Jonathan Taylor explores the connections between memoir and the nineteenth-century slave narrative.

In order to produce writing that is authentic and rich with detail, there are various types of wider reading and research that writers must engage with. Reading and research in Creative Writing can be broad, diverse, eclectic and (obviously) depends on the creative work being developed. It helps authors contextualize their own work within an 'intellectual, aesthetic, social or other context' (Morley 2007: 37) and might include:

- books by other writers that deal with similar subject matter;
- critical texts that explore the same subject matter;
- textbooks on theory, culture, society, history, philosophy and politics;
- newspapers, archives, articles and online resources; films, documentaries and images;
- real-world research, such as visiting locations and talking to people.

To give one example from the sample commentaries: here's the wider research that Shaindel Beers delved into in order to bring dimension and authenticity to her series of poems about pelicans:

I learned the science behind *dynamic soaring*. I learned about the orphaned pelican, Bigbird, in Africa, who was taught to fly by humans. My son was three years old at the time, and I took him to see the pelicans and wrote about his language acquisition as he tried to talk about them. I wrote about the history and taxonomy of pelicans and their place in myth and religion. I wrote about pelicans and climate change, the possible ruination of our environment.

As Beers demonstrates, research fulfils our innate curiosity *to know what we don't know*. It's absorbing, moving and can open up new directions and possibilities. As Edward Hogan writes: 'It's interesting, and perhaps under-appreciated, how much the very act of research can dictate the shape and content of a story' (2014: 61). Indeed, Beers's conscious research proved to be a portal into the unconscious: 'Without realizing it, I wrote about my impending breakup with my son's father. In my mind, then, in 2014, I didn't know it was happening, but reading those poems ten years later, all the signs were there'.

The best commentaries strike a fine balance between the personal and analytical, avoiding a mechanical approach to process (*first I did this, and then I did this* ...). It is the story *behind* the story and should be as engaging and rich as the creative work itself: 'At best, these essays are personal examples of creative nonfiction' (Morley 2007: 37). As with the creative work, the commentary is a separate narrative that also needs shaping and focus. There has to be a reason for writing it – there has to be something (whether an experience, a theory or an ideal) that is worth sharing with a reader. Some of the strongest commentaries have a particular research focus they're addressing (such as Dan Powell's examination of Susan Lohafer's 'preclosure theory' through the writing of his second short story collection), and in doing so will include a good number (if not all – depending on the commentary's word count) of the following 'ingredients':

- a brief reference to the inspiration/s that sparked the initial idea (an observation, research, personal experience, imagination);

- analysis of the creative process (incorporating discussion on how research and reading served to develop and shape the creative piece, revealing affinities, or otherwise, with other writers);

- inclusion of primary and secondary reading to underpin and enrich the discussion;

- awareness of the genre or form (in terms of aesthetics, subject matter, structure, etc. and how these considerations have been applied to the piece);

- the rationale behind key technical decisions made (choices about such things as form, structure, viewpoint, imagery, language, etc.);

- the key challenges and breakthroughs that changed the creative work, and *how*;

- key areas for editing and revising, and *why*;

- how the workshop process or tutor feedback influenced redrafting;

- identification of areas that may still require attention or development.

The above 'ingredients' will undoubtedly open up onto the wider contexts that inform our process as writers. Why was I drawn to a particular subject matter? How do my interests fit into the 'wider context of form, genre, culture, society, history'? (Darwin 2014). What did I learn as a writer and reader, and how will this new knowledge or understanding help me to move forward as a writer?

*

Some students may feel uncomfortable with the self-interrogation that this non-creative assessment requires, but as Liz Cashdan points out, 'its purpose has always been to actually help students improve their writing, so that what may have started out as exploration and intuition becomes establishment and understanding' (2017). Similarly, Tara Mokhtari suggests that: 'Aside from the academic requirements of critique writing, what you are actually doing is becoming cognisant of your creative process' (2019: 225).

Graham and Leach feel that 'Good reflective writing is a way of thinking: it's a dialogue with yourself .... Reflection makes you write about your writing and reading experiences and thus discover your opinions' (2014: 70). The commentary's more formalized process of reflection can help to nurture a writerly 'identity', while also serving to identify future writing goals. It's a tool that helps students to *think* like a writer, to 'understand the shaping and fledging of your abilities .... It may even help you realise them, and to fly alone' (Morley 2007: 37).

The critical commentary, then, fosters writerly independence and develops valuable skills for life outside of academia. As Darwin points out: 'writing a commentary isn't just the thing that makes a writing course academic; it does feed your development – your learning – as a writer .... And if you're interested in writing professionally in any way in the future', she suggests, 'then conscious, technical awareness is essential for learning to write what's wanted, to length and deadline' (2014). Likewise, David Morley links the reflective thinking that sits at the heart of the critical commentary to the business that published writers engage in once their writing is out in the world:

> Many writers in the real world like to explain themselves, as a form of setting up their stall, and for creating an audience that understands their approach and purpose .... They discuss their working processes; they advocate and opinionate; they make no secret of their influences, enthusiasms or motivations. You must practice at this mirror.
>
> (2007: 37)

Of course, many Creative Writing students go on to 'fly alone' and publish their work, and find themselves being interviewed – in magazines, online, at festivals, etc. – where they must respond to the curiosity of readers on their creative process and inspirations. In that way, the critical commentary is excellent practice for the future.

Works Cited

Allott, M. (ed.) (1965), 'II: Germination', in *Novelists on the Novel*, London: Routledge & Kegan Paul, pp. 118–20.
Brande, D. (1996), *Becoming a Writer*, London: Macmillan.

Cashdan, L. (2017), 'What Is the Point of a Reflective Commentary?', *The Open University*, 3 May. Available online: https://www.oca.ac.uk/weareoca/creative-writing/point-reflective-commentary/ (accessed 3 March 2025).

Cowan, A. (2018), 'The Rise of Creative Writing', *Writing in Practice*, Vol. 4, National Association of Writers in Education (NAWE). Available online: https://www.nawe.co.uk/DB/wip-editions/articles/the-rise-of-creative-writing.html (accessed 3 March 2025).

Cowan, A. (2024), *The Art of Writing Fiction*, Second Edition, London and New York: Routledge.

Cunningham, M. (2014), 'So You Want to Be a Writer ...', *The Guardian*, 14 March. Available online: https://www.theguardian.com/books/2014/mar/14/creative-writing-courses-advice-students (accessed 14 November 2024).

Darwin, E. (2014), 'Creative Writing Commentaries: Don't Know Where to Start?', *This Itch of Writing*, 12 March. Available online: https://emmadarwin.typepad.com/thisitchofwriting/2014/03/critical-commentary-on-your-work-dont-know-where-to-start.html (accessed 3 March 2025).

Ferrante, E. (2015), 'The Art of Fiction, No. 228', Interviewed by Sandro Ferri and Sandra Ferri, *The Paris Review*. 212, Spring. Available online: https://www.theparisreview.org/interviews/6370/the-art-of-fiction-no-228-elena-ferrante (accessed 14 November 2024).

Ford, R. (1998), 'Where Does Writing Come From?', in W. Blythe (ed.), *Why I Write*, London: Little, Brown, pp. 13–20.

Forster, E. M. ([1948] 1965), '"The Raison d'Etre of Criticism in the Arts," "III Novelists at Work: Effort and Inspiration"', in M. Allott (ed.), *Novelists on the Novel*, London: Routledge & Kegan Paul, pp. 144–58.

Graham, R., Leach, H. and Newall, H. (eds) ([2005] 2014), *The Road to Somewhere: A Creative Writing Companion*, Second Edition, Hampshire: Palgrave Macmillan.

Hemingway, E. (2020), 'Hemingway's Loveliest Lines from a Moveable Feast Reflect His Feelings on Writing Love and Navigating Dark Times', Cole Schafer, 20 March. Available online: https://www.coleschafer.com/blog/a-moveable-feast-quotes (accessed 7 April 2025).

Hogan, E. (2014), 'Writing Home', in K. Stevens (ed.), *Writing a First Novel: Reflections on the Journey*, Hampshire: Palgrave Macmillan, pp. 58–65.

King, S. (2021), 'FF Daily#339: Stephen King on How to Write Well', *Founding Fuel*, 5 April. Available online: https://www.foundingfuel.com/article/ff-daily-339-stephen-king-on-how-to-wr te-well/#:~:text=%E2%80%9CIf%20you%20want%20to%20be,has%20been%20done%20to%20you%E2%80%A6 (accessed 9 April 2025).

Kureishi, H. (2014), 'Something Given: Reflections on Writing', in K. Stevens (ed.), *Writing a First Novel: Reflections on the Journey*, Hampshire: Palgrave Macmillan, pp. 17–25.

May, S. (2007), *Doing Creative Writing*, London and New York: Routledge.

Mokhtari, T. (2019), *The Bloomsbury Introduction to Creative Writing*, London: Bloomsbury Academic.

Morley, D. (2007), *The Cambridge Introduction to Creative Writing*, Cambridge: Cambridge University Press.

Oates, J. C. (2004), *The Faith of a Writer*, New York: Ecco.

QAA Subject Benchmark Statement, Creative Writing (2019). Available online: www.qaa.ac.uk/docs/qaa/subject-benchmark-statements/subject-benchmark-statement-creative-writing.pdf?sfvrsn=2fe2cb81_4 (accessed 24 February 2024).

Stevens, K. (ed.) (2014), *Writing a First Novel: Reflections on the Journey*, Hampshire: Palgrave Macmillan.

Weldon, F. (1993), 'Harnessed to the Harpy', in C. Boylan (ed.), *The Agony and the Ego*, London: Penguin, pp. 179–94.

3

On Influence in Creative Writing

By Karen Stevens and Jonathan Taylor

In his essay 'Tradition and the Individual Talent', T. S. Eliot famously claims that 'no poet, no artist of any art, has his [sic] complete meaning alone'. Rather, the artist's 'significance, his appreciation is the appreciation of his relation to the dead poets and artists. You cannot value him alone; you must set him, for contrast and comparison, among the dead'. The writer exists in an ongoing literary tradition, having both a 'historical sense', while also being 'acutely conscious of his place in time, of his own contemporaneity' ([1919] 2000: 32–3).

For all its gendered and intellectually élitist language, Eliot's essay could stand as a kind of manifesto for certain aspects of Creative Writing, as it has been taught in higher education over the last fifty years. The assumption of most Creative Writing courses is that writers learn their craft by placing themselves within a literary 'tradition' (or perhaps multiple traditions), as well as their contemporary literary context – in other words, by reading what others have done before them, and are doing now, in their chosen form. Writers must be voracious readers: this is the assumption of most teachers and practitioners of Creative Writing. Author Stephen King speaks for a thousand others when he writes: 'If you don't have time to read, you don't have the time (or the tools) to write. Simple as that. Reading is the creative centre of a writer's life' (2000: 58). On this definition, writers are not lone geniuses who spring spontaneously as if from nowhere; rather, they learn their craft over time by studying and absorbing the work of other writers. Writers develop within a community of other – living and dead – writers. As Eliot suggests, 'no poet, no artist ... has his complete meaning alone'.

This process of learning from other authors is sometimes called 'Reading Like a Writer'. New authors read other authors, and learn from their techniques, their successes and their misjudgements. As Francine Prose writes in her excellent book on the subject,

> Like most – maybe all – writers I learned to write by ... reading books ....
> In the ongoing process of becoming a writer, I read and re-read the authors I most loved. I read for pleasure, first, but also more analytically, conscious of style, of diction, of how sentences were formed and information was being conveyed, how the writer was structuring a plot, creating characters, employing detail and dialogue .... And though it's impossible to recall every source of inspiration and instruction, I can remember the novels and stories that seemed to me revelations: wells of beauty and pleasure that were also textbooks, private lessons in the art of fiction.
>
> (2012: 2–3)

Prose presents an entirely positive view of literary influence, whereby the 'novels and stories' she reads provide 'private lessons in the art of fiction', which she then puts into practice in her own work. In Harold Bloom's words, this is 'the idea of literary influence as a seamless and friendly mode of transmission, a gift graciously bestowed and gratefully received' (2011: 7).

Arguably, many Creative Writing courses are informed by just such a benign, unproblematic model of literary influence. In this respect, Eliot's essay once again stands behind them as a sort of foundational text. Indeed, Eliot pushes the idea of influence as a 'gift graciously bestowed and gratefully received' almost to breaking point:

> One of the facts that might come to light ... is our tendency to insist, when we praise a poet, upon the aspects of his work in which he least resembles anyone else .... We dwell with satisfaction upon the poet's difference from his predecessors .... We endeavour to find something that can be isolated in order to be enjoyed. Whereas if we approach a poet without this prejudice we shall often find that not only the best, but the most individual parts of his work may be those in which the dead poets, his ancestors, assert their immortality most vigorously.
>
> (2000: 32)

For Eliot, influence is not only a positive thing: it also, paradoxically, constitutes an author's essential individuality. Influence and individuality are the same thing: when a writer is influenced most by 'the dead', they are somehow simultaneously at their most individualistic. It's a strange and counterintuitive argument, to which we'll return later.

*

If Creative Writing courses don't always pursue Eliot's arguments to their (il) logical conclusions, they still generally encourage students to acknowledge their literary 'ancestors'. In Prose's terms, they urge students to make public the 'private lessons' they receive from reading, prompting them to discuss and, indeed, expand their sources of 'inspiration and instruction'. One of the main places this happens is in the reflective or critical commentaries which most courses ask students to submit alongside their creative work. In these commentaries, students will frequently be asked to situate their work in relation to other texts, discussing their reading, inspirations and influences in detail. As Tara Mokhtari writes, a commentary

> helps you to better understand your creative writing in terms of ... where your work sits within your genre, and how diverse your literary inspirations are and what exactly you are learning from your readings .... [It] is basically there as a way for you to demonstrate ... to your ... teacher [that] ... you have done your readings [and] ... you appreciate that you are not writing in a bubble. You read widely and you can name the literature which inspires and informs your personal style.
>
> (2019: 223–5)

Similarly, David Morley argues that, as a student of Creative Writing, you should 'make no secret of [your ... influences, enthusiasms and motivations', such that, in commentaries, 'you ... give critical attention to your own writing' by discussing openly 'the affinities you may feel it has with the work of other authors – and by placing your work in any intellectual, aesthetic, social or other context you feel it should be seen in' (2007: 36–7).

All the sample commentaries included in this book give critical attention to the authors' own writing by discussing affinities with other texts. And not just literary texts: while Eliot's and Prose's emphasis is primarily on *literary* influence, the authors herein talk not only about texts in their chosen genres but also many other 'intellectual, aesthetic, social ... context[s]' which have informed their creative work. Prose provides an excellent framework for reflecting on direct and conscious literary influence, especially at the level of craft. Hers is an excellent starting point, even blueprint, for any writer reflecting on literary influence, and what they have learned from comparable primary texts. As the commentaries in this book make clear, though, it's also important to look beyond the immediate literary context to other influences on the creative work. 'As with all writers', writes Karen Stevens, 'I suck in influences from all of life (not just reading)'. Likewise, Shaindel Beers argues that

> writers ... should read widely – poets from the past, contemporary poets, world poets – and they should read about any topics that interest them. But they also need to look up from their books. They need to go outside. Notice the wildflowers, notice the songs of the birds, and beyond noticing them, *learn* them. Writers need to discover all they can.

For some academic subjects, the texts students draw on are limited to one or two disciplinary-specific areas; for Creative Writing, by contrast, the range of texts might encompass everything from contemporary literary works to the language of birdsong and wildflowers. If this might seem overwhelming, it's worth dividing up the kinds of texts which writers might draw on into different (if overlapping) categories. This can then help in structuring a discussion of textual influences in a commentary. These categories might include:

- Primary texts (i.e. contemporary or historical novels, short stories, scripts, poems, works of creative non-fiction, etc.)

- Creative Writing texts (i.e. works on craft, process and genre)

- Contextual texts (i.e. texts which inform the subject matter and content of the creative work)

- More general 'experiential texts' (i.e. anything that involves 'going outside', as Beers puts it: birdsong, wildflowers, memory, living, overheard conversations, adverts on billboards, and so on and so forth)

Most creative writers will draw on more than one of these categories at the same time, such that their 'textual affinities' are diverse, multifarious – eclectically intermingling, for example, poetry with birdsong (as in Beers's commentary), social realism with the symbol of an abandoned fridge (as in Karen Stevens's commentary), middle-grade fiction with Tony Blair's speeches (as in Joanna Nadin's commentary), or an experimental form of poetic autobiography with the language of American processed meat (as in Lila Matsumoto's commentary). In short, writers take inspiration from everywhere, feeding the literary tradition into the same machine with things like processed meat products, turning the handle, and seeing what kinds of sausages emerge as a result.

If literary sausages can be made with anything, inspiration coming from anywhere and everywhere, our influences are potentially limitless. Although as writers, we're often asked to name our influences, it's well-nigh impossible to circumscribe them – to draw a neat line round the influences which informed a particular work, including some, excluding others. As Prose admits. 'it's impossible to recall every source of inspiration and instruction', and many of the authors in this book would agree. Lila Matsumoto suggests that

> naming the influences of a piece of work seems to suggest that there is a one-to-one, explicit relation between two things. For me, determining the influence for my work is like peering into the nebulous soup that is the creative process.

The 'nebulous soup' runneth over: Jonathan Taylor argues for 'the widest possible idea of influence when it comes to Creative Writing …. We're both consciously *and* unconsciously drawing on a near-infinite wealth of pre-existing texts – both in our chosen genre and far beyond it'. He goes on to quote Rob Pope, who writes that

> for each of us there are many and various communities, traditions and cultures to which we relate … These span the dead as well as the living, the remotely absent as well as the immediately present. Influences therefore exist on a continuum that, in principle, is intrinsically plural and infinitely open.
>
> (2005: 96)

According to this definition, it's clearly impossible to name or even know all of the influences which stand behind a particular creative piece. A commentary can only select a few conscious influences on which to focus, while the rest of the infinite 'continuum' remains hidden from sight, much of it unknown even to the author. In that sense, Ernest Hemingway's famous 'iceberg theory' of fiction (1958: 183) applies equally to reflective writing, where most of a work's context remains hidden from view. It also means that the usual requirement for commentaries to reflect on influences – to situate creative work in relation to other texts – is both a vital and, philosophically speaking, impossible or never-ending task. As authors, we cannot trace all of our influences, many of which remain unconscious.

*

Some of our influences, though, only begin life in the unconscious – and then gradually emerge into consciousness as part of the writing process. The reflective-creative process, in this sense, can work like a 'royal road to the unconscious' (Freud [1899] 2000: 608), as Sigmund Freud famously termed dream interpretation. This is what Lila Matsumoto implies when she suggests that 'determining the influence for my work is like peering into the nebulous soup that is the creative process'. She goes on to argue that

> Temporal distance is necessary for me to critically attempt the question of influence; only hindsight lets me understand how an idea or something I read alchemised with other ingredients to have propelled me to begin writing, and what additional ingredients then sustained the text-in-becoming. I believe that influence can often be dormant: that after having read or experienced something, it sits for months and even years before that curiosity or compulsion is carried out.

A number of the commentaries included in this book claim something similar. Jonathan Taylor, for instance, writes that

> we tend to think of influence as formative, generative – something that pre-exists 'creation' – and no doubt that is, to some extent, true. But often I become conscious of influence retrospectively, as a secondary phenomenon, as if I'm writing towards it, rather than setting off from it. Influence can be a point of arrival as well as departure. Only when I look back on a draft as an almost-whole do its precursors emerge, uncannily, into consciousness – only then does it become clear to me which pre-existing narratives haunt my own.

Jemma Kennedy goes even further, talking about texts that somehow came to 'haunt' her creative process, even though she didn't know them before drafting her own play: 'I found myself wondering if somehow I'd also been influenced by a play I'd never seen. Was this even possible?' Theoretically speaking, the answer must be yes: Kennedy talks of a 'collective cultural consciousness' which speaks through her writing, and Taylor, not dissimilarly, suggests that 'a genre's pre-history … represents a kind of collective unconscious you draw on – and are influenced by – when you choose to write in that form'.

*

At the most fundamental level, our collective cultural consciousness is formed by the words and phrases we inherit and then put to use. We all draw on a pre-existing language, which has been marked and reshaped by a near-infinite number of texts before us. As authors who want to be read and understood by others, we can't invent our own language – even Anthony Burgess's *A Clockwork Orange* is really just a mash-up of English, Russian and Cockney Rhyming Slang – and hence, on a granular level, we are always appropriating words from others.

In this sense, influence is inevitable, inescapable and works on a micro, as well as macro, scale – both linguistically and structurally, both in terms of the phrases we use and the genres in which we write. As Julia Cameron suggests, 'All work is influenced by other work. All people are influenced by other people. No man is an island and no piece of art is a continent unto itself' (2016: 174). Roland Barthes says something similar, in rather more polemical terms, in his famous (some might say infamous) essay, 'Death of the Author':

> We know now that a text is … a multi-dimensional space in which a variety of writings, none of them original, blend and clash. The text is a tissue of quotations drawn from the innumerable centres of culture …. The writer can only imitate a gesture that is always anterior, never original. His [*sic*] only power is to mix writings, to counter the ones with the others.
>
> ([1967] 1977: 146)

Barthes's words here may seem stultifying, almost a kind of curse, for authors: originality is impossible, influence inexorable, overwhelming. And certainly, some of the authors in this book have, at times, felt besieged by influence. The assumption of Prose and others is that the 'ongoing process of becoming a writer' is unproblematically aided by reading, in what Bloom calls a 'seamless transition' from author to author. Yet influence can also be a matter of anxiety, as Bloom makes clear in his (influential) book, *The Anxiety of Influence* (1973).

One or two of the commentaries included here allude to Bloom's language and ideas: Kennedy, for instance, discusses what she calls the 'Anxiety of Influence in the Age of Authenticity' and her concerns that her own work is haunted (unconsciously) by earlier, well-known plays, such as Tony Kushner's *Angels in America*. This anxiety causes her to wonder if the originality of her own play has been compromised: 'Had my quest for emotional authenticity blinded me to a lack of *creative* authenticity?'

Similarly, David Swann talks about influence's double nature as something both vital and potentially overpowering. On the one hand, he quotes Jay Parini, who suggests that writers 'find a source of energy in a prior body of work and attach themselves to it' (2009: 89). On the other hand, he also quotes the author John Wain, for whom there is danger in 'breathing breathed air' (Firchow 1974: 323). Wain's language here reminds us, perhaps, that the word 'inspiration' originally meant to have air blown into us (and hence to inhale someone else's air), and the word 'influence' shares the same root as 'influenza'. Influence is something contagious, viral, that we inhale from another and which subsequently infects our creativity.

*

Still, if influence can be a kind of influenza, it generally seems to be a passing malady, which ends up strengthening the writer's immune system. Despite the anxieties and viral infections, all of the authors in this book ultimately see influence as beneficial to their creative practice. Influence is an essential and transitional stage the author has to go through – perhaps is always going through, with every new work – in order to create something worthwhile. Kennedy quotes essayist Adam Gopnik, who suggests that:

> Nobody ever finds their voice by shutting off their influences. You find it by imitating other people and then through the process of osmosis, of putting in those people, internalizing their sound. Suddenly, one day you wake up and you say, 'Oh, that doesn't sound like anybody else. That sounds like me'.
>
> (Gopnik 2023)

Through a 'process of osmosis', that is, an author finds their own voice by absorbing and then – somehow – transcending their influences.

One way of understanding this 'process of osmosis' might be by returning to Barthes. While, on the surface, Barthes *seems* to be suggesting that originality is impossible, he does admit that the author has one 'power', which is 'to mix writings, to counter the ones with the others'. In other words, the author's power, according to Barthes, consists of their ability to mix linguistic cocktails. This also seems to be the implication of many of the commentaries in this book: that creativity and so-called originality come from mingling influences, from mixing the language of processed meat with experimental poetry (as in Matsumoto's commentary), from synthesizing poetic influence with the language of birdsong and flowers (as in Beers's commentary), or from bringing together the image of a fridge abandoned on a lawn with socio-economic theory (as in Stevens's commentary).

According to Stevens, the 'socio-economic backdrop' (symbolized by an abandoned fridge on a lawn) and the 'central theory' (specifically, Richard Wilkinson and Kate Pickett's study of inequality, *The Inner Level*) were 'two sticks that rubbed together until a spark went off in my head'. In more general terms, Stephen King says something similar about his own creative process. He remarks that 'good story ideas' sometimes arise when 'two previously unrelated ideas come together and make something new under the sun' (2000: 18). Sometimes, as the commentaries in this book make clear, it's more than two. As Barthes might expect, originality ('something new under the sun') is often, it seems, a matter of bringing together seemingly incongruous ideas, images, voices and languages. In 'The Pleasure of the Text', he asks us to

> Imagine someone ... who abolishes within himself all barriers, all classes, all exclusions, not by syncretism, but by simple discard of that old spectre: *logical contradiction*; who mixes every language, even those said to be incompatible; who silently accepts every charge of illogicality, of incongruity .... Thus the Biblical myth is reversed, the confusion of tongues is no longer a punishment, the subject gains access to bliss by the cohabitation of languages working *side by side*: the text of pleasure is a sanctioned Babel.
>
> (1975: 3–4)

Barthes is talking about his ideal reader here, but his words could equally apply to many of the writers included in this volume, who find their own voices by mixing the seemingly incongruous languages of poetry, fiction, memoir, scriptwriting with science, philosophy, economics, political speech-writing, journalism, branding and so on. Eclecticism, for these writers, is pleasure, creativity and power. It is in this context, perhaps, that we can understand Eliot's notion that influence and artistic individuality are one and the same thing: individuality is nothing more – and nothing less – than the intermingling of many and varied influences. And given that we are all, during our lives, exposed to vastly differing influences, this means that we are all capable of producing an original cocktail out of them.

Works Cited

Barthes, R. (1975), *The Pleasure of the Text*, trans. R. Miller, New York: Farrar, Straus and Giroux.

Barthes, R. ([1967] 1977), 'The Death of the Author', in *Image, Music, Text*, trans. S. Heath, London: Fontana, pp. 142–8.

Bloom, H. ([1973] 1997), *The Anxiety of Influence: A Theory of Poetry*, Oxford: Oxford University Press.

Bloom, H. (2011), *The Anatomy of Influence: Literature as a Way of Life*, New Haven and London: Yale University Press.

Burgess, A. (1972), *A Clockwork Orange*, London: Penguin.

Cameron, J. (2016), *The Artist's Way*, London: Macmillan.

Eliot, T. S. ([1919] 2000), 'Tradition and the Individual Talent', in W. N. Herbert and M. Hollis (eds), *Strong Words: Modern Poets on Modern Poetry*, Tarset: Bloodaxe, pp. 31–8.

Firchow, P. (ed.) (1974), *The Writer's Place: Interviews on the Literary Situation in Contemporary Britain*, Minneapolis: University of Minnesota.

Freud, S. ([1899] 2000), *On the Interpretation of Dreams*, in *The Standard Edition of the Complete Psychological Works of Sigmund Freud*, trans. J. Strachey (ed.), 24 vols, IV, London: Vintage, pp. 1–630.

Gopnik, A. (2023), 'Steve Martin on Finding Your Authentic Voice', *ReThinking with Adam Grant* (series), TED audio collective, 4 May. Available online: https://podcasts.apple.com/us/podcast/steve-martin-on-finding-your-authentic-voice/id1554567118?i=1000611667002 (accessed 8 April 2024).

Hemingway, E. (1958), *Death in the Afternoon*, London: Jonathan Cape.

King, S. (2000), *On Writing: A Memoir of the Craft*, New York: Scribner.

Mokhtari, T. (2019), *The Bloomsbury Introduction to Creative Writing*, London: Bloomsbury Academic.

Morley, D. (2007), *The Cambridge Introduction to Creative Writing*, Cambridge: Cambridge University Press.

Parini, J. (2009), *Why Poetry Matters*, New Haven: Yale University Press.

Pope, R. (2005), *Creativity: Theory, History, Practice*, London: Routledge.

Prose, F. (2012), *Reading Like a Writer: A Guide for People Who Love Books and for Those Who Want to Write Them*, London: Union Books.

Wilkinson, R. and Pickett, K. (2018), *The Inner Level*, St. Ives: Allen Lane.

PART TWO

Sample Critical Commentaries

4

The Personal Is Always Political

By Karen Stevens

Two events in my family are periodically resurrected when me and my eldest son are teasing one another. His anecdote relates to my childhood, when I used to sneak downstairs to the kitchen late at night to steal Oxo cubes because I was hungry. My anecdote relates to a time when my son (then aged sixteen) woke up at a leisurely midday and announced that he would be making focaccia bread. *Focaccia,* I repeated, taken aback by the middle-classness of it all. Looking back, perhaps I shouldn't have been so surprised by my son's sudden inclination to take up artisan baking, but I now see this event provoked a moment of inner questioning: my children behave and hold aspirations we associate with the middle class – so did this mean *I* was no longer working class?

I come from a poor working-class background. In the mid-1990s, education offered me the social mobility that Tony Blair envisaged when he came into Downing Street just a few years later in 1997, with his vision that wider access to higher education would be the great social leveller. I suppose I'm living proof of Blair's vision back then, after making a career in academia. But I don't *feel* middle class – and if asked, would defiantly define myself as working class. As writer Durre Shahwar says, 'You can learn to navigate the middle-class spheres and even financially outgrow what would keep you in the working-class "bracket", yet the experiences that shape your formative years always stick' (2017: 77).

The impact of this 'in-betweenness' (as I think of it) is that I often suffer from imposter syndrome when engaged in predominantly middle-class environments, yet also feel distanced from my working-class roots. My feelings are not unique. In 1957, academic Richard Hoggart wrote in *The Uses of Literacy* about the 'uprooted and the anxious' ([1957] 1973: 291) – the working-class scholarship boy of post-war Britain who wanted to better himself through education but in doing so became 'the odd man out' ([1957] 1973: 302), no longer able to fit into his working-class community and too self-conscious to be comfortable with his middle-class peers. Much of my writing explores this psychic tension.

My recently completed short story collection, *Brilliant Blue* (2025), is set around the fictional Duncock Estate, loosely based on a sprawling council estate that I know well on the south coast of England. The great north-south divide still looms large in our consciousness, according to columnist Owen Jones: '[T]he North conjures up images of being downtrodden and impoverished .... The south, on the other hand, is a prosperous land of leafy suburbs' (2014). As I know from experience, however, there is much deprivation on the south coast, and I wanted to undermine this affluent southern 'myth' through my interconnected stories, in which many of the characters are living on the margins amidst financial and social uncertainty.

Author Elizabeth Strout says that 'when you write about people, you are writing about class. Time and place in history determine a great deal, and if you consider place to be a place in society, then that shapes a life as well' (2017). As with Strout's fiction, the stories in *Brilliant Blue* pivot around issues of class, and those moments when class lines are crossed or blurred and people become more acutely aware of their power and powerlessness within the hierarchies of class relations. This awareness is most consciously explored in my opening short story, 'Among the Crows', which will be the focus of discussion in this commentary.

Hanif Kureishi feels that 'To write is to be puzzled a second time by one's experience; it is also to savour it. In such reflection there is time to taste and engage with your own life in its complexities' (2014: 21). Write what you know is a controversial cliché, but perhaps it should not be quickly dismissed, for what we know does not only come from experience, but from what is central to us: our interests, obsessions, cares and preoccupations – 'those influences', Joyce Carol Oates points out, 'that come so early in childhood, they seem to soak into the marrow of our bones and to condition our interpretation of the universe thereafter' (2004: 13). I write and think about the world from a working-class perspective because this is where I come from. My background is fundamental to my writerly preoccupation with the British class system and, in particular, my interest in stories that make social commentary on the complexities of living in working-class environments.

Like Selina Todd, I believe that 'Class is a relationship defined by unequal power' (2015: 7), and the work of Ken Loach, Livi Michael and Elizabeth Strout are key influences for me in this respect. Their stories of working-class lives lay bare the inherent unfairness that exists in the social gap between poor and wealthy, exposing the attendant problems that come from social disadvantage: exploitation, marginalization, the dehumanizing effect of state bureaucracy and the struggle to achieve or be heard in an economic and social system where you have no influence or social stability. Like most people, I read in order to experience another reality and have come to see that those realities that make the deepest impression reflect something about myself, in some way. Writer Rebecca Mead believes that reading is where 'one finds oneself' (2022), and writing, I believe, is the place where one articulates one's history and identity, both consciously and unconsciously.

*

As with all writers, I suck in influences from all of life (not just reading), and the initial seed for my story 'Among the Crows' came to me many years ago, when a male friend relayed an incident of being hijacked outside a supermarket with his close friend after a football training session. The hijackers were strangers, a couple who insisted on being driven home with their shopping to the council estate where they lived, and my friend did as he was told because they were 'rough' (his word) and high on something, potentially dangerous. Nothing untoward happened and afterwards my friend and his football pal grew progressively distanced from one another until one day the friend left training and contact stopped. I was intrigued by the class dynamics at play in the hijack situation and fascinated by the men's unspoken, shared sense of emasculation (surely) that seemed to have played a part in the ending of their friendship.

I wanted to explore this friendship, and how the men's sense of masculinity had been so tested, but my characters wouldn't emerge in any meaningful way for years (such is the frustrating nature of creation) until I read Richard Wilkinson and Kate Pickett's book *The Inner Level*. Here was a thought-provoking exploration of the harmful psychic effects of inequality and how it leads to a tendency to define and value ourselves in terms of superiority and inferiority:

> Perhaps the most likely explanation of why inequality increases status anxiety across entire societies is because it increases the sense that people at the top of the social ladder are extremely important and those at the bottom are worthless, and, as money becomes more entrenched as a measure of people's worth, it makes us all more worried about where we come in the hierarchy.
>
> (2013: 35)

In the UK, the gap between poor and wealthy has grown exponentially due to political choices that favour neoliberalism. The Data and Analysis Census, year ending 2022, found that the median disposable income for the poorest fifth of the population fell by 3.8 per cent while the richest fifth rose by 1.6 per cent. Growing inequality has deepened class suspicion more acutely over the past few decades. The widening gap between rich and poor has fuelled class wars and divisions, even amongst those suffering in the same low socio-economic bracket. These divisions have been deepened by austerity and the government's hostile focus on immigration and the 'underclass' – a derogatory social descriptor that has gained political currency in the last few decades. In a neoliberal society that promotes individualism rather than collective action and shared identities, the assertion of sociologist and philosopher Zygmunt Bauman feels relevant: 'Present-day miseries are not synchronized .... Our sufferings divide and isolate: our miseries set us apart, tearing up the delicate tissue of human solidarities' (1999: 53–4).

This socio-economic backdrop and Wilkinson/Pickett's central theory were two sticks that rubbed together until a spark went off in my head. A disparate group of people – all struggling on the breadline to different degrees and unable to find shared identity – began to materialize in my imagination: Andy, the viewpoint character, who strims verges for the local council on a low income; Mac (Maciej), a Polish immigrant who works with Andy and is determined to make a better life for himself in the UK; and Becks and Scar Head, a couple who are barely surviving on Universal Credit and are forced to hunt rabbits with their dog because they don't have enough money to buy food every day.

Stories are about struggle. As writer Charles Baxter points out, a happy story is 'narratively sterile' (2008: 212) because stories about happiness 'deal with an activity successfully completed' (2008: 205). The best stories are in motion, and this is especially true of the short story because there's less space for 'easing in' or preamble. A short story must begin on the cusp of change, when things are in flux, disarray or conflict, in order to bring about a profound moment of realization for the central protagonist. My short story 'Among the Crows' is set at a point of disruption that offers a moment of clear-sightedness to Andy, who at the end of the story experiences an intense awareness of his loneliness, even though he is unable to fully comprehend it.

Andy and Mac are hijacked by a couple in Andy's car outside a supermarket. They must drive this couple to their home at the centre of the Duncock Estate, an area where Andy and Mac have been strimming verges for the council. It is a place that Andy finds alien and threatening, and his anxious state is ignited by an abandoned fridge, a prop taken from my own experience when visiting my relative on the housing estate I know well. On this occasion, I noticed that a fridge – door intact – had been dumped on the verge opposite and I experienced an irrational, almost threatening, sense that this estate was beyond the scope of conventional law and order. I fictionalized this intense feeling through Andy's perspective:

He sat on the verge and took in the council houses, their concrete walls bleached dirty-white from the sun. Objects poked out from the parched grass of a ramshackle garden opposite. A rusting fridge revealed its mouldy interior. A child the same age as his Cora could fit in there, closing the door to hide, suffocating within minutes .... Anything could happen here. He sensed it in the stillness, the lack of trees and plants, the biting looks of passers-by, their skins the same bleached colour as their houses. If he was jumped for the strimmer, they could have it; he wouldn't risk having his face slashed.

(Stevens 2025: 1–2)

Though Duncock is based on the place where my relative lives, my aim wasn't to recreate it faithfully through description – more to create a mood that would capture Andy's inner anxiety. As writer Chika Unigwe says, 'Setting is not just the time and place of a story, but also the mental landscape of the characters who inhabit a particular narrative. It is therefore often linked to mood or meaning' (2009: 58). Unexpected gifts (such as the dumped fridge) can lodge mysteriously in the writer's imagination, but it is the rational authorial mind which alters them to create meaning. This 'rational' process was not so rational in practice (as it turned out), but was an elusive, often dumbfounding process that led to many dead-ends and U-turns before the fridge gained symbolic significance and enabled thematic connections in the story. Andy's feelings of alienation and threat in the opening pages not only foreshadow the hijacking but also serve to express something about the powerlessness he experiences in his marriage, a complicated relationship in which Andy's wife both seeks to emasculate him and to invite him to dominate her. I wanted the exposition on Andy's marriage to broaden the story and to bring more depth to his character in order to help the reader understand why he behaves so passively when hijacked and why his gentle, uncomplicated friendship with his work colleague Mac is deeply important to him. E. M. Forster talks of 'flat' characters as 'constructed around a single idea or quality: when there is more than one factor in them, we get the beginning of the curve towards the round' (2011: 98).

*

Establishing the setting early on through Andy's perspective also served to seed the central theme of inferiority and superiority that had so captured my imagination, and this theme progressively develops in the story. Andy's concern about the rusty fridge prompts him into making judgments on the people who live in the 'dark heart' (Stevens 2025: 1) of Duncock, an area he considers to be more 'desperate and hostile' (2025: 2) than where he lives, on the outskirts. Here, Andy's need to feel superior is an attempt to suppress his irrational feeling of threat. Once hijacked, however, his outwardly submissive behaviour reveals his sense of inferiority when he does exactly as he is told and drives like 'a silent observer' (2025: 8). His outward behaviour is a survival tactic, as are his inner thoughts of superiority in comparison to his hijackers – 'Andy could see their poverty in his rearview, worse than his .... People who lived in the "dark heart" were loafers, though. Feral. The centre of the estate was a sinkhole' (2025: 6). This internal *othering* vilifies and relegates the hijackers to an underclass beyond the reach of civilized norms, at once setting up a moral and material distance between himself and the couple.

Joyce Carol Oates speaks of how our childhood experiences influence our interpretation of the world thereafter, but she also speaks of other influences – 'those that come a little later, when we ... have begun to be aware not only of the emotional power but the strategies of art' (2004: 13). In fiction, one such strategy which fascinates me is the act of Othering or being Othered. These are the moments that articulate our acute awareness of the differences that set us apart as inferior or superior. Indeed, the fiction of Elizabeth Strout and Livi Michael made a deep and lasting impression on me for their ability to powerfully explore the emotional impact of being Othered.

In *My Name Is Lucy Barton*, Strout draws on her protagonist Lucy's memories to tease out her understanding about what has caused her to always feel an outsider and an oddity, even though she has escaped from the isolation of her poverty-stricken childhood in Amgash, Illinois, to reinvent herself as a successful writer living in New York. Strout's first-person narration sets up a compelling intimacy and tension as Lucy's memories vibrate beneath and through her present situation, in which she is ill in hospital. She recalls how her college professor and partner used to drive her around what he considered to be a poor neighbourhood, asking with voyeuristic 'poverty-porn' curiosity, 'Is your house like that?' (2016: 27), and how her sophisticated New York neighbour once gave her a look of distaste that was 'so fast, so involuntary ... I had not yet learned the depth of disgust city people feel for the truly provincial' (2016: 39).

In *Under a Thin Moon*, Livi Michael explores how the disjunctions and hierarchies in language serve to reinforce inferiority and class difference. This is a novel of Thatcherism as experienced by poor working-class women on a run-down Northern housing estate, and a sense of powerlessness pervades the narrative as these marginalized women struggle to make ends meet. Laurie – a shoplifter who once had educational aspirations – is made to feel worthless at the DHSS office when she attempts to locate her missing giro. The indifferent, blank-faced clerks make her uncomfortably aware of how things work – that 'you needed money even to speak .... She listens to them on their terms, they translate her into theirs' (1994: 64). At university, 'When she tries to translate herself into terms her tutor can accept she hears always the jeering laughter of the people from her street .... When she tries to talk in the old way, their way, she sees always the resigned, dismissive faces of her tutors' (1994: 110).

Academic John Kirk says that to write about class is to write about 'feelings of belonging and un-belonging' (2009: 7). In both stories, the protagonists experience intense moments of self-consciousness when they are observed through the lens of middle-class normalcy and privilege, and this serves to heighten their awareness of their state of in-betweenness and sense of un-belonging.

In my story 'Among the Crows', the couple who hijack Andy and Mac experience similar feelings to Laurie within the intransigent and penalizing welfare system called Universal Credit. I wanted to show the couple's sense of powerlessness through their dialogue with each other when they talk about the recent hoop they must jump through in order to prevent another sanction. As writer David Lodge says, dialogue is 'the purest form of showing' (2012: 57) because it allows fictional characters to exist on the page, unmediated: '"Fuck the journal," Scar Head insisted, though Andy could detect a sort of helplessness in his voice. "I'm *not* doing it, Becks. They treat us like performing bears. They poke us with their electric prods and expect us to fucking dance for them!"' (Stevens 2025: 6). In *Consuming Life*, Bauman talks of how the underclass is viewed as:

> totally useless; as a nuisance pure and simple .... In a society of consumers – a world that evaluates anyone and anything by their commodity value – they are people with no market value ... they are the 'end is nigh' or the 'memento mori' sandwich men walking the streets to alert or frighten the bona fide consumers.
>
> ([2007] 2022: 124)

The hijackers must prove that they are actively engaged in job-hunting through the Universal Credit journal and that they are seeking to be 'valuable' through the official language of documentation. As with Laurie, they must listen and respond to officials on their terms only. They must log their work activities and completed tasks in order to comply with their claimant commitment. This process ultimately makes them feel inferior because it dispossesses them of their lived experience.

The characters Andy and Mac seemed to materialize from nothing, necessitating many hours of research into local council employment policy and Polish culture and immigration. The hijack couple, on the other hand, were influenced by a reality programme on Channel 4 called *Skint Britain: Friends without Benefits* (2019), which featured a clutch of residents from Hartlepool who became guinea pigs for the roll out of Universal Credit. The realities of this new system became apparent as they struggled to cope with this bewildering new government brainwave, which Amber Rudd, Secretary of State for Work and Pensions from 2018 to 2019, admitted had pushed more people into using food banks. As I watched *Skint Britain,* I felt angry that a man was reduced to weeping in a phone box after spending hours on hold to the benefits office, tortured by the soundtrack of Vivaldi's *Four Seasons.* I was appalled that a young couple had to go out with their dog to the local common to catch rabbits because they didn't have enough money to buy food every day. The young man was frustrated because he couldn't read and was required to attend interviews for jobs that were utterly inappropriate. The programme made me reflect on Ken Loach's ability in *I Daniel Blake* to capture the miserable failures of state bureaucracy and the dehumanizing effect on both government officials and claimants.

As with Andy's internal Othering, the hijackers need to express superiority within an emasculating bureaucratic system, and so they bait Mac by blaming immigration as the root cause of their financial hardship: 'You lot are why they switched over to Universal Credit. Before there was a drip, drip, drip. Now it's dry, mate. Sahara Desert dry. It's sanctions all the way, and it's killing us' (Stevens 2025: 7–8). Mac's response is to defend the Polish people from blame: 'I don't know anyone from Poland who is on welfare. We are hardworking people' (2025: 8). Mac is the underdog in this hijacking situation for the simple reason that he is foreign. He responds to baiting with calm civility, a survival tactic that leads to him being set up by Scar Head.

A quotation from psychoanalyst Alfred Adler in *The Spirit Level* stayed with me and served to develop Scar Head's actions:

> Behind everyone who behaves as if he were superior to others, we can suspect a feeling of inferiority which calls for very special efforts of concealment .... The greater the feeling of inferiority ... the more powerful the urge to conquest and the more violent the emotional agitation.
>
> (2018: 2)

Andy and Mac are lured into the couple's back garden on the pretext that Mac's knowledge of dogs will offer some answers as to why one of their dogs is sickly. Scar Head knows full well that the dog will attack as soon as Mac's back is turned. The cruelty shown to Mac is an extreme reaction to Scar Head's feelings of inferiority and powerlessness at the hands of government officialdom, and I was concerned that the couple may come across as caricatures – a clichéd representation of the underclass evolved through derogatory political rhetoric. I wanted to suggest another side that isn't just feckless, baiting and cruel through their decision to catch and grow their own food. I wanted to show that they are striving to be more self-sufficient in the face of ever-deepening poverty – a hint, I hope, of E. M. Forster's 'curve towards the round':

The plants were well tended, the leaves deep green. One of the plants had two delicate clusters of red flowers, a contrast to the grey of the earth and the walls and the concrete path running along the back of the house.

'Spuds, too, next year,' Scar Head said proudly.

(Stevens 2025: 11)

Mac and Andy have no choice but to go into the garden to see the couple's sickly dog, and Mac tells Andy: 'Once among the crows, sing as they do' (2025: 11). This Polish proverb is a common-sense call for social conformism in the face of an adverse and alien environment and is something Mac is practiced at in order to survive. Here, Mac imitates Scar Head's commanding manner: '"Hey!" Mac called over to Scar Head. "If you want me to look at dog, you must put others inside"' (2025: 11). In contrast, Andy remains a silent observer, unable to speak up and prevent the orchestrated dog attack that brings Scar Head such 'twisted pleasure' (2025: 11).

The hijackers own three dogs, and one is sickly because, as Mac points out, it is the 'underdog' (2025: 12) relentlessly bullied by the other two frustrated dogs. Writer Flannery O'Connor feels that 'In good fiction, certain of the details will tend to accumulate meaning from the action of the story itself, and when this happens they become symbolic in the way they work' (2014: 98). I hadn't realized that the dogs' hierarchical bullying instinct echoed Mac's own position with the hijackers until it was pointed out to me in workshopping. Virtually all writers operate with some kind of feedback on their work in progress, and this exploratory process is both helpful and endlessly interesting because it alerts me to other possible readings, pointing up conscious and unconscious elements that materialized in the writing process. I could now see how the dogs shuttled between realist detail and symbolic significance, and I developed this further by strategically endowing the male hijacker with dog-like traits:

Whenever the dogs bounded up, Scar Head booted them back and Andy's stomach quivered. They were dangerous things with heads like anvils, wiry fur, and stringy haunches. Dog versions of Scar Head, Andy thought, as he watched him gnawing on a knuckle.

(Stevens 2025: 10)

The job of fiction is to raise questions rather than offer solutions, and I resisted a moralistic discourse or liberal rationalization. Instead, the dog attack shifts Mac and Andy's perception of each other. Their subjugation at the hands of the hijackers has rendered them impotent in each other's eyes, and I wanted to suggest the resultant irreparable breakdown of their friendship through the final image of Mac limping away from Andy down the road – 'getting smaller and smaller, until he was just a speck' (2025: 14). As is the case in real life, there is no neat resolve; these people are simply responding to inequality in their own way, day after day. Writer David Gaffney suggests that 'The last line ... should leave the reader with something which will continue to sound after the story has finished. It should not complete the story but rather take us into a new place; a place where we can continue to think about the ideas in the story' (2012) – what writer Michael Trussler calls 'post-narrational projection' (1996: 571). I hoped that the characters' plights and interactions (submissive, cruel, imitative) and their suspicions and Othering would prompt questions in the reader about the broader political and cultural context that shapes our responses to one another and how this impacts our social cohesion.

*

I'm a working-class person who no longer lives a working-class life, and I began this commentary by talking about the psychic tension that arises from this state of 'in-betweenness'. I'm an in-betweener, yes. A visitor for evermore. Hoggart's 'odd man out'. But maybe it's a privilege to be able to visit two worlds. This tension, after all, is the creative pulse that ticks insistently through my writing. If the novel is more focused on society, then the short story is for the marginalized. I'm interested in the poor and disenfranchised, in the 'anxious and uprooted' – those people who Frank O'Connor refers to as the 'submerged population, unable to speak for themselves' (2003: 4).

Writing about these lives expresses something of my own experience while enabling me (and hopefully the reader) to understand, more clearly, that class is ultimately shaped by the unequal power relations we live with. Class is less visible than other social signifiers such as race and gender, and yet 'the gap between rich and poor is wider than it has been at any time since the early twentieth century' (Todd 2015: 367). This ever-deepening divide is perhaps supported by the loss of a solid working-class identity. Academic Kenan Malik says that 'Today, the old industrial working class ... has largely been unmade, politically marginalised and stripped of its social power. Few regard class as a fertile concept in historical thinking, fewer still as a foundation for progressive politics' (2024). It's not easy to rise up and unite against inequality in a society 'where our success, even our survival, is down to us' (Todd 2015: 399), and so we must keep talking and writing about class. As writer John Green says, 'Writing fiction is an inherently political activity because people – even imaginary ones – do not live in vacuums ... no work of the imagination is truly apolitical, because the world and our hopes for it are always part of our stories' (2014).

Works Cited

Bauman, Z. (1999), *In Search of Politics*, Cambridge: Polity Press.

Bauman, Z. ([2007] 2022), *Consuming Life*, Cambridge: Polity Press.

Baxter, C. (2008), *Burning Down the House: Essays on Fiction*, Minnesota: Graywolf.

Forster, E. M. (2011), *The Art of Writing Fiction*, Andrew Cowan (ed.), Harlow: Pearson.

Gaffney, D. (2012), 'Stories in Your Pocket: How to Write Flash Fiction', 14 May. Available online: https://www.theguardian.com/books/2012/may/14/how-to-write-flash-fiction (accessed 27 August 2024).

Green, J. (2014), quoted in '14 Quotes about Writing from John Green', by Mark Mancini, 15 January. Available online: https://www.mentalfloss.com/article/54511/14-quotes-abgout-writing-john-green (accessed 3 July 2024).

Hoggart, R. ([1957] 1973), *The Uses of Literacy*, Penguin Books.

I, Daniel Blake (2016), [Film] Dir. Ken Loach, UK: British Film Institute.

Jones, O. (2014), 'The North-South Divide Is a Myth – and a Distraction', *The Guardian*, 4 May. Available online: https://www.theguardian.cogm/commentisfree/2014/may/04/north-south-divide-myth-distraction (accessed 10 September 2024).

Kirk, J. (2009), *The British Working Class in the Twentieth Century: Film, Literature and Television*, Cardiff: University of Wales Press.

Kureishi, H. (2014), 'Something Given: Reflections on Writing', in K. Stevens (ed.), *Writing a First Novel: Reflections on the Journey*, Houndmills, Basingstoke and Hampshire: Palgrave Macmillan, pp. 17–25.

Lodge, D. ([1992] 2011), *The Art of Writing Fiction*, London: Vintage.

Malik, K. (2024), 'What a Legendary Historian Tells Us about Today's Working Class', *The Guardian*, 4 February. Available online: https://www.theguardian.com/commentisfree/2024/feb/04/what-legendary-historian-tells-us-about-contempt-for-todays-working-class-ep-thompson (accessed 30 August 2024).

Mead, R. (2022), quoted in '"Books Bring Us into Being": How Writing about Reading Became an Inspiring Literary Genre of Its Own', by Lara Fiegel, *The Guardian*, 13 August. Available online: https://www.theguardian.com/books/2022/aug/13/books-bring-us-into-being-how-writing-about-reading-became-an-inspiring-literary-genre-of-its-own (accessed 15 July 2024).

Michael, L. (1994), *Under a Thin Moon*, London: Minerva.

Oates, J. C. (2004), *The Faith of a Writer: Life, Craft, Art*, New York: Ecco.

O'Connor, F. ([1962] 2003), *The Lonely Voice: A Study of the Short Story*, Cork: Cork City Council.

O'Connor, F. (2014), 'Writing Short Stories', in S. and R. Fitzgerald (eds), *Mystery & Manners*, London: Faber and Faber, pp. 87–106.

Office for National Statistics, The Data and Analysis Census 2022: Average Household Income, UK: financial year ending 2022. Available online: https://www.ons.gov.uk/peoplepopulationandcommunity/personalandhouseholdfinances/incomeandwealth/bulletins/householddisposableincomeandinequality/financialyearending2022 (accessed 24 November 2023).

Shahwar, D. (2017), 'Navigating Space', in N. Connolly (ed.), *Know Your Place*, Liverpool: Dead Ink, pp. 69–77.

Skint Britain: Friends Without Benefits (2019) [TV programme] Channel 4, 13–27 February.

Stevens, K. (2025), *Brilliant Blue*, London: Barbican Press.

Strout, E. (2016), *My Name Is Lucy Barton*, St Ives: Penguin.

Strout, E. (2017), 'How Do We Become Aware of Class in America?', *The Washington Post*, 28 August. Available online: https://www. washingtonpost.com/entertainment/books/one-writers-life-elizabeth-strout/2017/08/25/35130bde-7b96-11e7-9d08-b79f191668ed_story.html (accessed 19 August 2019).

Todd, S. (2015), *The People: The Rise and Fall of the Working Class*, St. Ives: John Murray.

Trussler, M. (1996), 'Suspended Narratives: The Short Story and Temporality', *Studies in Short Fiction*, 33:4, 557–77.

Unigwe, C. (2009), 'Setting', in V. Gebbie (ed.), *Short Circuit: A Guide to the Art of the Short Story*, Cromer: Salt, pp. 57–66.

Wilkinson, R. and Pickett, K. (2018), *The Inner Level*, St. Ives: Allen Lane.

5

The Art of Persuasion

By Joanna Nadin

Maybe she's born with it; maybe it's Maybelline.

– Advertising Slogan, 1991

In the 2010s, this slogan, coined for the make-up brand Maybelline in 1991, was voted the 'most recognizable in the last 150 years'. It uses, among other things, a simple rhetorical device called *diacope* (the repetition of words or phrases with a small number of intervening words) and *isocolon* (successive phrases of relatively equal length and structure) to achieve its memorable effect. Close runners-up were Nike's 'Just Do It' (which employs *tricolon*, or what is commonly known as the 'rule of three'), and KFC's 'It's Finger-Licking Good' (*tricolon* and *assonance*, which uses the repetition of vowel sounds to form an internal rhyme). My point here is that we are well-used to the appearance of rhetorical devices in advertising, even if we are oblivious to their efficacy, and occasionally condescending about their effects, dismissing them as 'spin' or 'soundbites': the same insults that tarred New Labour's political campaigning during my years at Millbank and Downing Street. Whatever we think about them, we understand that they are used to 'move people', whether that's to the polling booth or the shops.

We are less used, perhaps, to noticing them in fiction, or at least understanding why they are there and what their function might be. And yet, like advertising, like political campaigning, my endgame as a children's writer is to 'move people', and to do it, like Maybelline, like Nike, like KFC, fairly subtly. To achieve that in *No Man's Land* (2021), as in all my writing, I turned to the 'art of persuasion'. This is the practice Aristotle set out in 350 BCE, delineating three key appeals or 'proofs': the character of the speaker (*ethos*), the logic of the argument (*logos*) and the emotions of the audience (*pathos*) (Lancaster 2015: 7).

Ethos: Creating a Believable Leader

No Man's Land is narrated by Alan, a ten-year-old boy whose mother died giving birth to his younger brother, Sam. While Sam preoccupies himself with 'Marvel and DC and dinosaurs' (Nadin 2021: 7), Alan worries about Albion, with its increasingly prohibitive government and alliance with a far-right America, a looming world war, and his father's role in all this. It opens with a post-narrative retrospective, setting out his recent realizations against the fears he held before the narrative began:

> I used to think I knew about heroes. That some wore fancy outfits and flexed bulging muscles and had special powers like invisibility or flight or flames from their fingertips. The others wore uniforms and fought for the country with guns and rockets, or carried babies out of burning buildings.
> It turns out not all heroes wear capes. And not all heroes carry guns.
> It turns out it's not so easy to tell them and the baddies apart, neither.
> 'Cause real life isn't like on the telly or in films. Villains don't go round cackling madly and flashing their tattoos. They come in pretending to be your friend and promising you stuff so you're tricked into thinking they're the good ones after all.
> And the real heroes? They can slip in and out without you even noticing. And fight with their wile and their wits and their kindness instead of weapons.
> And they might be skinny as a stick and dressed in a T-shirt and just a kid.
> But I didn't know that then.
> I just knew the world was changing.
> And I knew I wanted it to stop.
>
> (Nadin 2021: 3–4)

This, Alan's opening 'speech', in which he worries how hard it is to work out who's the hero, unwittingly sets out one of the key issues I had to grapple with in the genesis of the narrative and its protagonist. *Ethos* is the 'proof' of the character of the speaker to be a leader: someone reliable, whom the audience / reader can invest in. When Aristotle set out his 'proofs', they were based on observation, but we now know they can be rooted in neuroscience, and *ethos*, as speechwriter Simon Lancaster points out in *Winning Minds* (2015), is a proof that appeals to the instinctive brain.

In political terms, that appeal is often beyond words; it comes down to stance, stature, speed and tone of voice (even hair colour, if one of the oft-touted reasons for the defeat of Neil Kinnock in the 1987 general election is to be believed). When drafting a political speech, my *ethos* appeal would be twofold: giving the speaker authority while also suggesting to the audience they are 'one of us'. Thus, the speaker will prioritize their wants and needs. Biography is common here – a story from the speaker's past that aligns them with the audience, that reminds them that the speaker, too, is human and a 'bit like me'. This is a doubly useful tool because we also know from studies like Kubin, Puryear, et al. (2021) that personal experience is more effective in convincing a listener or reader than 'facts', and increasingly so in an area of 'fake news', when it is hard to tell what is fact and what is concoction; it is harder to dispute someone's personal 'truth'.

My job in *No Man's Land* was more complex, given there is no live speaker who can stand like Batman[1] and thus persuade the listener they are 'safe with me'. For a start, Alan is a ten-year-old child, so he lacks the experience that would lend him natural authority. He's also, as he observes himself, 'skinny as a stick' (Nadin 2021: 4) and his chief interest is, as he later sets out, coding, implying he is more 'geek' than 'jock': 'I like code. Because you don't have to be a Chosen One or have superpowers like e.g. melting death rays to work it out. You just need patience and concentration' (2021: 21). On top of that, this was to be a narrative in which the very concept of 'leaders' is refuted, a narrative in which collective action rather than a hero, in the Joseph Campbell[2] mould, might begin to save the world.

What I needed, then, was for readers to invest in the authority of Alan's narrative, despite his age and character. In part, this relies on *logos* appeals, which will be discussed in the next section, but in *ethos* terms, in this opening salvo, he confesses his own ignorance: 'But I didn't know that then' (2021) implying all that was said before was truth, and that the subsequent chapters will be Alan's reveal of this truth. He is also implicitly aligned with another adult 'leader' through the use of Michael Rosen's poem 'Fascism: I sometimes

---

[1] What has become known as the 'superhero stance' is an open pose in which the speaker stands with legs apart, chest out head up, effectively taking up more space. This open stance, famously adopted by several Conservative politicians in the 2010s, has been shown to convey a sense of power to onlookers as well as imbue the person in the stance with enhanced confidence (Carney, Cuddy and Yap 2010).

[2] Joseph Campbell, an American professor in comparative mythology, set out a twelve-stage structure of myth – 'the hero's journey' – that has become a 'how to' narrative template for myriad Global North novelists and screenwriters, and not just those dealing in myth and fantasy. It has recently been called out for its false suggestion that a single figure can 'save the world', most notably by writer and activist Toby Litt in connection to the climate crisis.

fear ... ' as an extended epigraph on page vii of the book. Rosen is a figure who is recognizable to many young readers (and their parents); he is both well-loved and renowned for speaking truth to power (British Library 2023). As such, my relief when Rosen kindly agreed to this usage was palpable. Alan further aligns himself with Rosen by riffing on his line 'Fascism arrives as your friend' (2021: vii) with his version replacing fascism with 'villains': 'They come in pretending to be your friend' (2015: 3).

This point also illustrates how I began to set Alan up as 'one of us', that is, a child the reader might recognize from class or even in themselves. 'Fascism', a term that may not be recognized by primary-age children, is replaced with 'villains', which almost certainly will. Alan also refers to himself being dressed in a 'T-shirt' and 'just a kid' (2021: 4), further aligning himself with the readers. Later he name-drops Marvel characters and the Batmobile (2021: 24) and reveals a penchant for Coco Pops (2021: 30), all recognizable, real products designed to frame Alan as 'like me' in the mind of the reader.

However, the 'who' of it – ensuring that Alan himself was 'like me' and trustworthy – is only part of the labour of rhetoric. The 'what' and 'why' of it was the next step, as I began to shape a story that would appeal not just to *ethos* – our instinct on character – but to the logical and emotional parts of the brain. And it is in these proofs of *logos* and *pathos* that we can really see rhetoric flex its (bulging) muscles.

Logos: Articulating a Believable Argument

Ask me my three main priorities for government and I tell you: education, education, and education.

–Tony Blair, *Leader's Speech*, 1996

The message of then-Labour leader Tony Blair's speech to the party conference in Blackpool in 1996 could hardly have been clearer. This pithy statement, which became, arguably, *the* soundbite of the Blair campaign, was followed by a biographical appeal to *ethos* – 'who' – and the 'why' of the argument:

I sometimes sit reading a newspaper, watching TV, and you look up and you see your children at a computer, and you marvel at what they can do, using that computer as easily as we would read a book. Yet we are 35th in the world league of education standards today – 35th. They say give me the boy at seven, I'll show you the man at 70. Well give me the education system that is 35th in the world today and I will give you the economy that is 35th in the world tomorrow.

(Blair 1996)

Then came the meat: the list of what Labour would do to change things: '[R]adical improvement and reform for our children; a teaching profession trained, able to stand alongside the best in the world and valued as such. No to Tory nursery vouchers, yes to proper nursery places for all our children .... Continual assessment, targets set, instant action where they are not met' (Blair 1996).

Blair's short, punctuated sentences combine plain speaking with passion. But it is the devices behind this that are where the real power lies. These 'invisible' tricks are what help make his argument appear logical, appear truthful. As Lancaster points out, while we may believe that you cannot judge a book by its cover, to our racing brains it is only appearance that matters. 'The logical brain does not have time to pause, scrutinize and test every piece of information that comes its way, weighing it up for truth and veracity; instead what it does is look for patterns .... That sounds right, so it probably is right. That sounds balanced, so it probably is balanced' (Lancaster 2015: 13). And by 'patterns', in speechwriting we simply mean repetition.

So in 'education, education and education', Blair uses repetition in the form of both *epizeuxis* (the repetition of a single word multiple times) and *tricolon*. He uses *tricolon* again: 'Continual assessment, targets set, instant action'. He uses *antithesis* (the juxtaposition of contrasting ideas in balanced phrases or sentences): 'No to Tory nursery vouchers, yes to proper nursery places for all our children'. Later he uses *anaphora*, a technique that repeats phrases at the start of successive sentences, declaring 'I vow that' a total of ten times in a row. He uses *diacope*, with another vow that evolved into the much-vaunted 'tough on crime, tough on the causes of crime' (Blair 1996). These repeats, these rhythms, all work on the audience's logical brains to convince them that what he's saying sounds right; ergo, it *is* right.

Alan isn't trying to get readers, or anyone in the novel itself, to vote for him; his is a longer game: to persuade readers that populism is dangerous, so that by the time they do come of voting age, this idea has been seeded. But his voice is still littered with these devices that help me convince the reader that what he's spelling out explicitly in the opening and less so in the subsequent narrative – fascism is bad, but sometimes villains are hard to spot – is logical and therefore true.

Tricolon

We remain the wealthiest, the most powerful, the most respected nation on earth.

– Barack Obama, Presidential Farewell Address 2017

'Three', sang De La Soul, 'is the magic number'. And how. 'When we present arguments in threes', says a playful Lancaster, 'it creates the illusion of completeness, certainty and conviction' (2015: 21). He goes on, explaining that one fewer lacks impact, any more risks sounding 'overegged, unbalanced, hyperbolic and even a little bit bonkers' (2015). Speech also, I know from my own political days, becomes less memorable the more items or ideas are added. So, as well as writing in threes, I would always urge my ministers to focus on three key 'take-aways' and three only.

In political speeches, we hear threes consistently, from Blair's 'education, education, education' Leader's Speech in 1996 to his 2001 version, in which he painted Osama Bin Laden as 'supported, shielded and given succour by the Taliban regime'; from Barack Obama's speech at Nelson Mandela's memorial: 'when the night grows dark, when injustice weighs heavy on our hearts, when our best-laid plans seem beyond our reach' (2013), to his pithier Presidential Farewell, quoted above, which ends with the catchphrase 'Yes, We Can' (2017), harking back to his time on the campaign trail.

Threes abound in advertising ('Beanz Meanz Heinz', 'A Mars a day helps you work, rest and play', Rice Krispies: 'Snap, crackle and pop') as well as in films (*The Good, the Bad and the Ugly*; *Tora! Tora! Tora!*; *Everything, Everywhere, All At Once*), fairy tales (three wishes, three bears, three little pigs) and elsewhere in fiction, including in *No Man's Land*, in which there are roughly 125 instances of 'threes' in just 262 pages. For example, there are myriad occurrences in the opening chapter quoted above: 'wore fancy outfits and flexed bulging muscles and had special powers', 'wile and wits and kindness', 'skinny as a stick and dressed in a T-shirt and just a kid' (Nadin 2021: 3–4). Later, the fascistic political movement is the 'AAA' or 'Albion-America Alliance' (2021: 15), and Sam's volley of questions comes in triplicate: 'Is it holiday? Is it Benidorm? Will I be sick?' (2021: 35). Longer lists, too, tend to threes, though these may be harder, at first, to spot: 'And he shut himself in the airing cupboard for half an hour, and went to school in wellies and did a wee in the bath, all for a game' (2021: 34). Visibility, though, isn't the point; our brains still unwittingly detect that rhythm and ascribe to it a rightness that in turn suggests truth.

Diacope, Isocolon and Antithesis

The world thanks you for sharing Nelson Mandela with us. His struggle was your struggle. His triumph was your triumph.

– Barack Obama, *Speech at the Memorial of Nelson Mandela* 2013

While they may not have the 'completeness' of threes, couplets do have some impact, at least when used cleverly, for example, in the form of diacope, isocolon or antithesis. So, alongside all the threes, we can also see the power of two in Obama's speech above and in Blair's 'No to Tory nursery vouchers, yes to proper nursery places for all our children' (1996). In the opening to *No Man's Land*, Alan points out that 'not all heroes wear capes. And not all heroes carry guns' (Nadin 2021: 3). Later, he paints the tension in his classroom with 'No one moved a muscle. No one said a word' (2021: 12). Both of these examples from the novel use anaphora as well, employing the same phrases at their outset, creating another satisfying repetitive effect that makes our brains 'see' rightness.

Anaphora and Epistrophe

If Margaret Thatcher wins on Thursday:

I warn you not to be ordinary.
I warn you not to be young.
I warn you not to fall ill.
I warn you not to get old.

– Neil Kinnock, Campaign Speech, 1983

In 1983, the Labour Party under Michael Foot was in disarray, its general election manifesto famously described by one of its own MPs, Gerald Kaufman, as the 'longest suicide note in history' (Bates 2017). But not everyone had given up. Two days before polling, then-MP for Bedwellty Neil Kinnock addressed supporters in Glamorgan. 'I warn you', he told them. 'I warn you that you will have pain, when healing and relief depend on payment' (Kellner 1992: 7–8). He went on to repeat that phrase, 'I warn you' a further nine times at the head of lengthy sentences, even before the fourfold appeal quoted at the opening of this section. Labour lost the election, but four months later Kinnock was elected party leader, and that speech has, rightly, become celebrated among party members and rhetoricians alike, including me.

Deliberately following Kinnock's lead, I used *anaphora* extensively in my political writing and continue to do so in fiction. In addition to the instances mentioned in the previous section, *anaphora* is used in the opening chapter of *No Man's Land* with a repeat of the phrase 'It turns out' (Nadin 2021: 3). It's used again on page 32 with a triple repeat of 'If I'd known' (which is also, thus, a *tricolon*). Two of those three repeats also end in the phrase 'begged [X] to let me stay', a sister technique known as *epistrophe* (the repetition of phrases at the end of successive sentences or clauses), and the combination of which is known as *symploce*. As I write this, I regret not lifting and riffing on Kinnock's 'I warn you', replacing Thatcher with Trump and Farage. I will endeavour, instead, to work it into the follow-up novel, which will take a similarly dystopian setting but pit climate crisis rather than fascism as the antagonist that children must battle.

Alliteration

There is an oft-quoted 'rule' for writers that we should 'always avoid alliteration' (the repetition of letters or syllables at the beginning of successive words), presumably on the grounds that, as a rhetorical trick, it's a bit 'obvious' or even 'basic'. As a speechwriter, I tended to obey the rule on the grounds that I didn't need it, relying instead on *assonance*, which I discuss below. As a writer for children, I dismiss it as piffle, knowing, as I do, that young readers consciously revel in and even seek out these 'right' patterns, whether that's the repetition already mentioned; the rhyme to be found in Donaldson's picture books like *The Gruffalo* (1999), *The Snail and the Whale* (2003) and *Stick Man* (2008); or even, yes, *alliteration*, which is why *No Man's Land* indulges in the trick.

In the opening we have 'flight or flames', 'babies out of burning buildings' and 'skinny as a stick' (Nadin 2021: 3–4). Later we have the 'Albion-America Alliance' (2021: 15); the word 'Resistance' feels 'dangerous and dirty' (2021: 17); the river is 'sleepy and still' (2021: 197); and in the bunker, at the climax, time feels 'stretched out and strange' (2021: 254).

All this said, building again on my political experience, it is *assonance* that really sings in this text, appearing more often even than threes, with instances on almost every page.

Assonance

And those who hope that the Negro needed to blow off steam.

– 'I Have a Dream', Martin Luther King, 1963

Martin Luther King's 1963 speech at the National Mall on the March for Jobs and Freedom is remembered largely for the repeated motif 'I have a dream' Inevitably, though, there are other rhetorical 'repeats' to be seen, including the assonance in the above passage that allies 'those' with 'hope' and 'Negro', as well as 'needed' with 'steam'

In political writing and in all my fiction, along with threes, this is my go-to trick – in fact I use it instinctively now in almost every spoken as well as written sentence, regardless of audience. What appeals is that it is so discreet as to be almost invisible to the eye and ear, unlike, perhaps, alliteration, but as ever there is a quiet 'rightness' to it that the brain registers anyway. So in the opening chapter of No Man's Land, we can see 'wore' matched with 'uniforms' and 'fought'; we can see 'tricked' matched with 'thinking'; we can see 'fight' matched with 'wile' and 'kindness' (although it pains me on rereading that 'wits' interrupts this instance) (Nadin 2021: 3–4). As I reread now, I can spot usage on almost every page, but some favourites would be: 'the stink of his pits' (2021: 241); 'Modern things. Proper things' (2021: 185); and 'mutters and muffled hushing' (2021: 255).

Others

There are other useful repetitive devices – *consonance* (the repetition of consonant sounds in two or more successive words), *anadiplosis* (in which the last clause of one sentence is repeated at the head of the next), *ploce* (a general term for the repetition of a word), for example. But here I want to move on, as Alan's narrative depends on more than sounding 'right'. As I mentioned earlier, facts – or the appearance of facts – don't win an argument anymore. Luckily, there is more to the devices of repetition set out in this section. On top of suggesting that what is being said is logical, and therefore true, the more obvious ones also 'move' us; they work on our emotional brain, tripping the wires that release a cocktail of chemicals, and appealing to our *pathos*.

Pathos: Moving the Reader

Pathos is the reason I pursued a career in politics. Unlike my devoted colleagues in the Millbank policy unit, the 'what' and 'how' of change, beyond knowing it came from Labour, didn't really interest me at that point. What I was passionate about, though, was conveying that change in such a way that it moved people.

This epiphany occurred during my postgraduate study, after a screening of documentary maker Jeffrey Tuchman's 1992 short *The Man from Hope*, a promotional TV film introducing Bill Clinton to the voting public. I left the lecture theatre in tears, convinced he was the solution to America's ills, wishing I wasn't British and could vote for him, and convinced too that this was what I wanted to do: to move voters in such a way that they would vote in a specific way. Crucially, I knew, from this singular experience, that achieving that went beyond logic, and into the realms of cultivating strong emotion. Back then, my sense was instinctive. Now I know that specific characters, sentences and scenes click certain neurotransmitters in our brains, releasing an addictive cocktail of chemicals: oxytocin and serotonin, cortisol and adrenaline, and dopamine.

Oxytocin and Serotonin

Oxytocin – the 'love' drug – is produced when we identify with whoever is speaking or being depicted (Lancaster 2015: 125). So, by making Alan likeable, by making him 'one of us' from the very first page, I should have tripped that chemical wire already. Specific words and phrases can also produce oxytocin, as well as serotonin, a 'happy' drug. 'Me', 'you', 'your', 'us' and 'our' are all what Lancaster calls 'word bombs' or 'shortcuts to emotions' (2015: 154–5), along with 'great' and 'love'. In the opening chapter, Alan slides from first into second person, using 'you' and 'your' three times in quick succession, 'pretending to be your friend and promising you stuff so you're tricked into thinking' (Nadin 2021: 3). I believe that 'home' is another 'word bomb', and it is no coincidence that this is the final word of the novel: 'And this, now, is home' (2021: 263).

Cortisol and Adrenaline

Cortisol and adrenaline are the 'stress' hormones, produced in moments of danger or dilemma. While many of us actively avoid these in 'real life', in the 'safety' of fiction they can be addictive. So, I place Alan in danger, for example, when he has to steal back his phone (Nadin 2021: 186) and then goes on the run with Sam (2021: 190), and later, when he goes into hiding in the bunker (2021: 253). I also give him dilemmas, for example, when he has to decide whether or not to let Noah tattoo him (2021: 160) and then whether or not to agree to Paris's demands to take her with him (2021: 252).

Dopamine

I have a dream that one day on the red hills of Georgia the sons of former slaves and the sons of former slave owners will be able to sit down together at the table of brotherhood. I have a dream that one day even the state of Mississippi, a state sweltering with the heat of injustice, sweltering with the heat of oppression, will be transformed into an oasis of freedom and justice. I have a dream that my four little children will one day live in a nation where they will not be judged by the color of their skin, but by the content of their character. I have a dream.

– 'I Have a Dream', Martin Luther King, 1963

Dopamine – another 'happy' drug – is what's triggered through repetition, chemically rewarding the astute listener or reader who can begin to predict its appearance (Lancaster 2015: 38). That is a large part of the power of Martin Luther King's 'I have a dream' speech, with its repeating motif that, after a while, provides a hit every time we hear it (2015: 19). This is all the more impressive when you discover that this section of King's speech was entirely unscripted; he was riffing on old material following a call-out from gospel singer Mahalia Jackson to 'Tell 'em about the dream, Martin' (Collins 2017: 275). King, a Baptist minister, knew that this kind of repetition could sway a congregation. So too, as discussed earlier, did Kinnock with his bleaker 'I warn you'. My aims are less urgent (and impressive) but just as deliberate: dopamine is what I am trying to provoke with every instance of *anaphora* in *No Man's Land*.

Dopamine is also what we're chasing when we hope for – indeed expect – what has become known as a 'Hollywood ending' to a film or novel: that neat resolution and pay-off to the three- or five-act structure (Lancaster 2015: 125). In politics, this can be complicated by the desire to avoid the kind of Aristotelian catharsis that moves us emotionally, but in such a colossal purge that we don't feel any further need for action. As a former Brecht devotee,[3] hoping to – albeit in the distant future – move readers to fight fascism, knew I had to avoid this purge while also giving readers enough of what they wanted to avoid dissatisfaction with the novel itself. So, while Alan and his family are safe, allowing the reader to feel that brief hit of relief, his friends are not safe – Noah is missing, Paris is left behind, Maggie's wife Laura is still imprisoned – and the world is not safe:

---

[3]Twentieth-century German dramaturg Bertolt Brecht, in an anti-Aristotelian move, sought to avoid his audience's identification with the narrative and their eventual catharsis using a technique that became known as the 'alienation effect' (Willett (ed.) 1978: 78).

I don't know if the world will go back to how it was before war, before Albion, even. I don't know if I'll see Ahmed again or Mrs King or anyone from then.

But if we don't, then it wouldn't be the end of the world.

Because that's just it. War is still raging – we can hear the guns sometimes, over in Plym Mouth: Albion firing at Europe over the water; them firing back – but the world is still going. It's coping, somehow.

(Nadin 2021: 262)

There is no neat resolution here; this fictional world is not saved by a singular hero, especially not a now-eleven-year-old boy. But there is palpable hope. Like Almond, I am proud to be a 'hope hunter' and believe that middle-grade books, while they can lead readers into the darkest of rooms, must also show them the chink of light that might lead to escape. Here, that chink of light, that hope comes in the form of collective action, which is building a new 'way to live' in this fractured world: 'Because all of them believe, like we do, that we're better together' (2021: 262). Through this, I am suggesting that, perhaps, collective action in the real world might prevent us ever getting to this point at all.

Conclusion

So, has it worked? Does the abundant use of rhetoric in *No Man's Land* mean we might see this collective action in the future? That the world might, actually, be saved?

Without the immediate and clear evidence offered by a polling booth, it is, of course, impossible to say. The influence, though, is clear, and, I believe, relevant. Speechwriters learn from story-makers – along with Simon Lancaster, I have taught the use of fairy tales to Whitehall staff as a way to connect their ministers to an audience's collective memory – and we story-makers can learn from speech in return. There are ways to lift our prose and move our readers that go beyond plot and character and can serve a purpose beyond pure entertainment. There are some that might question the legitimacy of this – as I have mentioned before, rhetoric is habitually dismissed at best as 'spin', at worst as cynical manipulation – and these are children we are 'manipulating', of course. But is it cynical? Rhetoric is everywhere, after all, and I believe *No Man's Land* is not a book with a sinister agenda. It is a book that encourages empathy and tolerance (indeed, it was included in the 2023 Empathy Lab collection, which promotes books that cultivate empathy in young readers). It is a book, despite its bleak narrative, about the best of humanity. It is also a book that gave me a voice at a point in my political life when I felt voiceless and hope when I felt hopeless. If it can inspire even just a handful of readers, its means are more than justified.

Works Cited

Aristotle (2018), *The Art of Rhetoric*, Oxford: Oxford University Press.

Bates, S. (2017), 'Sir Gerald Kaufman Obituary', *The Guardian*. Available online: https://www.theguardian.com/politics/2017/feb/27/sir-gerald-kaufman-obituary (accessed 10 October 2023).

Blair, T. (1996), *Leader's Speech*. Available online: http://www.britishpoliticalspeech.org/speech-archive.htm?speech=202 (accessed 10 October 2023).

Blair, T. (2001), *Leader's Speech*. Available online: https://www.theguardian.com/politics/2001/oct/02/labourconference.labour6 (accessed 10 October 2023).

British Library (2023), *The PEN Pinter Prize 2023: Michael Rosen*. Available online: https://www.bl.uk/events/the-pen-pinter-prize-2023-michael-rosen (accessed 12 October 2023).

Carney, D., Cuddy, A. and Yapp, A. (2010), 'Power Posing: Brief Nonverbal Displays Affect Endocrine Levels and Risk Aversion', *Psychological Science*, 21:10, 1363–8. Available online: https://pubmed.ncbi.nlm.nih.gov/20855902/ (accessed 12 October 2023).

Collins, P. (2017), *When They Go Low, We Go High: Speeches that Shape the World – And Why We Need Them*, London: 4th Estate.

Kellner, P. (1992), *Thorns and Roses: Speeches of Neil Kinnock 1983–1991*, London: Radius.

Kubin, E., Puryear, C., Schein, C. and Gray, K. (2021), 'Personal Experiences Bridge Moral and Political Divides Better than Facts', *PNAS*, 118:6. Available online https://www.pnas.org/doi/10.1073/pnas.2008389118 (accessed 12 October 2023).

Lancaster, S. (2015), *Winning Minds: Secrets from the Language of Leadership*, New York: Palgrave Macmillan.

Leith, S. (2012), *You Talkin' to Me? Rhetoric from Aristotle to Obama*, London: Profile Books.

Nadin, J. (2021), *No Man's Land*, Preston: UCLan.

Obama, B. (2013), *Speech at the Memorial of Nelson Mandela*. Available online: https://obamawhitehouse.archives.gov/the-press-office/2013/12/10/remarks-president-obama-memorial-service-former-south-african-president- (accessed 10 October 2023).

Obama, B. (2017), *Farewell Address*. Available online: https://obamawhitehouse.archives.gov/farewell#:~:text=Let%20me%20tell%20you%2C%20this,fear%20but%20something%20to%20embrace (accessed 10 October 2023).

Rosen, M. (2015), 'Fascism: I Sometimes Fear ... ', in *Don't Mention the Children*, Ripon: Smokestack Books. Available online: https://smokestack-books.co.uk/book.php?book=110 (accessed 11 April 2025).

Willett, J. (1978), *Brecht on Theatre*, London: Methuen.

6

On the Genealogy of Memoirs

Influence, Revenge and Ressentiment

By Jonathan Taylor

Tout comprendre, c'est tout pardonner .... To understand is to forgive. Or maybe not.

– Blake Morrison, *As If* (1997: 239)

1

In my second memoir, *A Physical Education: On Bullying, Discipline and Other Lessons* (2024), I set out to write about the uses and abuses of power in education, interweaving my own experiences with literary criticism, sociology and philosophy. One of the first things I wrote for the book was this scene:

> It's January 1985. I'm eleven. We're lined up on the school football pitch, ankle-deep in slushy brown snow. It's -2 degrees and raining ice .... We're shivering in shorts, white t-shirts ... and football boots with studs in. I've got plastic studs on my boots, but others like Danny Beaker – who ... is a good foot taller than me – have got metal spikes. There are a couple of punctures in the tops of my football boots from ... when Danny stamped on them ....

[The teacher] ... inevitably [chooses] ... the giant Danny Beaker as captain of one team, a second Godzilla-like boy as captain of the other. They take turns to nominate who they want on their teams. I'm ... last .... Godzilla II ... doesn't even bother to call my name, merely rolls his eyes .... He slouches over to the centre spot ... and waits for Sir to blow the whistle. Godzilla II's holding his balls, jiggling on the spot, ... his vaporous speech bubble presumably saying: *Get on with it, sir, before these freeze off.*

Sir's rather allegorical name is Mr Yorwin. He's dressed in a brown sheepskin knee-length coat, woolly tracksuit bottoms, and is smoking a cigarette .... 'Taylor,' he grunts out of the side of his mouth, 'get your arse in gear' ....

I jog over to him: 'Sir, please, can't we wear ... ?' But he cuts me off.

'Don't be a poof, Taylor. You don't need yer tracksuits. You'll warm up on the pitch if you play proper' ....

Mr Yorwin blows his whistle. Danny Beaker is immediately thundering down the pitch ... towards me. I ... can't decide which way to jump, to get out of his way. In the end, indecision wins the day, and I stay put. He dribbles the ball round me, round half a dozen other half-hearted defenders, and scores the first of the afternoon's seventeen goals ....

Meanwhile, Mr Yorwin has turned his back on us, as if in disgust, and is vacating the field. He's striding towards his shed, where he'll sit smoking for the next half hour or so, ... with the electric fire on. We watch his retreating back enviously, smoky speech bubbles mingling again: *Why the hell are we out here freezing our arses off?*

(2024: 1–3)

Eventually, the game disintegrates because of the cold. All the boys gather round and collectively plan to rebel on Mr Yorwin's return:

By the time Mr Yorwin finally emerges from his shed, and strides back to the pitch, ... we're not even pretending to play – just hugging ourselves, hovering, waiting for him. Only Danny Beaker is away, down one end of the pitch, scoring goals by himself, on auto-pilot ....

Meanwhile, near the centre spot, Mr Yorwin is ... scowling at us, puffing on his cigarette .... 'What?' he asks. 'Why aren't ye lazy gits playing?' ....

Now he's here, in front of us, all too real, no-one is saying anything ....

So I step forwards, shaking, stammering: 'Sir ... it's too c ... c ... cold, *Sir.* Honestly, Sir. We're ... we're *bloody* freezing here. Gonna get ill. I think ... we *all* think we should go in.'

He glowers at me over his cigarette: 'Taylor, did you just swear at me?'

I'm suddenly angry: 'Yes, Sir. But it is *bloody* freezing and we've had enough …. It's not fair. You're a bloody … *tyrant, Sir.*'

He … glares over my head at the others: 'Is this just Taylor's opinion, or do you *all* wanna go inside?'

No-one speaks. Without turning around, I can feel the opposition behind me melting away to slush. There are a few half-hearted mumbles ('Shurrup, Taylor, you'll get us all done in') ….

Mr Yorwin turns back to me. 'So it's just you, Taylor?'

'No it isn't … wasn't,' I say, exasperated. I look around at the others for a moment: 'Tell him.' Some shake their heads, others turn their noses up at me ….

Mr Yorwin flicks away the stub of his cigarette. 'Too cold, my arse. You've got no backbone, Taylor. Spineless, that's your problem' …. He blows on his whistle, waves Danny Beaker over: 'Gimme the ball.' Danny reluctantly … passes it to Mr Yorwin. Mr Yorwin throws it … at me …. 'Your centre kick,' he says, and turns towards his shed. The boys take his place, close in on me: 'Haha,' they snigger, 'no backbone. Spineless. Taylor the Invertebrate.'

The names echo through the remainder of the game and into the changing rooms …. [They] follow me around for the rest of the day, and – off and on – for the next few years.

Sticks and stones may break my bones, but names will never hurt me: everyone knows that old rhyme's a lie …. The names [though] didn't hurt the high-school-me so much as the very idea that *I* was the spineless one …. I … kept trying to explain to the others: 'But, look, *I'm* the one who stood up to Yorwin, … while you Judases shrank away, went back on what you'd said. And yet somehow *I'm* the invertebrate.' It seemed so unfair.

(2024: 5–8)

2

On a miniature scale, that sense of unfairness isn't a million miles away from what Friedrich Nietzsche calls, in *On the Genealogy of Morals*, '*ressentiment*': the envious hatred of the weak for the strong. For Nietzsche, 'the powerless, the oppressed, … suppurate with poisonous and hostile feelings' towards their oppressors, and their 'hatred grows to take on a monstrous and sinister shape, the most cerebral and most poisonous form' ([1887] 1998: 24, 19).

This is the 'vindictive cunning of impotence', which gives rise to 'a truly great policy of revenge, of a far-sighted, subterranean revenge which unfolds itself slowly and thinks ahead' ([1887] 1998: 30, 21). The policy consists of a full-scale 'slave revolt in morals', which 'begins when *ressentiment* itself becomes creative and ordains values: the *ressentiment* of creatures to whom the real reaction, that of the deed, is denied and who find compensation in an imaginary revenge' ([1887] 1998: 22). Ultimately, over two thousand years, the slave revolt is successful, and

> the 'masters' are done away with .... This victory might also be seen as a form of blood-poisoning .... The 'redemption' of humanity (from the 'masters', that is) is proceeding apace; everything is visibly becoming more Jewish or Christian or plebian (what does the terminology matter!).
>
> ([1887] 1998: 21)

Notwithstanding Nietzsche's dubious 'terminology', his model of a slave revolt has its roots in an earlier and more abstract paradigm – namely, G. W. F. Hegel's 'Master and Slave Dialectic', in the *Phenomenology of Spirit*. According to Hegel, the master-slave (or 'lord and bondsman') relationship is inaugurated by a 'life-and-death struggle', in which a stronger 'self-consciousness' overcomes a weaker one ([1807] 1977: 113). The latter is forced to capitulate and is subsequently enslaved. Over time, however, the relationship between master and slave is reversed: through 'work' and 'fear of death', the slave 'acquires a mind of his own', while the master is reduced to a 'servile consciousness':

> Just as lordship showed that its essential nature is the reverse of what it wants to be, so too servitude in its consummation will really turn into the opposite of what it immediately is .... The bondsman realises that it is precisely in his work ... that he acquires a mind of his own ... [and] freedom.
>
> ([1807] 1977: 117–9)

Hegel's and Nietzsche's models share the same teleology or 'consummation', whereby the weaker slave-consciousness eventually inverts the hierarchical relationship with the master. The difference between the two models is in how the consummation is achieved: for Hegel, the slave-consciousness discovers a sense of independence through work and fear; for the more cynical Nietzsche, slave morality wins its long-held grudge-match because of superior cunning, 'the cleverness of the lowest rank, which even insects possess (insects which, in situations of great danger, ... play dead) ... thanks to the forgery ... of impotence' (1998: 30).

3

As a fellow 'invertebrate', I feel a nagging sense of identification with Nietzsche's cunning insects. This sense of identification came into focus while drafting *A Physical Education*, as Hegel's and particularly Nietzsche's models of the master-slave relationship started haunting me.

This often happens: as I approach the end of a first complete draft of something, I gradually become aware of the inspirations, intertexts or 'influences' (to use the word in the broadest sense) that lurk behind it. We tend to think of influence as formative, generative – something that pre-exists 'creation' – and no doubt that is, to some extent, true. But often I become conscious of influence retrospectively, as a secondary phenomenon, as if I'm writing towards it, rather than setting off from it. Influence can be a point of arrival as well as departure. Only when I look back on a draft as an almost-whole do its precursors emerge, uncannily, into consciousness – only then does it become clear to me which pre-existing narratives haunt my own.

Such narratives can be literary, critical or philosophical. It might seem strange to name Hegel's and Nietzsche's philosophies as 'influences' on a memoir. I subscribe, though, to the widest possible idea of influence when it comes to Creative Writing. When we write, I think we're both consciously *and* unconsciously drawing on a near-infinite wealth of pre-existing texts, both in our chosen genre and far beyond it. As Rob Pope suggests,

> for each of us there are many and various communities, traditions and cultures to which we relate .... These span the dead as well as the living, the remotely absent as well as the immediately present. Influences therefore exist on a continuum that, in principle, is intrinsically plural and infinitely open.
>
> (2005: 96)

On this continuum, it would seem arbitrary to separate so-called Creative Writing from other types of texts. So philosophy might indeed influence memoir, for example.

This seems to me even more likely given the 'creative' aspects of Hegel's and Nietzsche's work. Philosophy, in these instances, is also Creative Writing: their descriptions of master-slave relationships are works of creative non-fiction, paradigmatic narratives, for all Hegel's abstract language and Nietzsche's dubious political, religious and ethnic terminology. In this sense, their influence on my memoir is, I think, as much about shared narrative forms, as it is about language – stories haunting stories.

Initially, I wasn't sure quite why their narratives were haunting me – though the answer was obvious, really, once I re-read the draft of my opening chapter. Hegel and Nietzsche are telling philosophical stories about an archetypal power struggle, while I was telling very specific stories about personal bullying. There is, of course, a big difference in scale here. Nietzsche's text, in particular, has a vast historical sweep, covering over two thousand years, while I was writing about my experiences as a British schoolchild in the late 1970s and 1980s. As well as a temporal mismatch of scale, there's also a political one: clearly, I was by no means a slave, in either Hegelian, Nietzschean, or literal terms. I was a relatively privileged, white, middle-class boy, attending a fairly standard comprehensive school in the UK. Invoking Nietzsche's ideas on *ressentiment* and slave revolts, in this context, might seem like bringing to bear a philosophical-sledgehammer on a memoir-walnut.

Having said that, I think the strength of Nietzsche's and Hegel's archetypal stories inheres in their ability to describe very different contexts – to encompass everything from the macro- to microcosmic, everything from chattel slavery to the mundane micro-powers that operate between people in, say, a school or university. As regards Hegel, for instance, I write in the memoir that

> it's not a matter of saying [that] … slave driving, headmastering, bullying, tyrannising … are the same …. [Rather] what Hegel's model allows us to do is to trace commonalities between very different kinds of bully-victim relationships, without equating or comparing them. Hegel's abstract model … points up recurring patterns – … struggles, threats, pacts . . – which are shared by bully-victim relationships, across divergent contexts.
>
> (2024: 35)

If Hegel's model, in this sense, constitutes what might be called a 'trans-contextual' type of knowledge, memoir, by contrast, represents a purely contextual, subjective, empirical knowledge – at least ostensibly, given its micro-focus on personal experience. Both forms are (I believe) valid and complementary means of understanding power relations, and what memoir – and Creative Writing in general – can do is to explore abstract theories in context, observing how macrocosmic ideas work (or break down) on a micro-scale. Creative Writing might be likened to the science experiment which proves, disproves or complicates a hypothesis. Maybe influence works like that sometimes, too: influence is the initial hypothesis which a creative writer experiments on, tests out in (new) practice.

In writing *A Physical Education*, Nietzsche's and Hegel's models emerged as overarching hypotheses, which shared certain territory with my own memoir, if only in a metaphorical sense. I came to recognize that the three very different narratives had things in common – that they echoed each other in subtle and not-so-subtle ways. In light of that recognition, I could then go on to reshape the memoir, so that it both self-consciously echoes and departs from the two pre-existing narratives. I wanted to acknowledge frankly the influence of the Hegelian-Nietzschean models, and to diverge from them. In *The Anxiety of Influence*, Harold Bloom – himself influenced by the philosopher Lucretius – talks of the way poets 'swerve' from their predecessor's models ([1973] 1997: 42); and, in writing my memoir, I felt both the magnetism of the philosophical narratives and the need to swerve away from them. In other words, if influence is sometimes a point of arrival rather than departure, it might equally be an iceberg to swerve round rather than a safe harbour in which to dock.

And not only an iceberg: perhaps influence also works a little like *ressentiment*, such that Creative Writing sometimes represents a 'reaction' against a dominant model or author, a kind of slave revolt or overturning, a moment when the writer swerves away from a domineering predecessor. After all, Bloom names Nietzsche as one of the 'prime influences on [his] ... theory of influence', and *On the Genealogy of Morals* as 'the profoundest study available ... of the revisionary ... strains in the aesthetic temperament' ([1973] 1997: 8).

4

For me, *On the Genealogy of Morals* represented a warning, an iceberg, that I didn't want to hit head-on. I was writing about my own experiences of bullying, so I realized the book was in danger of becoming – or seeming like – a rehearsal of grudges, an exercise in Nietzschean *ressentiment*. It's well known that people who experience childhood bullying often suffer from long-term psychological effects, including resentment and a desire for revenge. As Ellen Walser deLara suggests in her book *Bullying Scars*, 'bullying ... can have serious and lifelong implications', that are not 'left behind at graduation .... Victims can experience lifelong depression, anxiety [and] ... post-traumatic stress disorder' (2016: 112–3).

Having written a whole memoir about bullying, it would be disingenuous of me to deny such 'lifelong implications' on my part, even if I make no claims for a self-diagnosis of post-traumatic stress disorder. The book itself is a sign of the long-term effects of bullying. The challenge I set myself, though, was to write about experiences and effects without (too much of) a sense of *ressentiment* towards the people involved.

As I say, this challenge came into focus as I completed the first through-draft of the opening chapter. The obvious danger was that the chapter might sound bitter, might seem like an act of belated revenge on those concerned – a 'far-sighted, subterranean revenge which unfolds itself slowly', given that the scene is set over thirty-seven years ago. 'Revenge is a motive not often confessed to [in memoir writing]', writes Patti Miller, 'but ... people may feel bitter ... and want to punish those who have hurt them. Such motivations have an unpleasant way of distorting the writing' (2017: 8). It was precisely that sort of distortion I was keen to avoid in my own memoir, as far as possible.

One way of doing this, I decided, was to talk about my motivations openly. It's one of the strengths of the memoir form, as I've discussed elsewhere (see Taylor 2021: 75–91), that the author-narrator can step outside a scene and address its implications directly. This goes for influences as well: once you become aware of them, you can acknowledge them explicitly in a memoir. In *A Physical Education*, I decided to confront my philosophical influences, and the shadows they were casting, in the text itself. Hence, towards the end of the first chapter, I added a short passage disavowing Nietzschean *ressentiment*, in a sort of textual-evasive-manoeuvre. In doing so, I was acutely aware that any such disavowal of bitterness might be taken as a sign of its opposite, as so often happens in everyday conversation (*I'm not bitter, but ...*). Still, for what it's worth, I appended the following disclaimer:

I'm not writing this memoir to sting or bite back Mr Yorwin, ... or my other long-time-ago classmates. I don't want this story to be an exercise in what Friedrich Nietzsche calls '*ressentiment*' – the revenge of the weak ... on the Danny Beakers or Mr Yorwins of the world .... I don't want this to be memoir-as-*ressentiment* .... [Memoir] too readily becomes criticism of people, rather than texts, systems, organisations, which validate certain patterns of behaviour.

(2024: 15)

I do think the memoir form in general is prone to the distortion of *ressentiment*. This is, to some extent, inevitable: feelings of resentment, guilt and loss are intertwined with our memories from the earliest age; and, simply by reconstructing these memories on the page, a memoir is enacting a kind of retrospective revenge on the past, getting one over on it, as it were. 'All writing is revenge', claims Reinaldo Arenas (1999: 118) – and, as many critics have said, the desire for belated revenge is an all-too-common, perhaps (in sublimated form) near-universal, motive in autobiographical writing. Marion Roach Smith, for instance, writes that 'it would be impossible to count up just how many people over the years have come into my [memoir] class hell-bent on writing a revenge tale' (2019: 22). Similarly, William Gass asks: 'Are there any motives for the enterprise that aren't tainted with conceit or a desire for revenge? .... To have written an autobiography is already to have made yourself a monster' (2017).

If I don't wholly agree with Gass in this regard, it's still useful for a writer to be aware of the worst accusations that might be levelled at them – and most memoirists know they are vulnerable to accusations of monstrous egotism, conceit, resentment and vengefulness. In fact, what Gass doesn't acknowledge is that memoirists themselves often use this awareness to help shape and refine their work: working as they do in the most self-conscious of forms, memoirists write in ways that (try to) pre-empt these sorts of criticism. I attempted to do this in a later chapter of *A Physical Education*, where I set out to describe more recent experiences of workplace bullying. Both structure and content of the chapter were affected by an awareness that I might seem to be exacting revenge on my one-time manager (whom I flippantly – or, if you prefer, *bitterly* – call 'Prof. Caligula'). I added this near the start of the chapter:

> It was always my intention ... to write about Prof. Caligula, and what happened to me when she was my boss – to tell the story of the most sustained, vicious bullying I have experienced .... I thought writing about it – years later – might exorcise some professorial ghosts .... I wanted to give a full blow-by-psychological-blow account of my then-manager's behaviour ....
>
> But now ... I've ... gone off the idea. For a number of reasons ....
>
> [These include] the ... feeling that such a description would be rather unedifying .... I never wanted this book to be an act of vengeance on school or workplace bullies ... [though] I am all too aware that revenge on the past, however sublimated or displaced, is a feature of most, if not all, memoirs.
>
> That brings me to the [next] ... uglier reason for not describing my experiences with Prof. Caligula in detail – a reason that no doubt constitutes a contorted, paradoxical form of revenge: the revenge, that is, of omission .... I'd like to respond [to my ex-boss] *à la* Carly Simon: *You're so egocentric, no doubt you expected this chapter to be about you.*
>
> (2024: 165–7)

So even omission can be a form of revenge. *All writing is revenge*: whether conscious or unconscious, explicit or sublimated, monstrous or paradoxical, revenge seems to be an almost-inescapable element of memoirs – even if that revenge is on the past as a whole, rather than a specific individual. It's most patently apparent in the sub-genres of so-called misery memoirs or survivor memoirs, which gained huge popularity in the wake of Dave Pelzer's

A Child Called It (1995), and which typically recount a narrator's process of overcoming an abusive childhood. Such memoirs have a lot in common with Hegel's model, moving as they usually do from a situation of powerlessness, to the authority (*author*-ity) of the present-day memoirist, who now writes or rewrites the past. As Hegel might expect, the memoirist has triumphed over past trauma, and those who inflicted it, through the 'work' of writing. This is what Judith Barrington memorably terms the 'triumphalist imperative' of many memoirs (2002: 58). As G. Thomas Couser notes, a pattern common to many memoirs is 'the rhetoric of triumph, as manifested in the popularity, and thus the prevalence, of narratives of overcoming ... [and] triumph over adversity' (2017: 203).

Of course, there is a difference between, on the one hand, a memoir which charts the narrator's 'triumph over adversity' in general and, on the other, a memoir which is about overcoming human adversaries (for example, abusive parents or bullies). Still, the difference is not quite so wide as it might seem. Felicity James and Julian North suggest that 'life writing [is] ... a dynamic expression of relationship within social networks, ... rather than ... the consecration of individual identity' (2017: 134), and it's clear that, however individualistic a form memoir might appear, all autobiographical writings necessarily involve significant others, alongside the narrator. So all memoirs bear traces of the dynamic relationship between the (first-person) protagonist and antagonists familiar in fiction.

One of those antagonists might be the earlier self of the narrator. Sometimes 'triumph over adversity' means overcoming a *past* self. As is well known, the central 'self' of a memoir is usually divided, whereby the narrator-protagonist looks back on an earlier self, who is both the same *and* different. As Micaela Maftei suggests, 'something like a splitting of selves is required to feature within the [autobiographical] text while constructing it'. Because of 'the passage of time ... the writer writing is not ... the same person who lived the events being described ... encouraging a dissociation between the author of the memoir and the central figure within it' (2013: 59, 67–8). Similarly, James Olney writes that there is often a 'great emotional and intellectual divide [in] ... autobiography, giving an ironic ... distancing to the past' – and this results in a 'kind of ... semi-comic irony, exercised at the expense of a younger self', a 'self-mockery' (1984: 198–9).

I've always considered this self-irony important in memoir as one way of undercutting self-aggrandisement. In writing *A Physical Education*, though, I found there was a balance to be struck: too little irony, and the descriptions of my (unexceptional) experiences of bullying might appear self-indulgent, overblown; too much irony, and I might overly distance the events described, draining them of any emotion apart from humour – to the point that I might seem to be turning bullying into a joke, which it certainly is not. In other words, I couldn't use irony to 'triumph' over past events *too* much, in case the adult perspective drowned out the child's. Somehow, the challenge was to balance irony with immersiveness, my adult's perspective – and concomitant awareness that my childhood experiences were 'relatively tame' – with the child's-eye view. I addressed this issue in a couple of places in the memoir:

> Nothing is relativistic to a child – who, for the most part, lacks points of comparison beyond their own perspective – and it's all too easy ... to forget how intensely children feel .... These experiences might seem trivial in hindsight. Yet adults often ... forget or repress their own childhood terrors, ... patronising their own younger [selves]: ... *Why on Earth did that upset me so much back then? It all seems so trivial, laughable.*
>
> (2024: 46, 142–3)

In my memoir, I didn't want to patronize my younger self too much, and I didn't want to stage the linear, quasi-Hegelian narrative of triumph over adversity, so much as the coexistence and intermingling of the two. After all, as I point out, 'it was as a grown-up, in the workplace rather than school, that I had my worst experience of bullying' (2024: 46). So any kind of straightforward teleology, whereby my adult self-patronizes, takes revenge on, or triumphs over, my younger self, wasn't really possible for me anyway. The 'triumphalist imperative' wasn't an option.

5

Intra-personal, interpersonal and intergenerational forms of revenge are all features of one of the founding texts of the memoir genre, Edmund Gosse's *Father and Son*. I want to talk in detail about Gosse's memoir because it seems to establish common narrative patterns in memoirs, which memoirists since have both assimilated and subverted. Both assimilation and subversion are, of course, types of influence: as Bloom suggests, to take on a pre-existing narrative pattern and subvert it is as much a matter of influence as simply echoing it.

The narrative pattern of *Father and Son* has become familiar to readers, if only through its many imitators. It is cast as a 'spiritual struggle' ([1907] 2004: 4) between an overbearingly religious father and oppressed son. By the end of the book, the narrator has gained independence from his domineering father and the latter's religion – just as Hegel's slave eventually gains independence from the master. As Gosse writes of himself (here in third person):

> No compromise ... was offered; no ... truce would have been acceptable. It was a case of 'Everyth ng or Nothing'; and thus desperately challenged, conscience threw off once [and] for all the *yoke* of his 'dedication', and .. he took a human being's privilege to fashion his inner life for himself.
>
> ([1907] 2004: 186: my italics)

In throwing off the *'yoke'* of his dedication to his father's religion, Gosse is clearly also throwing off the yoke of filial slavery.

If there is a Hegelian undercurrent to this narrative, there is also an Oedipal one. I've discussed this elsewhere (see, for example, Taylor 2019: 7, 126–39), as have many other critics. Deborah Nord, for example, suggests that the father-son struggle in Gosse's memoir echoes the work of 'many [earlier] Victorian autobiographers', which stage 'what would later come to be understood as Oedipal struggles' (2014: 87). Something similar might be said of Nietzsche's and Hegel's narratives – namely, that the struggles they describe between masters and slaves are implicitly Oedipal. And conversely, the Oedipal struggles described by modern psychoanalysis bear traces of Hegelian and Nietzschean narratives of power.

For psychoanalyst Jacques Lacan, both the master-slave relationship and the Oedipal struggle are 'pregnant with ... cunning tricks (*ruses*)' (1977: 308). While, for Hegel, the slave gains independence through work, for Nietzsche and Lacan, the son-slave undermines his subjugation through trickery. Both methods of subverting hierarchy co-exist in Gosse's memoir. On the one hand, Gosse sounds rather Hegelian (and Victorian) when he claims that his later work as a young writer provides him with a feeling of independence: 'I was gaining the reliance upon self ... which come[s] naturally to a young man ... who earns his own living and lives his own life' (2004: 183). There's a definite sense towards the end of *Father and Son* that Gosse junior's independence is something *earned* through hard work.

On the other hand, there is also a different, subtler model of independence threaded throughout the narrative – one based on trickery, ruses, laughter. Whatever he claims later on, Gosse doesn't just work his way out of spiritual dependence; he also continually undermines it from within, using tricks, deception, even dirty jokes. Some of these are his own 'subterfuges', his own 'hypocritical ingenuity in drawing [his] ... Father's attention away' from the 'terrible subject' of religion; some of the tricks are concocted in 'covert collusion' (2004: 181–2) with his stepmother. As Freud and Lacan might predict, there is an Oedipal complicity between stepmother and son, that undermines paternal authority. The stepmother is seen to 'aid and abet' the son's schemes, 'producing incongruous themes, likely to attract ... Father aside', from his sermonizing, 'with a skill worthy of a parlour conjurer' (2004: 181).

Conjuring tricks, covert collusion, subterfuges – these all stand in the stead of direct confrontation. While still a child under the legal protection of his father, Gosse junior feels he can't rebel openly, so he sees trickery as his only option: 'the dilemma was now before me', he claims, 'that I must either deceive my Father in such things or paralyse my own character .... I was docile, ... I was anything but combative; if [only] my Father could have persuaded himself to let me alone, ... to leave my subterfuges ... unanalysed' (2004: 177–82). This is Nietzschean *ressentiment* – non-combative, docile, deceptive: 'the *ressentiment* of creatures to whom the real reaction, that of the deed, is denied and who find compensation in an imaginary revenge'.

My own memoir, too, includes instances of trickery, where the weak exercise a non-combative revenge on the powerful – specifically, where pupils play tricks on bullies or teachers. While I myself was, by and large, too terrified for subterfuge, I was surrounded by other children who did try and subvert – at least temporarily – the teachers' authority, and what I call 'the rule of the cane' (2024: 115). The relationship between teachers and pupils is 'pregnant with ... cunning tricks (*ruses*)', even when teacherly authority is upheld by brute force, as it was in the 1970s and early 1980s. In one chapter, for example, I describe how a friend I call 'Carrot Hair' undermines a teacher's authority with a 'big lesson-destroying hoax' (2024: 96). He pretends that there's a thread unravelling his school jumper, and asks the myopic Mr Trog to cut it:

Mr Trog['s] ... concentration is fully focussed on the non-existent thread. He tries again and again with the scissors – snip, snip, snip – each time, leaning in closer, squinting through his thick glasses .... 'I can't seem to get it,' he says, exasperated ....

'No good,' says Carrot Hair. 'I'm doomed, sir. My mother's going to belt me one.'

Mr Trog ... glances up at the class: 'Can anyone else help us?'

A couple of big boys ... step forwards: ... 'Anything to help a mate out, Sir.' Elsewhere in the classroom, ... one girl shouts out helpful advice, while Mr Trog snips again at the thread: 'You're missing by a mile, Sir! .... Up a bit! Warmer! Colder! Oh, you're dead hot, Sir!' The whole lesson is collapsing around us – which, of course, is the aim of the enterprise ....

The two volunteers take turns with Mr Trog's scissors .... 'Oh dear, Sir, missed it,' says one ... now snipping Mr Trog's notes by mistake – now trying to snip his tie: 'Oops, sorry, Sir.'

(2024: 94–5)

There are various carnivalesque moments like this dotted throughout my memoir, where a Mr Trog's disciplinary power is challenged, or temporarily overturned, through trickery, and it struck me, while writing *A Physical Education*, how common such moments are in autobiographical narratives in general. No doubt this is partly because autobiographies and memoirs so often involve 'narratives of overcoming', where an initially weak narrator (such as a disempowered child) attempts to gain some kind of independence, a modicum of power – and feels that the only way to do so, at least at first, is by resorting to trickery.

6

Something similar might be said of an earlier genre of autobiographical writing – namely, the nineteenth-century slave narrative, where narrators often use trickery to survive slavery. Slave narratives are simultaneously Hegelian – in that they typically chart the protagonist's emancipation from the master-slave relationship through violence, escape and work – and Nietzschean, given that they also celebrate moments of subversion, subterfuge and trickery. As Harriet Jacobs writes in her *Incidents in the Life of a Slave Girl*: 'Who can blame slaves for being cunning? They are constantly compelled to resort to it. It is the only weapon of the weak and oppressed against the strength of their tyrants' ([1861] 2016: 88). There are 'numerous similar slave narratives', Mikko Tuhkanen points out, 'that show the necessity for, and even celebrate, trickery and dissemblance' (2009: 93).

This means that the slave narrative has a lot in common with another narrative form, which was prevalent among antebellum slaves: the trickster tale. As Peter Dorsey suggests, 'The slave narrative depicts the successful journey from slavery to freedom', and this narrative arc is often 'modelled on the "trickster tale"' (1993: 75). 'In [such] ... folk-tales', John Blassingame writes,

the slave gave full play to his wish fulfilment ... especially in those involving animals. Identifying with the frightened and helpless creatures, so similar in their relations to the larger animals to the relationship of the slave to the master, the slave storytellers showed how the weak could survive.

> Especially in the Brer Rabbit tales, the hero ... always defeated the larger animals through cunning.
>
> (1979: 24)

Likewise, James C. Scott argues that, 'within ... [the] veiled context' of the trickster tale, 'the slave could identify with the protagonist, who managed to outwit ... his more powerful enemy .... Identifying with Brer Rabbit, the slave child learned ... that ... success depended on ... deception and cunning' (1990: 164).

In many different incarnations, the trickster tale has a very long history, from Aesop, to picaresque narratives, to Brer Rabbit folk tales, to Chaplin movies, Tom and Jerry cartoons, and British sitcoms like *Porridge*. Maybe even Nietzsche's *On the Genealogy of Morals* might be read as a strange philosophical offshoot of the trickster tale. Through writing *A Physical Education*, I've come to think this wider tradition might also encompass, or inform autobiographical writings – from slave narratives to modern memoirs. The trickster tale tradition is a cultural strain from which the modern memoir developed, via the slave narrative.

To put this another way: a genre's prehistory, it seems to me, represents a kind of collective unconscious you draw on – and are influenced by – when you choose to write in that form. Hence, I believe that in writing my memoir, I was indirectly influenced by the trickster tale without necessarily being aware of it at the time: again, influence comes into consciousness in retrospect.

7

Actually, I think *retrospect* is the number one trick played by memoir: the modern memoir form is trickster-tale-plus-time. The disempowered narrator wins out eventually through patience, through a waiting game, through the trick of 'playing dead' (Nietzsche 1998: 30) over long periods. 'The man of *ressentiment*', writes Nietzsche, 'has a perfect understanding of how to keep silent, how not to forget, how to wait', developing – as has been seen – 'the secret black art of a truly great policy of revenge, of a far-sighted, subterranean revenge which unfolds itself slowly and thinks ahead' (1998: 24, 21). This is the far-sighted, black art of memoir-writing. Gosse junior claims he was 'anything but combative' during his childhood, but the writing of the memoir itself, many years later, stands retrospectively in place of that combativeness. It is 'compensation' for 'the real reaction', at the time, 'that of the deed'. Likewise, in writing a memoir about bullying, I am potentially responding to *physical* violence decades later with *verbal* violence.

This belated verbal violence is the ruse of memoir: it bides its time, waits till the antagonist is unable to respond physically, being too old or faraway or, for that matter, dead. Blake Morrison implies as much in his recent memoir, *Two Sisters*, where he suggests that 'You can't write an honest memoir when the subject is alive. At any rate I can't. Death is the only permission' (2023: 7). As Ian Jack bluntly puts it: 'To be frank, it helps [in memoir] if the subject is dead' (2006: 11). In more theoretical terms, Lacan suggests that the slave wins out eventually when he 'finds his alibi in the death of the Master. But what about this death? He quite simply waits for it' (1977: 308). In memoir, waiting and writing converge in a 'great policy of revenge', as the 'slave' writes back to the 'master', who can no longer respond. The memoir, in this sense, is sometimes a trick played on the dead.

Although, of course, that's not always the case: sometimes, antagonists are still very much alive and able to answer back. The slave-masters in antebellum America certainly were when ex-slaves wrote their narratives. Even when they were writing from the free states, the ex-slaves were running a life-and-death risk by disseminating their memoirs. They did not wait till the masters were all dead, or until slavery was abolished, but rather wrote back to the system while it was still, directly or indirectly, disempowering them and other Black Americans. Their narratives were vitally important ways of answering power back, of trying to undermine a whole system that still oppressed them.

8

If, in Nietzschean terms, that sounds like *ressentiment*, of the revenge of the oppressed on the strong, then perhaps *ressentiment* isn't always such a bad thing. The slave narrative and its sister genre, the trickster tale, both suggest to me a more positive way of understanding *ressentiment*, whereby the cunning of the weak is of critical importance in challenging oppression. By becoming aware of the influence of trickster tales and slave narratives on the form in which I was writing, I have also developed a more sympathetic attitude towards so-called *ressentiment*. That is, by coming to understand the prehistory of memoir, I've gained an enhanced understanding of *ressentiment*, as a far more emotionally and ethically ambiguous concept than previously. Nietzsche himself is characteristically ambivalent about *ressentiment*: while his language seems, for the most part, critical of the weak, and is moreover tainted with anti-Semitism, he does admit that 'human history would be a much too stupid affair were it not for the intelligence introduced by the powerless' (1998: 19).

This 'intelligence' is frequently expressed through writing, and particularly autobiographical writing – in slave narratives, trickster tales, and later in family memoirs, survivor memoirs, memoirs addressing ethnic, religious or political forms of oppression. Yes, memoirs might often seem 'tainted with ... a desire for revenge', but – despite Gass's claims – this doesn't necessarily make the memoirist a 'monster'. There may be good reasons why the disempowered need their say, why they need the weapon of autobiographical writing – as was obviously the case for slaves in nineteenth-century America. Critic Rosemary Hill sounds like Nietzsche when she suggests that, 'like poison, the revenge memoir is a weapon of the weak. A person unlikely to prevail in an open fight will naturally resort to indirect methods. This is often the case for women' (2020). Such indirect methods might be of vital importance to the oppressed.

Of course, I'm well aware that I'm not writing a memoir as an ex-slave or as a woman. As I said earlier, I'm a white male from a (basically) middle-class background who went to a fairly ordinary comprehensive school in the Midlands. So *ressentiment* would certainly seem far less justified on my part than, say, it is for the narrator of a slave narrative. My perspective is obviously very different, to say the least. In this sense, I think it's just as important to acknowledge differences, disconnections, disjunctions between one's own writing and one's influences, as it is to be aware of what they have in common.

Because of that difference in perspective (and privilege), I decided I still wanted to avoid – as far as possible – any sense of interpersonal *ressentiment* in the book. But *ressentiment* towards wider systems of disciplinary power, in which we are all, to a lesser or greater extent, victims, seems a much more valid 'policy'. In fact, I think this is really what slave narratives are concerned with, too: they are expressions of *ressentiment* towards the slaveholding system as a whole, as opposed to specific individuals – however dreadfully individuals might behave within that system. Jacobs states explicitly that it is the 'system of violence and wrong' that is her principal target: 'Slavery is a curse to the whites as well as to the blacks .... Yet few slaveholders seem to be aware of the widespread moral ruin occasioned by this wicked system' (2016: 49). Other slave narratives stake similar claims: in relation to *The Narrative of Sojourner Truth*, for example, Kimberly Rae Connor points out that the author 'makes it clear ... that she does not attribute the cruelty inflicted upon slaves to any innate sin on the part of individuals, but rather on the corporate sin of the slave system' ([1850] 1994: 76).

Something analogous might be claimed even of that most individualistic of memoirs, *Father and Son*, despite its utterly different social and political context. At a climactic point in the narrative, Gosse junior admits that, for all the personal criticism of his father, the main 'antagonist' of the piece is not really Gosse senior, but the latter's religious system:

There occurred to me the reflection ... what a charming companion, what a delightful parent ... my Father would have been ... if it had not been for this stringent piety which ruined it all .... Evangelical religion ... divides heart from heart. It sets up a vain, chimerical ideal, in the barren pursuit of which all the tender, indulgent affections, ... all that enlarges and calms the soul are exchanged for what is harsh and void and negative.

(2004: 183)

If this is *ressentiment*, it is *ressentiment* against a system, a religious ecology, rather than a particular person. Perhaps that is really how Nietzsche uses the term, too: he discusses *ressentiment* in relation to classes or groups (the *ressentiment* of Jews for Rome, of priests for warriors, of lower orders for aristocrats and so on), rather than individuals. I think there is an important lesson here for the memoirist, which I learned while writing *A Physical Education*, and which helped me finish it. Maybe *ressentiment* is inevitable in a memoir, but *ressentiment* aimed at individuals is mere vengeful bitterness, and doesn't achieve any kind of wider understanding. By contrast, *ressentiment* towards organizations, ecologies, systems, which serve to disempower individuals – whether they are slaves or masters, children or teachers, victims or bullies – might be much more insightful.

I decided I wanted to make all this clear in my own memoir – that I was primarily writing back to what is sometimes called the 'ecology' (Smith 2019: 38–42) of bullying, rather than specific individuals therein. So this is what I added, towards the end of the first chapter:

I don't want to criticise Mr Yorwin .... He was merely part of a system, with its own set of assumptions (about competitiveness, stiff-upper-lipped masculinity, the weather and so on); and compared to other members of that system, he was relatively mild, really ....

We were all part of that system, and hence all equally vulnerable to [criticism] .... 'I guess we are all guilty of everything', writes American author William Burroughs; and no doubt my ex-classmates might cite other lessons when I myself was on the opposite side .... We can all be bullies, all victims, and sometimes both at the same time.

(2024: 15–6)

Works Cited

Arenas, R. (1999), *The Color of Summer: Or, the New Garden of Earthly Delights*, trans. A. Hurley, London: Penguin.

Barrington, J. (2002), *Writing the Memoir: From Truth to Art*, Portland: The Eighth Mountain Press.

Blassingame, J. W. (1979), *The Slave Community: Plantation Life in the Antebellum South*, Oxford: Oxford University Press.

Bloom, H. ([1973] 1997), *The Anxiety of Influence: A Theory of Poetry*, Oxford: Oxford University Press.

Burroughs, W. S. (1995), *My Education: A Book of Dreams*, Harmondsworth: Viking.

Connor, K. R. ([1850] 1994), *Conversions and Visions in the Writings of African-American Women*, Knoxville: The University of Tennessee Press.

Couser, G. T. (2017), 'Signifying Selves: Disability and Life Writing', in C. Barker and S. Murray (eds), *The Cambridge Companion to Literature and Disability*, Cambridge: Cambridge University Press, pp. 199–211.

deLara, E. W. (2016), *Bullying Scars: The Impact on Adult Life and Relationships*, Oxford: Oxford University Press.

Dorsey, P. A. (1993), *Sacred Estrangement: The Rhetoric of Conversion in Modern American Autobiography*, Pennsylvania: Pennsylvania University Press.

Gass, W. H. (2017), 'The Art of Self: Autobiography in an Age of Narcissism', *Harper's Magazine*, 7 December. Available online: https://harpers.org/2017/12/the-art-of-self/ (accessed 4 January 2022).

Gosse, E. ([1907] 2004), *Father and Son: A Study of Two Temperaments*, M. Newton (ed.), Oxford: Oxford University Press.

Hegel, G. W. F. ([1807] 1977), *Phenomenology of Spirit*, trans. A. V. Miller, Oxford: Oxford University Press.

Hill, R. (2020), 'Gosh, What Am I Like?' *London Review of Books*, 42:24, 17 December. Available online: https://www.lrb.co.uk/the-paper/v42/n24/rosemary-hill/gosh-what-am-i-like (accessed 14 December 2022).

Jack, I. (2006), 'Introduction', *Granta 95: Loved Ones*, 95, 11–14.

Jacobs, H. ([1861] 2016), *Incidents in the Life of a Slave Girl*, New York: Open Road.

James, F. and North, J. (2017), 'Writing Lives Together: Romantic and Victorian Auto/biography', *Life Writing*, 14:2, 133–8.

Lacan, J. (1977), *Écrits: A Selection*, trans. Alan Sheridan, London: Tavistock.

Maftei, M. (2013), *The Fiction of Autobiography: Reading and Writing Identity*, New York: Bloomsbury.

Miller, P. (2017), *Writing True Stories: The Complete Guide to Writing Autobiography, Memoir, Personal Essay, Biography, Travel and Creative Non-fiction*, London: Routledge.

Morrison, B. (1997), *As If*, London: Granta.

Morrison, B. (2023), *Two Sisters*, London: Borough Press.

Nietzsche, F. ([1887] 1998), *On the Genealogy of Morals: A Polemic*, trans. Douglas Smith, Oxford: Oxford University Press.

Nord, D. E. (2014), 'Victorian Autobiography: Sons and Fathers', in M. DiBattista and E. O Wittman (eds), *The Cambridge Companion to Autobiography*, New York: Cambridge University Press, pp. 87–101.

Olney, J. (1984), 'The Uses of Comedy and Irony in Autobiographies and Autobiography', *Yeats*, 2, 195–208.

Pelzer, D. (1995), *A Child Called 'It'*, Deerfield Beach: Health Communications.

Pope, R. (2005), *Creativity: Theory, History, Practice*, London: Routledge.

Roach Smith, M. (2019), *The Memoir Project: A Thoroughly Non-Standardized Text for Writing and Life*, New York: Grand Central.

Scott, J. C. (1990), *Domination and the Arts of Resistance: Hidden Transcripts*, New Haven: Yale University Press.

Smith, P. K. (2019), *The Psychology of School Bullying*, Abingdon: Routledge.

Taylor, J. (2019), *Laughter, Literature, Violence, 1840–1930*, Basingstoke: Palgrave Macmillan.

Taylor, J. (2021), 'Scenes of Judgement: Genre and Narrative Form in Literary Memoir', in M. Moore and S. Meekings (eds), *The Place and the Writer: International Intersections of Teacher Lore and Creative Writing Pedagogy*, London: Bloomsbury, pp. 75–91.

Taylor, J. (2024), *A Physical Education: On Bullying, Discipline & Other Lessons*, London: Goldsmiths.

Tuhkanen, M. (2009), *The American Optic: Psychoanalysis, Critical Race Theory, and Richard Wright*, Albany: New York State University Press.

7

'The Community of Sorrow'

Searching for Harmony in a Fragmented Novella

By David Swann

What follows is an attempt to analyse the creative process behind my 'novella-in-flash', *Season of Bright Sorrow* (Ad Hoc Press 2021), which I wrote during several Covid lockdowns, in collaboration with the artist, Sam Hubbard.

*

The project flickered into life after Sam approached me to suggest a joint project, but its roots stretched back twenty-five years, to an event I witnessed while working in a prison. Entering the jail, I crossed paths with a distraught young mother, who was escorting two tiny, frightened kids from the gate. They'd been refused entry through an issue with the mum's papers – and the children would now travel miles home, on several buses, without seeing their father.

*

It was the elder daughter who haunted me. She must have been about five – a pale, skinny lass whose clear, blue, truthful eyes ached with hunger.

*

The novella that emerged was about a troubled girl, closing in on her teens, who'd been cast adrift in a decaying seaside resort with her alcoholic mother. Her name was Lana, and she'd recently been moved by the authorities into a crumbling boarding house, closer to the jail where her father was imprisoned for murder.

*

The plight of that child outside the prison had been simmering in my imagination for decades, I realized. Sadness, anger and curiosity drove me as I wrote. Had she overcome the odds stacked against her? Was she flourishing or had she faltered? How wide and deep was the prison's shadow?

*

Years on, the strength of the emotion surprised me – and gave me a sense of purpose. I think this is the first key ingredient in any creative project: that it *matters* to the writer. In this commentary, I will describe several moments of darkness when I worried that I was lost. In those moments, it was my faith in the emotional core of the book that kept me going. As a writer, you can make doubt your friend, as long as you possess the conviction that the heart of the writing is fully and authentically yours.

*

Bonni Goldberg: 'Writing, like any spiritual undertaking, has many paths, but only one direction – deeper' (1996: xi).

*

Before I get carried away, allow me to briefly signpost where this commentary is going. In the opening half, I'll complete this brief introduction to the book, and define key terms associated with flash fiction. Afterwards, I'll ·demonstrate how a tingling encounter with Mary Robison's very short story, 'Yours', influenced my outlook upon flash fiction and gave me a model to aspire to. Finally, I will analyse how I sought a coherent shape for the individual flashes that make up my 'novella-in-flash'.

*

Wait, though. 'What's a "novella-in-flash"?' This was the reaction of several friends and relatives when they found me showboating after publication. For those unfamiliar with my microscopic literary empire, I'll offer a few baggy definitions.

*

Put simply, 'flash fiction' is short! The Bridport Prize limits its word length to 250 words, the Bath Flash Fiction Award to 300. However, there are contests and publications for stories of six words, and fifty, and … well, you get the drift. 'To offer a complete, hard-edged definition [of flash fiction] is virtually impossible', writes Tara L. Masih (2009: XI) – but she fixes on length as the form's most reliable index and identifies 250 to 1,000 words as the customary range.

*

Word counts are vital to the form, as Masih indicates. But, if applied too early in the creative process, I find they can clutter one's path. My natural inclination is to write long, then cut later. When starting a piece, I turn the focus from numbers to words and simply 'view the constriction of time and space as a need for urgency and profundity' (Brown 2009: 69). I also do my best to heed the warning of Ron Carlson: 'Key is to stop before you mess up page two' (2009: 156). A one-page wonder is a lovely thing.

*

Fred Chappell: '[Flash fiction] inhabits a larger world which it must take pains to imply' (1986: 227).

*

Except … the flashes in a 'flash novella' *are* part of a larger world, even if that world happens to be fragmented. Because the writers of 'flash novellas' build their fictional worlds from individual flashes – and those individual flashes form the 'chapters'/sections of their books. Again, various models exist, and other flavours are available, but when *Season of Bright Sorrow* won the Bath Novella-in-Flash Award, it met the publisher's criteria: a book not longer than 18,000 words, with no single 'chapter' exceeding the 1,000-word limit.

*

Why a flash novella, though?

*

Does your life feel like a realist nineteenth-century novel, with a seamless, linear plot that makes sense? I remember an occasion at university when middle-class friends were discussing where they were from and where they were going. My silent reaction: 'Wow, they have a *plot!*' As a working-class person who infiltrated the middle class, my own life has usually felt more like a blizzard of moments.

*

For Michael Loveday, flash novellas capture the 'fragmented quality in human experience and identity' (2022: 6) that pervades twenty-first-century life, while answering our need 'for some grand overarching narrative for the world – and our place in it' (2022: 6).

*

Meg Pokrass: 'I do not believe that life as it is being lived has a "narrative arc" – and if it does, it does not become clear until a person has gone' (2014: 51).

*

I suspect the vulnerability of the 'novella-in-flash', as a form, attracts me, too. Editing a flash is like performing heart surgery on a butterfly. There's so little to cut into and so much that can go wrong. And when those tiny pieces are set end to end in a sequence, they slip and slide over each other, so that you start to doubt the order, and sometimes the whole project.

*

But how satisfying it is when you get the right pieces in the right places, as Denis Johnson does in *Jesus' Son* (1993), Meg Pokrass in *Here, Where We Live* (2014) and Mary Robison in *Why Did I Ever* (2001), and …

*

No matter how we explain the emergence and appeal of the novella-in-flash, one of the challenges for a writer entering this territory is clear As Michael Loveday argues, it's a question of balancing the fragmentation of the individual flashes against the sense of 'a coherent whole' (2022: 3), so that the novella is 'more than a miscellany of diverse stories' (2022: 9). Or, as Abigail Beckel and Kathleen Rooney put it, the flash novella must trade on 'the concision of the individual pieces and the way they connect, breathe, and build into a larger narrative' (2014: XV–XVI).

*

As above, so below. Like the novella-in-flash itself, you will have noticed that this commentary is fragmented. I'm hoping that the 'rhyme' in approach allows me to mimic certain qualities of the flash novella, especially the angles, collisions, segues and juxtapositions that become possible when writers try to arrange very short chapters into a meaningful sequence. A 'commentary-in-flash' also has the potential to activate white spaces between sections, making the ellipses and omissions 'speak' – just as they might if the fragments of a novella are carefully arranged.

*

There is, of course, a danger that the commentary's fragmentations prove disruptive. I've decided to settle with this because it's the same risk run by novellas-in-flash. Above all, I'm hoping that a 'commentary-in-flash' *dramatizes* the key creative challenge I'm identifying here – namely, the need to balance fragmentation against flow.

*

William Gass: 'Nowhere do we need order more than at an orgy' (1979: 8).

*

David Shields: 'The main question collage artists face: you've found some interesting material – how do you go about arranging it?' (2010: 117).

*

Joe Moran: '[A] flowing voice comes through suggestive arrangement, not coercive connection' (2019: 194).

*

Although the novella-in-flash has found its time, it's been around for a good while. For example, see *Mrs Bridge* ([1959] 2012) by Evan S. Connell and *Play It as It Lays* ([1970] 2011) by Joan Didion. Perhaps we could include Kurt Vonnegut's *Slaughterhouse-Five* ([1969] 2000), too. Its fragmentations echo the obliteration of an entire city – and the disintegration of Billy Pilgrim's shell-shocked mind. Form and content feed each other, becoming parts of a luminous whole. To many on first encounter, Vonnegut's scrambling of outer space and the Second World War is as disorientating as stumbling into a free-jazz gig. But there's an ordering principle buried inside the novel that I will return to later – a principle that allows Vonnegut to achieve a balance between fragmentation and flow and which keeps readers orientated (even if they don't consciously realize that they are!).

*

Like Billy Pilgrim in *Slaughterhouse-Five*, I will now come 'unstuck in time' (2000: 19) and backtrack even further to illuminate some of the terms I'm using.

*

Ever since the 1560s, our word 'flash' has come from the sky, in the sense of a 'sudden burst of light' (*Online Etymology Dictionary*), but the word has older connotations and seems to have sprung from the ground in ancient sources, where it meant to 'swell or well up' (ibid.), as water might from a spring or a rupture in a pipe.

*

Wherever it comes from – whether the ground or the sky – there is a suggestion of suddenness. At various times, I've heard the stories referred to not only as 'flash' and 'sudden fiction' but as 'blasters', 'Bird-in-the-Hand narratives' and 'one-page wonders'.

*

When it comes to classification, or a name for the form, does it matter, really? On first encounter with the perfect, yearning 776 words of Mary Robison's 'Yours', the last thing I needed was a definition. I just wanted to read it again, amazed by its ability to hold so much content while retaining the sense that it had floated into my hands on some autumn draught.

*

'Yours' is set near Halloween, in Virginia, on a 'twig-and-leaf-littered porch' (Robison 1983: 95), where a couple with homely, somewhat Bohemian tendencies are carving the pumpkins that will stare inscrutably out at us in the final line.

*

The pumpkins are used, first, as props to suggest contrasts and differences in the recently wed couple: 'His four pumpkins were expressive and artful .... Allison's four faces were less deftly drawn, with slits and areas of distortion' (1983: 96).

*

Later, the lanterns allow Robison to dig beneath the scene's delicate, candlelit surface, and release the story's final stream of emotion. After the husband meets the artful gaze of his pumpkins, he experiences an awful longing

> to get drunk with his wife once more. He wanted to tell her, from the greater perspective he had, that to own only a little talent, like his, was an awful, plaguing thing; that being only a little special meant you expected too much, most of the time, and liked yourself too little. He wanted to assure her she had missed nothing.
>
> (1983: 98)

*

But it's too late, of course – as in any story worth its salt. For the truth that's been hiding in plain sight ever since the story's second word 'struggled' (1983: 95) is now revealed: although she is half her husband's age and viewed by his suspicious relatives as a gold-digger, Clark's young wife is dying, and the pumpkins will be the last thing the couple ever share.

*

As swiftly as it began, the story ends, still in motion, in the following tantalizing lines: 'Clark was speaking into the phone now. He watched the jack-o'-lanterns. The jack-o'-lanterns watched him' (1983: 98). That's it – no moral, no consolation, only the inscrutable facts, and their temporary, barely touchable beauty, as the world hurtles relentlessly onwards.

*

It's a story about loss and grief, of course. But more than that, too. Close to the midpoint of 'Yours', the husband peers across the ravine behind the couple's home. There, away from the lanterns, the neighbours have extinguished their lights, so Clark's view is the 'nothing' (1983: 96) of the valley that separates his house from theirs. That's where Robison's story truly lives: in the ravine – out there, beyond the lights, in that uncrossable space, where words founder in the darkness that stretches between us all.

*

Kurt Vonnegut: 'There are too many of us and we're all too far apart' (2017: 883).

*

Chekhov understood, of course. The small, intimate domestic spaces in 'Yours' are full of vast, ordinary distances – distances very difficult to bridge. In Chekhov's 'The Kiss', a shy soldier rushes back from his first (accidental) kiss, wanting to convey the epic, heroic narrative to older colleagues. But when he finally spills his burning secret, the pals barely react – and the story takes only seconds to relate, in words that shear the event of its wonder (1994: 183).

*

It's thirty years since Robison's story floated like a leaf into my life – and the memory of that first encounter burns just as bright, even now. Most of the qualities I continue to treasure in very short stories were revealed to me right there, right then.

*

First: consider time. Or its lack. A flash fiction is tumbling headlong towards its ending as soon as it begins. Robert Frost: 'Like a piece of ice on a hot stove the poem must ride on its own melting' (1973: 501).

*

With time melting, there's little room for the past. In 'Yours', Robison delivers a few blunt lines of on-the-nose exposition and uses a domestic prop (a letter) to trigger information from the backstory. But, as soon as she's established the suspicions in Clark's family, she returns to the porch. 'Yours' maintains its scene-based focus on several specific moments, carefully selected from the same day, and presents them in linear fashion.

*

That poor husband, longing to share the contents of his heart with his dying wife. Robert Olen Butler: 'A short short story, in its brevity, may not have a fully developed plot, but it must have the essence of a plot: yearning' (2009).

*

As far as the lighting goes, we don't always need a flash from a meteorite or a bomb. As in 'Yours', a few spluttering candles may be bright enough. Frank O'Connor: 'since a whole lifetime must be crowded into a few minutes, those minutes must be carefully chosen indeed and lit by an unearthly glow' (1963: 22).

*

In another sense of the word, 'Yours' isn't flashy at all. The language is plain, and most of the narration is unhurried. True, the story ultimately engulfs us in a terrible transition, but, in the build-up, Robison dwells on the sensory experience of the pumpkins. Like all fiction, flash follows two contradictory trajectories: the line of the narrative and the line of the senses. Without immersion in its sense-based detail, we might not feel the story under our feet. But too much surface detail could slow the tale's momentum. So it's another balancing act: between depth and direction.

*

The leaves and lanterns aren't mere details, included for their own sake. An image is more than a detail. Details become images when they are entangled with a story's themes and arranged into meaningful patterns. In strong fiction, images in the setting are usually doing metaphorical work and contributing to theme and character. 'Yours' is a good example. The autumnal props and setting are inseparable aspects of the story's elegy for the dying wife. As images, they create an inevitability in the wife's fate and in the husband's longings. A detail is a lonely, isolated thing. An image loves company.

*

The best flashes illuminate their subjects – and cast shadows that extend beyond the characters and the narrative frame. Without Clark's final upwelling of emotion, 'Yours' would remain a beautiful story, but its shadows might not creep out quite so far.

*

Finally, consider what isn't – or can't be – said. A flash makes the white spaces speak.

*

Well, get me. Those are some of the things I'm aiming to achieve whenever I write a flash …

*

... although I chose not to burden Sam Hubbard with my lofty pretensions when he contacted me during lockdown to suggest a joint project. Instead, I listened as he proposed drawing tiny pencil illustrations to accompany a series of six- or nine-word stories. Sam's idea: to create a book just about big enough for field mice to read.

*

A neglected demographic, I agreed. And, yes, I *did* want to co-create a tiny book like that.

*

But have you ever tried writing a six- or nine-word story? The experience put me in mind of Blaise Pascal's supposed apology for writing a long letter: he didn't have time to write a short one.

*

Defeated by the microscopic scale of Sam's plan, I sent him flash fictions of a conventional length (100 to 500 words), and he emailed me drawings – and, just like that, unexpectedly, we were off. As the project evolved, we took it in turns to provide prompts. Sometimes a drawing would arrive that forced me to bend the story in an unexpected direction (for example, I built the increasingly key character of the old beachcomber out of Sam's drawing of a hat). Or I drove Sam mad with ridiculous requests. ('Could you draw something that's both a lion and a duvet, please, Sam?').

*

My imagination insisted that the book's images should be drawn from Morecambe Bay, a seaside place in northern England where I'd once lived. As a setting, it offered me the small share of 'menace' that Raymond Carver recommended (1985: 26). The bay's quicksands, fogs and tides can be scary, and provided metaphors appropriate for the protagonist, Lana, who has been cut off from her old life, and is sinking in the new one.

*

I had a *where*, then – and I hoped it chimed with the 'spirit of the characters' (Herzog 2002: 81). But *who* was this child?

*

Characterization is rarely singular. Even the shipwrecked, solipsistic Pincher Martin has crustaceans as companions when he scales that ridiculous rock in Golding's hallucinatory short novel, *Pincher Martin*. So I gave Lana company: a mother wrecked by drink, an old beachcomber who's got his own grief-stricken reasons to roam the sands – and Archie, a rogue acquaintance who's also troubled by the absence of a father. The book's been criticized for going off-piste with the fatherless Archie, and I get that – it diverts attention from Lana, perhaps an issue in a very short novel, where there's little room for digression. However, I've always liked an observation I read once, perhaps by Flaubert – although I can no longer trace the quotation. The gist: when you're trying to evoke exactly how blue the sea is, forget all that 'azure' and 'cerulean' nonsense – and, instead, describe a freshly tarred road parallel to the water. In other words, Lana was more like Lana when I set her next to Archie, just as an ocean grows bluer when it's placed beside a jet-black road.

*

While working on the cast of characters, I understood what the young girl lacked: a functioning family and a safety net. She was alone in a strange environment, with little security. Once you identify fears and absences in a character's life, you're close to understanding their yearnings.

*

Robert Olen Butler: 'I yearn for self, I yearn for an identity, I yearn for a place in the universe, I yearn to connect to the other' (2005: 41).

*

With abstract thematic concerns slowly taking shape at the back of my mind, it was a question now of steeping myself in the book's atmosphere and of using the senses to bring the story-world to life. Each day, I went off to my allotment shed and did everything I could to stay in the zone.

*

For me, the 'zone' is best thought of as a fruitful and mysterious mood. It often has no rhyme or reason, and can remain elusive for weeks, or vanish all at once, but I know it when I enter it. I do everything I can to sustain the mood, often by floating through vague memories of books I love, and whose effects I yearn to emulate. As John Wain says, in an interview by Peter Firchow, there is danger in 'breathing breathed air' (Firchow 1974: 323), so it isn't a case of direct influence. Rather, I agree with Jay Parini, who describes 'the influence of the precursor ... [being] subtle and almost invisible .... Poets find a source of energy in a prior body of work and attach themselves to it: not unlike cables to a battery' (2009: 89). Parini borrows the term 'aura' from Walter Benjamin: 'often there is no specific poem from which a new poem arises; rather, the poet's aura ... against which the new poet struggles to superimpose a competing aura' (2009: 89).

*

Except, inconveniently enough, there *was* a specific novella on this occasion – *The Summer Book* by Tove Jansson, a book of linked, impressionistic short stories about a grieving girl rubbing up against her irascible grandmother on a tiny island. I'd read the book a few months before Sam Hubbard contacted me, and had remained beguiled by its acute perceptions of an often-unbeautiful setting, and by its guarded ration of warmth – qualities achieved through an understated style, full of droll humour. In certain Scandinavian editions, Jansson's *The Summer Book* contains pencil drawings, too – very different from Sam's, but equally resonant. The serendipity appealed to me.

*

Our allotment shed proved fruitful. Alone during lockdown, and bathing in Jansson's aura, I assembled a pile of flash fictions, strong on character and setting. Situation, too – that's a biggie. I'm forever hunting out connections and disconnections, or meetings and partings, or births and deaths. These, Claudia Hunter Johnson argues, are the 'tidal' forces that drive powerful stories (2005: 3). Johnson takes issue with the (male) idea that conflict, alone, is the driver. Rather, she proposes a narrative model in which conflict and connection become 'complementary forces' (2005: 5), so that conflict's link to power and dominance is balanced against connection's concern with 'the ties between us' (2005: 4). Although I prefer the word 'struggle' (arguably, a richer term than 'conflict'), I set my sights on similar dynamics.

*

So far, so good. Yet, when reading through those early fragments, I struggled to detect an overarching story. Laid side-by-side on my writing desk, the first dozen flashes reminded me of the swarms of jellyfish I'd observed at times in Morecambe Bay. True, they carried a fair old sting and possessed some weird, alien beauty – but their threads drifted off in all directions, and not a single spine between them.

*

These jellyfish of mine had drifted in partly because of the piecemeal method of construction, as Sam and I traded emails, and partly because I'd been concentrating on character and setting, that is, on depth at the expense of direction. Plus, I'd been writing out of the excitement of entering the new territory of a flash novella – particularly as it offered a 'rhyme' with the lives I was describing. My characters were falling to pieces, so a fragmented narrative seemed appropriate …

*

… but where was the flow?

*

If you're after a narrative spine, John Yorke's *Into the Woods* is a good place to start. In it, Yorke describes his realization, working as a young BBC script-reader, that 'the biggest point of drama, the supreme ordeal, was in the middle of the film' (2013: 55). At *Titanic*'s midpoint, the ship sinks. Halfway through *The Godfather*, Michael becomes a murderer. These, Yorke says, are 'the point(s) from which there's no going back' (2013: 58).

*

Nevertheless, Yorke remained puzzled. Most storytelling models seemed to suggest that enormous moments like these should come later and form the story's climax.

He solved the puzzle for himself, first by conceiving five-act structures – and then by feeding character flaws into the equation. In doing so, he understood that the midpoint crisis acts as a pivot. For Yorke, stories start by dislodging a character from their familiar world, and propelling them into a deep, dark wood. What they discover in the midpoint ordeal, far from home and hearth, is the key that offers them a route to survival – and to change and growth. But they don't yet know what to do with that key, or which lock it will fit.

*

So: a story begins by dramatizing the hero's search for a key – and then later shows us the consequences of its discovery. Huge events happen at the midpoint because they open up the story's second half, where the protagonist's flaws will meet their greatest test. In the crisis that stems from, say, a shipwreck or a killing, the protagonist will be destroyed unless they prove that they are capable of the change that their ordeal is offering them.

*

John Yorke: 'How they develop that knowledge forms the underlying subject matter of the second half of the film. A well-designed midpoint has a risk/reward ratio: a character gains something vital, but in doing so ramps up the jeopardy around them' (2013: 59).

*

My favourite book is Homer's *Odyssey*, in which our hero wades home at the midpoint. In the first half, we've experienced his fitful journey to Ithaka and wondered whether he'l make it. In the second half, we're asking if he'll survive the perilous homecoming to reunite with his family.

*

Time and again, I found similar turning points. In *Pulp Fiction*, the injection that saves Uma Thurman's character is administered halfway through the film – appropriate in a story about resurrection (and whose flashback ending restores dead characters to life).

*

Slaughterhouse-Five, next – a flash novella in all but name, since it's smashed into fragments by the war that's left its protagonist, Billy Pilgrim, 'unstuck in time' (2000: 19). Re-reading Vonnegut's brief novel, I spotted something that had previously eluded me (duh!). Although it feels like free jazz, *Slaughterhouse-Five* is anchored by a bassline that cements its broken fragments. Billy Pilgrim's random voyages through time and space are set against the war scenes, which remain stolidly, boringly linear. There s order at the orgy.

*

Something else, too. Previously, I'd nursed some vague intuition that Vonnegut's novel was a warning about man's inhumanity to man. Now, I saw it pivoted around Billy's encounter with the pulp sci-fi writer, Kilgore Trout, which is placed exactly at the midpoint. After meeting Trout, Billy gains the metaphors that transport his mind to another dimension, where he's free from the war – an echo of Vonnegut's discovery that the incorporation of science fiction would allow him to break free from damaging clichés associated with war novels. If it can be summarized, I'd say the book's message is that we can be saved, but only by our imaginations.

*

Could Lana's imagination save *her*? Inspired by Vonnegut, I went back over my novella, searching for moments that dramatized Lana's imagination in action. Time and again, I found myself circling the scene when she encounters a spider in the grotty boarding house bathroom – and where she speculates on the spider's mind. I was acting on a hunch rather than following any storytelling logic, and therefore I still struggle to articulate exactly why this moment kept nagging at me. Perhaps it marked a convergence of many thoughts and feelings that had brought the novella into being. Or maybe the interaction with the spider allowed me to access Lana's mind, and to sense what she was thinking while she thought about the spider. For whatever reason, that scene gave off some mysterious heat. I sensed an opportunity to dig there, and to work out what the spider wanted from me, and why it was in the story.

*

The scenes in which Lana studies the spider had been fed by an enjoyable conversation I'd had on a hike with the philosopher, Helen Steward. Helen is fascinated by spiders and with the clues their behaviour might provide about free will and determinism. When a spider makes its web, how free is it in its choices and decisions? Now it occurred to me that this was the right question to be asking in a book concerned with prison – and with the webs and cages that threaten a prisoner's loved ones.

*

There was now a key, maybe – but I'd no idea how to get home yet.

*

Two and a half thousand years ago, roughly around the time when I started work on this commentary, Aristotle waded into his own bay, the lagoon behind his house, and cut up his first fish. In doing so, he was acting exactly as he did later when dissecting tragic stage plays – searching for what they contained, how they worked and how the separate pieces interacted.

*

For Aristotle, a tragedy's most important organ was the plot, with character in second place and theme or thought in third. The other three organs (language, music, spectacle) followed, making up the famous six-part hierarchy that creative types still quarrel over.

*

Aristotle: 'Every drama alike has spectacle, character, plot, diction, song and reasoning. But the most important of them is the structure of the events .... Tragedy is not an imitation of persons, but of action and of life .... So the events, i.e. the plot, are what tragedy is there for, and that is the most important thing of all' (1996: 11)

*

For my own part, after teaching it to writers for years, I've decided that Aristotle's list is best understood as a conversation, not a league table. Rather than relegating and promoting the individual items, it's more effective to treat them as dynamic, interconnected equals, all serving the same body, and all regulated by the theme, which is the heart of the story, pumping blood to the spine of the plot and the brain of the character.

*

Theme can be useful to consider when you're trying to turn a pile of flashes into a coherent novella. *What's the story about?* By that, I don't mean tell me the plot. I mean: describe what's at the heart of the story and why that matters.

*

In contemplating theme and heart, we enter territory neatly summarized by John Gardner, who suggests that 'theme is elevated critical language for what the main character's main problem is' (1985: 52). This was now my preoccupation. Lana was troubled by her father's absence, of course – but was that her *main* problem?

*

It helped to engage with ideas from Lajos Egri, who expresses Gardner's statement in more detailed, dynamic terms. Egri prefers to think of theme as the story's 'premise' (2004: 2), which he suggests is both the container and engine of a successful story. For him, the premise needs three ingredients: 'character, conflict, and resolution' (2004: 28). And that holy trinity should be concentrated into a single sentence. For example, based on my interpretation earlier, we might summarize the principle of *Slaughterhouse-Five* as being: 'Only the imagination will save us from slaughter'. Here, the imagination belongs to Billy Pilgrim. His conflict is suggested by the word 'slaughter', but the word 'saves' holds out for the possibility of a transcendent outcome. There we go, then: character, conflict, conclusion.

*

With this in mind, I sifted through the series of disconnected flashes I'd created in collaboration with Sam and realized that dangers lurked in the fairly vivid sense of stasis I was evoking. Of course, that's how it goes in real life – especially for hard-pressed individuals facing massive, intransigent forces. Like Lana, they can get stuck in the mud, unable to move.

*

But a story is 'upon a time' and therefore must deal with change. If it doesn't deal with change, it can be something else. Something strange. Something beautiful. But it isn't a story.

*

Joan Silber: 'Time is always in some ways the subject of fiction' (2009: 8).

*

I understood now that Lana would need to break free from her victimhood in the mud – and that it would be the spider that sparked the change. If I placed the creature early in the story (Swann 2021: 15), that might establish a living connection between the spider and Lana. And, then, if I wrote a new flash in which the spider vanished, and I positioned this discovery at a fruitful point in the narrative (2021: 85), Lana might sense that it was possible to copy the spider, and to escape her own web. Thus began another bout of 'plotting', the verb that creates the noun of the 'plot'.

*

At school, I had a history teacher obsessed with the Ems Telegram, the spark that led to the inferno of the Franco-Prussian War. Although his constant references to this fateful communication bewildered me at the time, they became useful to me now, as a metaphor. Because, like that fateful telegram, the spider was only a trigger – and, without the right combustible ingredients, it would have nothing to burn. In other words, I needed an event at the story's midpoint that would help us to see *why* Lana yearns to follow the spider ... and what's at stake for her in the decision to leave or stay ....

*

If John Yorke was right, that the centre of a narrative requires a big moment of change, I decided to confront Lana with a shocking midpoint discovery. In early drafts, I'd shown Lana reading letters from her incarcerated father, but later I'd cut those scenes, to make the daughter's disconnection total. No letters, no phone calls, nothing ....

*

Now I saw that I could reinstate one of those letters but make it a surprise discovery, prised from the grip of Lana's drunken mother. In other words, Lana's disconnection wasn't quite what it seemed. Her Dad *had* been writing to her, but the letters were always ripped to pieces and thrown into the bin by her Mum, in a misguided but hopefully understandable attempt to shield the daughter from his malign influence.

*

When Lana and I stumbled upon that ripped-up letter in the bin, I knew we both had our midpoint – and that it had arrived through the revelation of a secret, as is often effective in storytelling. Lana was able, now, to peer deeper into her disconnection, just as I was free to stand above her, with an aerial view of her story-path.

*

The first half of the story had been asking: 'Can Lana survive without her father?' The second half would dramatize her reaction to the discovery that he was still trying to connect with her (even if in a weak, self-absorbed fashion). The first half of *The Odyssey* dramatizes the hero's journey, and the second half shows him arriving home as a stranger. My novella inverts that structure. We start with the stranger, Lana, coming to town. And, after the midpoint, we follow her dangerous journey to reunite with family – a journey that I hoped would offer the 'risk/reward ratio' described by John Yorke (2013: 59).

*

In connecting the theme to the novella's overarching narrative, I'd refined what the book was about. Sure, it's concerned with prison, and injustice, and post-industrial life, and ... a million other things, as stories always are. But, at its heart, the book is about Lana's battle to control the story of her own life, and to defy the narratives passed down by prison and poverty. Until she heads out into the bay's wilderness, Lana has dutifully followed the directions of her mother. But the restrictions have made her helpless. If she fails to write her own script, she will never gain the sense of 'meaning, unity [and] purpose' that Dan P. McAdams says is vital in creating a 'healthy adjustment to threatening life events' (1993: 6, 49).

*

Now, at last, Lana understands what the story is telling her: 'You'll always be lost unless you find your own path'. As a premise, this seemed to meet Egri's requirements. It had a character (Lana), a conflict (lost), and a conclusion (a path of her own).

*

Lest this sound like the same individualistic guff that's killing our planet, I'd like to stress that Lana finds her path through the connections she forges with strangers in her new environment: the old beachcomber and his wife, the wayward Archie, and Lana's schoolteacher. In their own ways, all these characters offer the 'ties' (2005: 4) that Claudia Hunter Johnson identifies as a corrective force against myths of individual power and dominance. What I was after in *Season of Bright Sorrow* wasn't so much individual redemption, as the establishment of a 'community of sorrow', to use Cormac McCarthy's term (1993: 238) – a frail alliance of the wounded, rooted in grief and suffering, but reaching beyond it, into a more hopeful future.

*

That's why I named the novella as I did. For some religious scholars, early spring is the 'season of bright sorrow', a time of both hunger and hope, when our larder is at its lowest, but the sun is shining again over the fields.

*

Now that I'd located the heart of the book, I still didn't know if it would be any good, of course. For there's a lot more to a book than its structure. The ultimate aim of art is to put goosebumps on an unborn stranger's skin. But no reader ever shivered at the mere fact of a theme or a turning point. It's just as the Pixar screenwriter, Andrew Stanton, argues in his excellent TED Talk: we must make the reader care (2012). Otherwise, no matter how well-structured a story is, it fails.

*

Still, I had confidence and direction now. I thought I could finish the novella – because I knew what it was about and where it was going.

*

Like living creatures, stories exist 'upon a time'. The one enormous thing that unites us all, as human beings, is time and its changes – and the fear and excitement that these things stir. We were all born once. All babies and teenagers. And we'll all die one day (so it goes). And, along the way, we'll move house and town, and try our best to deal with new places and situations, and strangers, and jobs, or the lack of them. And we'll tell stories to make sense of it all – because a good story's not just trying to reflect life, but to shape its complexity, and to offer points of recognition for the reader. A well-told story is a thought experiment that helps us to deal with our changes.

*

Wonder, too. I agree with Andrew Stanton (2012) that the best stories contain wonder. In a story like 'Yours', which is full of tragedy and disconnection, we might sense the wonder of the well-made. And maybe this craftsmanship will inspire us, as writers, to search for – and share in – the sense of harmony that arises when we go deep into the creative process and do our work well.

Works Cited

Aristotle (1996), *Poetics*, trans. M. Heath, London: Penguin.

Beckel, A. and Rooney, K. (eds) (2014), 'Introduction', in *My Very End of the Universe: Five Novellas-in-Flash and a Study of the Form*, Brookline: Rose Metal Press, pp. VII–XX.

Brown, R. (2009), 'Making Flash Count', in T. L. Masih (ed.), *Field Guide to Writing Short Fiction*, Brookline: Rose Metal Press, pp. 68–75.

Butler, R. O. (2005), *From Where You Dream: The Process of Writing Fiction*, J. Burroway (ed.), New York: Grove Press.

Butler, R. O. (2009), 'A Short Short Theory', *Narrative Magazine*, Spring 2009. Available online: https://www.narrativemagazine.com/issues/spring-2009/nonfiction/short-short-theory-robert-olen-butler#:~:text=It%20has%20been%20traditional%20to,essence%20of%20a%20plot%3A%20yearning (accessed 30 September 2024).

Carlson, R. (2009), 'On Writing Short Fiction', in T. L. Masih (ed.), *Field Guide to Writing Short Fiction*, Brookline: Rose Metal Press, pp. 155–7.

Carver, R. (1985), *Fires*, New York: Collins Harvard.

Chappell, F. (1986), 'The Tradition', in R. Shapard and J. Thomas (eds), *Sudden Fiction: American Short-Short Stories*, Layton: Gibbs M. Smith, pp. 227–8.

Chekhov, A. (1994), *Early Stories*, trans. P. Miles and H. Pitcher, Oxford: Oxford University Press.

Connell, E. S. ([1959] 2012), *Mrs Bridge*, London: Penguin Modern Classics.

Didion, J. ([1970] 2011), *Play It as It Lays*, London: Fourth Estate.

Egri, L. (2004), *The Art of Dramatic Writing*, New York: Touchstone.

Firchow, P. (ed.) (1974), *The Writer's Place: Interviews on the Literary Situation in Contemporary Britain*, Minneapolis: University of Minnesota.

Frost, R. (1973), 'The Figure a Poem Makes', in G. Geddes (ed.), *Twentieth Century Poetry and Poetics 2nd Ed.*, Toronto: Oxford University Press, pp. 498–501.

Gardner, J. (1985), *On Becoming a Novelist*, New York: Harper & Row, Colophon.

Gass, W. (1979), *On Being Blue*, Manchester: Carcanet.

Goldberg, B. (1996), *Room to Write*, New York: Jeremey P. Tarcher/Putnam.

Golding, W. (2005), *Pincher Martin*, London: Faber and Faber.

Herzog, W. (2002), *Herzog on Herzog*, P. Cronin (ed.), London: Faber and Faber.

Homer (1991), *The Odyssey of Homer*, trans. Richmond Lattimore, New York: HarperCollins.

Jansson, T. (2003), *The Summer Book*, London: Sort Of Books.

Johnson, C. H. (2005), *Crafting Short Screenplays That Connect*, Second Edition, Oxford: Focal Press.

Johnson, D. (1993), *Jesus' Son*, New York: First Harper Perennial.

Loveday, M. (2022), *Unlocking the Novella-in-Flash: From Blank Page to Finished Manuscript*, Bath: Ad Hoc Fiction.

Masih, T. L. (ed.) (2009), 'In Pursuit of the Short Short Story: An Introduction', in *Field Guide to Writing Flash Fiction*, Brookline: Rose Metal Press, pp. XI–XXXVIII.

McAdams, D. (1993), *The Stories We Live By: Personal Myths and the Making of Self*, New York: Guildford Press.

McCarthy, C. (1993), *All the Pretty Horses*, London: Picador.

Moran, J. (2019), *First You Write a Sentence: The Elements of Reading, Writing and Life*, London: Penguin.

O'Connor, F. (1963), *The Lonely Voice: A Study of the Short Story*, Cleveland: The World Publishing.

Online Etymology Dictionary. Available online: https://www.etymonline.com/word/flash (accessed 5 June 2024).

Parini, J. (2009), *Why Poetry Matters*, New Haven: Yale University Press.

Pokrass, M. (2014), 'Breaking the Pattern to Make the Pattern: Conjuring a Whole Narrative from Scraps' [essay], and *Here, Where We Live* [flash novella], in A. Beckell and K. Rooney (eds), *My Very End of the Universe: Five Novellas-in-Flash and a Study of the Form*, Brookline: Rose Metal Press, pp. 45–98.

Pulp Fiction (1994), [Film] Dir. Quentin Tarantino, USA: Miramax/Jersey Films/A Band Apart.

Robison, M. (1983), *An Amateur's Guide to the Night*, New York: William A. Knopf.

Robison, M. (2001), *Why Did I Ever*, New York: Counterpoint.

Shields, D. (2010), *Reality Hunger*, London: Penguin.

Silber, J. (2009), *The Art of Time in Fiction: As Long as It Takes*, Minneapolis: Graywolf.

Stanton, A. (2012), 'The Secrets of a Good Story', TED2012, February. Available online: www.ted.com/talks/andrew_stanton_the_clues_to_a_great_story?subtitle=en (accessed 10 September 2023).
Swann, D. (2021), *Season of Bright Sorrow*, Bath: Ad Hoc Fiction.
Vonnegut, K. (2000), *Slaughterhouse Five*, London: Vintage.
Vonnegut, K. (2017), 'Adam', in J. Klinkowitz and D. Wakefield (eds), *Complete Stories*, New York: Seven Stories Press, pp. 878–83.
Yorke, J. (2013), *Into the Woods: How Stories Work and Why We Tell Them*, London: Penguin.

8

The End Is Never Where You Think

How Preclosure Theory Turned *Finally* into a Collection of Short Fiction Obsessed with Ending and Not Ending

By Dan Powell

My ideas for a story or collection of stories typically grow from some inciting idea or image or phrase that nestles in my thoughts. Once there, the idea gathers other often disconnected ideas or images or phrases together in that strange liminal space between brain and notebook until the vague shape of what it is I am aiming to write about emerges. The creation of my second collection of short fiction, *Finally*, did not begin with anything approaching this process. The writing of these stories began instead with a single key influence: the desire to apply the reader response theory of preclosure to my writing process and explore how using a preclosural writing methodology might affect my writing process and the resulting work.

Preclosure and the Short Story

I was first exposed to Susan Lohafer's examination of 'Preclosure and the American Short Story' in her monograph, *Reading for Storyness* (2003: 55–70). In this research, Lohafer moves away from close focus upon the ends of stories, a dominant trend in short story research of the time, and instead examines the way in which narratives build *towards* closure. Lohafer defines preclosure as 'those points in a narrative where *readers* feel the story *could* end' (2003: 58, original emphasis). In individual and group reader studies, Lohafer tasked participants with reading various short stories and identifying which sentences might mark a point at which that narrative could end. Analysing the results of these studies, Lohafer identifies the whole text, sentence and word-level signifiers at work within the selected sentences that suggest closure to the reader, as well as whether a consensus of preclosural sentence selection exists across groups of readers for each text.

Lohafer argues that the arrangement of each preclosure moment, one after another, is 'one of the most powerful ways in which short fiction packs much in little' (2003: 53). Each preclosural sentence, Lohafer asserts, marks the end of a putative story within the overall narrative, with each short story hosting multiple putative narratives. Furthermore, each putative story heralds a shift in terms of genre, theme, and mood, with each shift contributing to the polyphonic quality of the final story marked by each story's final, closural sentence. As a story is read, each previous putative story collides with those that come next and reverberates back through those that have come before, generating a spiralling momentum of closure that builds until it impacts with the story's final closure sentence.

Reading her work as an author of short fiction, I could not help but wonder if preclosure was present in my own stories. Looking back over the stories in my debut collection, *Looking Out of Broken Windows* (Powell 2014), I discovered numerous preclosure sentences packed with the same whole text, sentence and word-level closural signifiers that Lohafer identified in the various reader studies included in *Reading for Storyness* (2003). The preclosure sentences in my work also marked out putative stories that successively shifted the genre, theme and mood of each story, just as Lohafer describes.

The stories in my debut collection, written and published years prior to my first reading of Lohafer's research, were not consciously constructed using preclosure and putative stories. Yet I had clearly employed preclosural sentences and staging in the crafting of my short fiction as a means of crafting polyphonic short narratives with a clear closural momentum. Were these preclosural elements present in my work a product of my story sense as a reader rather than products of my story craft as a writer, or were they simply elements hardwired into the structure of fiction generally and short fiction specifically?

Throughout her work, Lohafer states that the preclosural sentences identified in a story and the putative stories they frame are of uncertain origin. As Lohafer explains, 'it is hard to say in what way these putative stories "exist," whose story sense they encode, and what ends they serve' (2003: 52). The selection of preclosure points by a reader appears independent of the text, drawing on the reader's 'inherited and learned strategies for recognizing storyness' (2003: 4). Equally, the generation of preclosure points and putative stories during the crafting of the work must also draw on an author's own inherited, internalized and learned strategies for recognizing storyness.

Developing a Preclosural Writing Methodology

Following my reading of Lohafer's research, the central question that I found myself returning to was not the question of authorship itself, however. In response to discovering this ghost in my writing machine, I was instead deeply curious as to what the effect might be if I were to write stories while intentionally and consciously employing preclosure to craft a short story. Looking at Lohafer's analysis in 'Preclosure and the American Short Story' (2003: 55–70), I realized that the structural and linguistic trends she identified in her preclosural data analysis of the stories could be used to generate a preclosural writing frame to follow when drafting a story. This idea, to use the data from a preclosural reading analysis of a cohort of short stories to develop a preclosural methodology of writing in the form, became the central goal of my doctoral thesis.

Using Lohafer's preclosural study of the American short form as a template for my own analysis, I defined four periods within the development of the British short story between 1800 and 2015 and selected twenty stories from within each period. I then identified the preclosural sentences within those stories and the closural words (such as 'end', 'death', 'never'), closural grammatical structures (such as grammatical recursion, inversion and repetition) and whole-text-level preclosural signals (such as narrative reversals, circularity or shifts of perspective) present within each identified preclosural sentence. From this data, I was able to identify the trends of preclosural signal use within each of my defined periods, at the word, sentence and whole text level and developed a pair of preclosural writing frames for each of my four periods. The first frame in each pair utilized the most prevalent preclosural signals of the period, while the second frame utilized the least prevalent preclosural signals. As a control experiment, I also decided to write a third story within each period without using a frame to explore what impact my writing with such an overt focus on preclosural staging and signal usage might have on my more typical writing process and the stories I produced.

Writing Using the Preclosural Frame

At the first draft stage, I found the frame provided a prefabricated closural structure within which narrative tonal shifts emerged on the completion of each putative story. Within this narrative space I remained free to imagine, select and shape the story content elements as I saw fit, with the writing frame operating as a writing prompt or formal constriction that might be used by any writer, particularly poets, albeit a heavily researched and perhaps overly elaborate one, not unlike the kinds of constriction employed by oulipo[1] writers. In my doctoral thesis I describe how the frame itself operates as 'something akin to the sculptor's maquette' (Powell 2021: 209). Like a maquette, the preclosural writing frame provides a structural shape or scaffolding to the creative elements, a shape that supports the initial act of creation but can be removed towards the end of the writing process, once the narrative is able to stand unaided by the frame.

As a second benefit, I found my preclosural writing methodology also highlighted similarities that exist between the reading process and the writing process. In reader response theory, Iser (1972) and Ingarden (1973) describe how, when reading, each sentence within a story reveals a narrative horizon which simultaneously modifies the narrative described within the previous sentences and is itself modified by all successive sentences. Iser explains how each sentence of a text 'opens up a particular horizon, which is modified, if not completely changed by succeeding sentences' (1972: 283), revealing the mechanics of sentence-by-sentence reading as an 'active interweaving of anticipation and retrospection' (1972: 287). The reader simultaneously looks out upon the new horizon provided by each sentence while retrospectively amending the understanding gained throughout the narrative's previous sentences. Ingarden encapsulates the nature of this continual modification of perspective that takes place during the reading process, describing how 'the literary work actually has "two dimensions": the one in which the total stock

---

[1]Oulipo, short for *Ouvroir de littérature potentielle* (which translates as 'workshop of potential literature'), is a group of predominantly French-speaking writers who employ constrained writing techniques or prompts as a method of generating new ideas and writing methodologies when crafting new literary works. These constraints often utilize mathematical rules or other similar structures to disrupt the writing process and inspire new ways of writing.

of all the strata extends simultaneously and the second, in which the parts succeed one another' (1973: 12), with the reader shifting between these two dimensions throughout the reading process.

This constant modification of narrative horizons is not limited to the act of reading; it also takes place within the act of writing. My use of the preclosural frames exposes that same foundation of interweaving anticipation and retrospection as a fundamental part of the writing process. The preclosural writing frame required that I consider each preclosure point, each narrative horizon, each shift from one putative story to the next, and focus explicitly and deeply upon the shifts between anticipation and retrospection taking place at these preclosural points. This deep reflection upon the workings of anticipation and retrospection within a short story is what author Ron Carlson is describing when he asserts that the short story author must be attentive to each successive sentence she writes to 'figure what could be earned by what has gone before' (2007: 68). It is through this engagement with anticipation and retrospection that the writer stays 'alert and open to the possibilities that emerge as each sentence cuts its way into the unknown' (2007: 14).

I was engaged in this same process of anticipation and retrospection throughout the writing of my debut collection, but that process was implicit. In using the preclosural frame when writing the stories in *Finally*, I transformed this implicit process into an explicit one that promoted a greater and more explicit reflection on the interweaving of anticipation and retrospection. This led to another benefit of my preclosural writing process: the creation of more robust first drafts for the stories in the collection. In my prior writing, my stories had always required large amounts of structural redrafting before a story achieved its final shape and structure. By contrast, when redrafting stories written using the preclosural writing frame, very little structural reorganization was required. The preclosural writing frame accelerated my discovery of the overall closural structure of each story, just as Lohafer's preclosural reading method accelerates a reader's understanding of the closural structure of a short story.

Writing using the frame did generate one major problem, though. When redrafting the stories in *Finally*, I realized that the final closure moments dictated by the writing frame of the stories brought some of the stories to an end that was either drawn out or premature. In six of the stories, the final drafting process required that I remove the final closure moment dictated by the writing frame. In doing so, I cut paragraphs and even entire scenes from the endings of my stories 'Fugue', 'The Ghost Boy', 'The Present Continuous', 'Dissolution', 'The Notificator' and 'The Living Child', compressing elements of each penultimate and final closure moment together to create a new final closure moment. The structure of these six stories was otherwise untouched, and the stories still point towards that original final closure moment. The only difference here is that my originally intended final closure moment occurs in 'a hypothetical *continuation* of the narrative world created by the text, a postnarrational existence' (Trussler 1996: 571, italics in original) that projects beyond the final full stop of each given short story.

My short story 'Dissolution' perhaps provides a clear example of this process in action. In this story, a sixteen-year-old girl narrates the story of how her mother, a woman struggling with her mental health, sets up an easel and a tent on the flat roof of their house and spends weeks up there attempting to paint the perfect sky. The young narrator takes over the running of the house and the care of her younger siblings while bringing meals up to her mother and trying to coax her down from her perch on the roof. One day it rains heavily, and the narrator witnesses her mother's face blur as if the rain is washing away her face along with the painting on her easel. Under cover of the tent, the narrator sees her mother's face return to normal and decides her strange vision must be the result of stress. A week or so later, her mother's state worsens when the narrator's absent father returns to the house to collect the last of his things and he refuses to even speak with her mother. That night, it rains heavily again. The next morning, the narrator returns to the roof and finds only a puddle of paint, shapeless and indecipherable, as if her mother had somehow simply washed away in the rain. In the original unpublished draft of the story, the ending reads:

> I stood there then, beside what was left of our mother and looked out, past her easel. The sky seemed suddenly frozen, the bright blue of its expanse tinged grey and white where what few clouds remained hung unmoving, and I stood still, staring deep into its breadth, its height for I don't know how long, half expecting to find whatever it was she had been looking for suddenly revealed, but there was nothing but empty sky spreading out above in all directions, and I might have stood there searching forever if one of you hadn't called my name from where you stood on the front step in your pyjamas, hadn't asked me again, Is Daddy home?
>
> (2019)

In the final draft, the ending comes a half paragraph earlier, with the narrator left staring into the sky.

> Crouched there, beside all that remained of her, I looked away, out past the easel. The sky seemed suddenly frozen, the bright blue of its expanse

tinged grey and white where the few remaining clouds hung unmoving. I stared deep into its breadth, its height for I don't know how long, half expecting to find whatever it was she had been looking for suddenly revealed, but above me hung nothing but empty sky.

(2021: 156)

In this newer, shortened version of the final scene, the return of the children and their question are both pushed outside the text and into the postnarrational projection. The heightened sense of isolation, with the narrator alone on the roof, looking out into the empty sky, is a stronger image on which to leave the story. Eventually, somewhere beyond the new final full stop of the story, the younger siblings will still arrive home, will still be asking if Daddy has come home, and the narrator will still have to explain that now Mummy has gone too. But this is left for the reader to experience in the postnarrational projection suggested by the story.

Of the remaining six stories, three demanded the addition of a further putative story to bring their narrative to a suitable conclusion. I produced these extensions to the narratives of 'The Other Woman', 'The Ghosts of Leonard Harriman' and 'The Möbius Band' by employing the inverse of the process used with the previous six. Here, instead of transferring the final closure moment to a story's postnarrational projection, I brought each story's postnarrational projection into the finished text itself.

Disregarding or amending the use of the writing frame in this way might appear to break the main rule of my project: to create stories using guidelines on closural signal use derived from my reading analysis. I would argue that this is not the case. My selecting more appropriate positions for ending these stories sits well within the parameters presented in Lohafer's theory. Remember, Lohafer defined preclosure as 'those points in a narrative where *readers* feel the story *could* end' (2003: 58, original emphasis). When writing and redrafting these stories, I was discovering the points of preclosure much as a reader does, revealing each successive horizon through a process of anticipation and retrospection, just as Iser and Ingarden describe. I brought each narrative horizon into being by shifting between the simultaneous dimensionality of the text and successive dimensionality of the sentences. In the editing I simply took these acts a step further, discovering not only where the story *could* end, but where the story *should* end. This switching up of my preclosural methodology to allow the narrative to end exactly where the writer feels it should, rather than breaking the rules of my project, was itself the natural extension of my transforming Lohafer's reading methodology into a writing methodology.

The Uncanny Effect of the Preclosural Writing Method

The influence of preclosure did not end at the writing process, however. Early in the crafting of the collection, it became clear that my preclosural process was influencing the *type* of stories I was writing. Across all twelve stories in *Finally* the key uncanny tropes of the double, temporal disruptions and repetitions, *déjà vu*, premature burial, death and ghosts all feature prominently. This emergence of the uncanny occurred even in stories where my initial ideas for the narrative did not itself suggest any kind of uncanny element. The first story in the collection, 'The Other Woman', was intended to be a realist story focusing on a woman who discovers her husband has another wife and family in another town. It was only halfway through writing the first draft that I realized the 'other woman' in the narrative was a double of the main character. This unplanned and unprompted diversion into uncanny territory emerged only as I wrote the words 'The woman in the doorway was like a reflection, … same build, same height, same features as Rachel' (2021: 63). 'What Used to be a Human' also began as straightforwardly realist story of adultery, this time between two women, but instantly morphed into the narrative of a woman who engages in an extramarital affair with a synthetic life form as I typed the words: 'I reach my hand to your skin; it is cool but not cold. You do not feel like a machine, I say' (2021: 71). In 'The Notificator', the narrative shifts from a realist story about a mechanical public noticeboard introduced into London in the 1930s into a ghost story, when, three quarters of the way through the first draft, the narrator suddenly sees the ghost of a character who died earlier in the narrative: 'Then, this morning, as I walk between my flat in Bow and the gallery in Whitechapel, I see Frank. I hurry after him, but he remains always some distance ahead' (2021: 126). The narrator finds it strange that the figure does not hear his calls and, despite how fast he follows, always remains the same distance away. Finally, the true ghostly nature of the figure the narrator is following is revealed when the narrator follows him into a dank and shabby antique shop: 'As he turns to face me, my breath catches in my throat. The revealed Rückenfigur figure before me is not Frank at all. The face of the thing before me is a blur of greyed oil paint, its eyes dank hollows, its mouth a silent howl of ecstatic torment' (2021: 127).

These transformations, from realist narrative into uncanny tale, occurred over and over during the crafting of the stories in *Finally*, and while I certainly embraced the uncanny as the distinct mode of the collection at times, I only consciously intended to write uncanny tales in the case of three of the stories,

'Fugue', 'The Ghost Boy' and 'The Ghosts of Leonard Harriman'. Despite my initial intentions, in nine of the twelve stories, and, notably, in the writing of the first three stories undertaken during the project, the uncanny arose unbidden during the writing of each story's more realist first draft.

I concluded that this irruption of the uncanny within the stories was a direct result of applying preclosure theory as my primary influence. The short story form specifically, and narrative more widely, is itself preoccupied with the uncanny. This preoccupation comes from narratives' need for an ending, with that ending being itself a kind of death. As Tzvetan Todorov explains, 'Narrative equals life, absence of narrative equals death' (1977: 74). The power of 'the end' is greatly magnified when operating within the compressed closural staging of a short form narrative. The brevity of the short story generates a density of preclosure that amplifies the relationship between preclosure, final closure and death. If, as Bennett and Royle assert, 'the uncanny is aligned with death' (2009: 42) and the short story is also aligned with death, the third point of this triangle of theory is that the short story is also aligned with the uncanny. The sheer weight of uncanny short stories that exist across all literary traditions, both temporal and geographical, supports this assertion, as does the origin of the short form in folklore, fairy tale and ghost story.

Preclosure itself is a key generator of the sense of the uncanny that pervades the short form. The main closural signals that Lohafer identified in her preclosural analysis of the American short form were circularity, emotional/ cognitive reversal, image recursion, alliteration, use of multiple abstract and negative terms, and structural recursion. In my own analysis of British short stories, I found a similar trend towards the use of the key closural signals identified by Lohafer, signals that overtly generate repetition of structure, grammar and imagery within a text. The compulsion to repeat that sits at the core of Freud's uncanny (2003b) seems also to sit at the core of the short story form. These repetitions at the core of the short story form are themselves further emphasized by the combination of the form's brevity and the density of the closural signals operating within the short narrative space.

The short story then is repeatedly ending and not ending throughout the reading (or writing) of a brief span of text. This is itself a kind of doubling as 'In order to construct a plot, the end must present the same terms as the beginning, although in a modified relation' (Todorov 1977: 60). Each preclosure and final closure point is simultaneously similar, presenting 'the same terms as the beginning', and different, presenting those same terms in a 'modified relation' to what has gone before or will come after. The uncanny doubling effect of repeated endings within the dense closural structure of the short story turns each point of closure within a story, whether preclosure or final closure, into an ambiguous moment that is simultaneously closural and anti- closural. Final closure, with its inevitable pushing out into a postnarrational projection that takes place in the mind of the reader, is also distinctly anti-closural and shares this ambiguity. Even the opening of a story is ambiguous, as it inevitably suggests a prenarrational projection that precedes the first sentence of the story. Sandwiched as it is between prenarrational projection and postnarrational projection, the short story is effectively all middle. Which means that the short story form, at its very core, is entirely preclosural.

If the short form is both uncanny and preclosural, then it must also be true that preclosure theory itself, with its focus on circularities, repetitions and endings, is an uncanny theory. My preclosural writing methodology is therefore also an uncanny methodology that heavily yet implicitly influenced my production of such overtly uncanny short fictions. While engaged in this creative research, my use of the preclosural writing frame pushed my previously unconscious consideration of preclosural staging firmly into my conscious writing process, even as my previously conscious consideration of subject matter, genre and application of key tropes moved into my unconscious process. The irruption of the uncanny into what I had intended to be straightforwardly realistic tales occurred inadvertently.

It was only after completing the collection that I realized the stories shared the same uncanny fictional world. Re-reading the work I was surprised to see settings recur, some obvious (the village of Heptonstall in Yorkshire being the inspiration for the setting of both 'The Ghost Boy' and 'The Möbius Band') and some implied (the antique shop in the closing scene of 'The Notificator' also being the shop where Leonard, a character who discovers he is himself an uncanny double of a real person, purchases the letter opener that plays a key part in the closing of his story, 'The Ghosts of Leonard Harriman'). Isolated houses haunt the fictional landscape of the stories in Finally, uncanny artworks feature in multiple stories, and the otherwise realistic settings that feature across the stories are themselves brimming with uncanny energy due to their repeated depictions as 'landscapes partially emptied of the human', a key trope of eerie and uncanny fiction, according to Mark Fisher (2016: 11). This repetition of uncanny elements within the twelve stories in Finally is not merely limited to generic uncanny tropes. Iterations of the uncanny specific to these stories also recur and repeat throughout individual stories and across the collection as a whole.

This 'compulsion to repeat … to repeat the repressed matter as an experience in the present' (Freud 2003a: 56) is, of course, the axle on which Freud's concept of the uncanny spins. The repetition of ending that occurs through use of preclosural staging is a fictional mirror of this compulsion to repeat, as repressed narrative matter surfaces and resurfaces. The same-yet-different moments of preclosure each generate a sense of déjà vu, itself an uncanny trope. And this compulsion to repeat goes beyond the fiction itself. The writing process itself is a compulsive repetition, with the writer compelled to return to key images, ideas and themes, revisiting and revising each scene, uncovering further repressed matter within a story.

My preclosural writing methodology intensifies this repetition. My analysis of the eighty British short stories selected as my sample required that I read them repeatedly to uncover both the explicit and implicit preclosural elements layered within each story. While creating my database of preclosural signals, I was repeatedly exposed to a density of closural signals that create repetitions within a text: circularity, structural recursion, syntactic recursion, image recursion, intrareferential motif, multiple closural words, multiple abstracts and alliteration. My use of the preclosural frames also mandated a repeated use of the same key closural signals in modified arrangements across the twelve stories. Writing these stories, I presented the same preclosural terms and structures over and over, in a way that mirrors and reinforces Todorov's assertion that 'the end must present the same terms as the beginning, although in a modified relation' (Todorov 1977: 60). This overt and explicit approach to preclosural staging had an exaggerated impact upon the content, themes and ideas within the story, resulting in the exaggerated, repetitious, and, for the most part, unintentional emergence of the uncanny, both generic and specific within each story. And this effect itself compulsively repeated, with each successive story presenting an uncanny narrative at once similar to what has gone before, in its use of themes, images and closural signals, and yet different, in its arrangement and use of these elements. As well as revealing that the short story form, preclosure and the uncanny combine to form a triangle of symbiotically linked elements when crafting short fiction, my preclosural methodology directly influenced the very nature of the stories I ended up producing.

The Ghostly Influence of Kafka-Time

Following completion of the twelve stories and the detailed commentary that formed the rest of my thesis, I felt that I had identified all the key influences at work within *Finally*. It was only some months after completion and submission of my thesis that I discovered a further, unintended yet unequivocal influence on the stories. While reading Michael Hofmann's introduction to his translation of Franz Kafka's *Metamorphosis and Other Stories*, I was suddenly struck by how closely the stories in *Finally* employ what Hofmann describes as 'Kafka-time' (2007: xi). According to Hofmann, Kafka-time consists of three co-substantial paradigmatic moments: 'On the one hand, it is almost always too late in Kafka .... On the other hand, the end has not yet happened .... And then there is perhaps the truest or most illusory moment, the middle moment, the Zeno moment, the infinite possibility of infinitesimal change' (2007: xi–xii). This illusory moment, as Hofmann describes it, is the moment where Kafka ends his stories, leaving both character and reader suspended in an ending that is intensely imminent and yet never truly arrives.

All twelve stories within *Finally* conform to Hofmann's model of Kafka-time. Each protagonist is faced with a profound change in their lives that will alter both how they see themselves and how their world will operate moving forward. As each story opens it is already too late for each character to avoid the profound change that approaches. The imminent end is almost upon each character but has not yet happened. And just as, according to Hofmann, the imminent endings never arrive in Kafka's short fiction, the imminent endings of the twelve stories in *Finally* also fail to arrive. Zeno's paradox of motion 'asserts the non-existence of motion on the ground that that which is in locomotion must arrive at the half-way stage before it arrives at the goal' (Aristotle 1984: 404). This is the paradox of motion at play within stories that conform to the model of Kafka-time. The middle moment that Hofmann describes within Kafka-time, the Zeno moment of endlessly moving towards ending but never being able to arrive, is a key dynamic of the short story form and is itself the product of preclosure at work in the short story. Each preclosure point within a short story is a step halfway towards an imminent ending that never arrives, even with the supposed final closure moment of the story's final sentence.

'Not the Fall' is the story in *Finally* that perhaps best exemplifies my unintentional use of 'Kafka-time'. Its narrative centres around Palmer, a middle-aged philosophy academic, husband and father, and closeted gay man. In the story's prenarrational projection, Palmer is shocked when he discovers his daughter, Lisa, is dating Adam, a younger man Palmer was previously involved with. The story opens some months following this revelation and takes place during Lisa and Adam's engagement party. The narrative that plays out in the final text not only clearly presents each of the three paradigmatic moments of Kafka time but also presents them in the order Hofmann describes them.

First, it is clearly too late for Palmer even as the story opens, as he literally arrives late to his daughter's engagement party. With the wedding fast approaching, time is running out for Palmer to do something to save his daughter from suffering the same long-term deception and betrayal to which he has subjected his own wife. More than this, it was already too late for Palmer when his daughter first brought Adam home, already too late when Palmer embarked upon his short affair with Adam some years before. These events all point forward to an inevitable moment when Palmer will have to be honest with his wife and daughter about his sexuality and his extramarital activities.

Clearly, the end for Palmer has repeatedly not yet happened. Since before the story opens, he has been constantly approaching the end in increments, while equally desperate to avoid it. This illusion of motion continues throughout the story. First, Palmer builds up the courage to approach Adam. Hesitantly, Palmer begins to cautiously navigate the confrontation. He tries discreetly to get Adam alone so they can talk openly. Finally, when all else has failed, Palmer marches Adam onto the balcony outside the function room. In this final conversation all movement stops as Adam refuses to call off his engagement to Lisa and threatens to 'out' Palmer in an act of mutually assured destruction if Palmer says anything to Lisa. Surely here, as Palmer tries to shove past Adam in a bid to reach Lisa and reveal all that has been repressed, the tensions within the story must finally come to light. But Palmer's forward motion is halted. Unable to physically overcome the younger man, Palmer is instead sent reeling backwards over the balcony railing. This moment at the end of the story presents the truest and the most illusory moment of Kafka-time, as Palmer's fall from the balcony becomes governed by Zeno's dichotomy:

> In the unlikely event of his survival, Palmer would perceive his fall to have lasted at least a third longer than the 5.71 seconds it takes for a man of his weight to accelerate down the 160 feet to the pavement below. With a top speed at impact of 103 feet per second or 70 miles per hour, survival would be impossible, though, and anyway, Palmer certainly did not think such things as he fell.
>
> Instead, flashing at speeds far greater than any his body might reach, even at impact, Palmer's panicked brain fixed once more upon Zeno's Dichotomy. Before his body could reach the pavement below, it must first fall halfway. Before it could reach halfway, it must first travel a quarter of the distance. Before a quarter it must travel one-eighth. Before one eighth, one sixteenth. Thinking of the fall in this way, the moment of impact could only arrive after the completion of an infinite number of tasks. Which is, as Zeno maintained, an impossibility.
>
> (Powell 2021: 161–2)

In this 'middle-moment' of Kafka-time, Palmer is suspended within Zeno's dichotomy. And 'Not the Fall' ends here, with Palmer falling infinitely in the middle-moment of 'Kafka-time', clinging desperately to the concept that 'All motion is an illusion … as he made his infinite and impossible way toward the pavement' (2021: 162).

It is pleasingly strange to me that all the stories within *Finally* conform to Hofmann's model of 'Kafka-time'. The ghostly influence of 'Kafka-time' clearly depends on much that is inherent in short fiction. The idea that it is 'almost always too late' is true of all short stories, with their beginning taking place prior to the first sentence in the story's prenarrational projection. The idea that 'On the other hand, the end has not yet happened' is also central to the short story, as ending is always imminent. And the way the short story tends to defer its ending, pushing it out into the postnarrational projection, leaves the form typically presenting a middle moment full of 'infinite possibility of infinitesimal change' that promises an ending that never quite arrives. I would argue then that Kafka-time is better defined as short story time. In the short story, it is almost always too late, and yet the imminent end has not yet happened. And in the short story, in particular the short story that utilizes the kinds of open or epiphanic endings that the form has embraced since the advent of modernism, ending itself plays out in a potentially infinite progression of moments that defer ending.

In the end, my writing of *Finally*, heavily influenced as it was by preclosure theory and the uncanny effects of writing in the short story form, was equally heavily influenced by the concept of Kafka-time. The narrative horizons described by Ingarden and the interweaving of anticipation and retrospection generated with each successive preclosural sentence are themselves repeated 'middle moments' present within Kafka-time. Each one is a small step towards an ending that never fully arrives. Equally, the compulsion to repeat at the heart of the short story, discussed by both Freud and Todorov, is simply the 'illusory moment, the middle moment, the Zeno moment, the infinite possibility of infinitesimal change' (2007: xi–xii) of Kafka-time described in slightly different terms. The way a short narrative is repeatedly ending and not ending, turning each point of closure into an ambiguous moment that is equal parts closural and anti-closural, is Kafka-time in operation.

The data from my preclosural study of the British short story (2021) and Lohafer's preclosural study of the American short story (Lohafer 2003: 55–70) both support the view that the short story form is predisposed to the repetition and deferral of endings consistent with what Hofmann describes as the middle-moment of 'infinite possibility of infinitesimal change'. Both my own study and Lohafer's reveal a trend within the contemporary and twentieth-century story to promote closural signals of perspectival shift, circularity and emotional/cognitive reversal, all of which create a narrative that spirals around ending without truly connecting with or arriving at an end.

With preclosure, it is always almost too late yet simultaneously not the end; after all, each preclosure point is always a moment that might be an ending but is not. And with preclosure, the end of the short story rarely, if ever, presents a conclusion, preferring instead to present a moment that suggests a path to that ending, a path made up of a potentially infinite progression of moments that never quite reach the end. Kafka-time is short-story-time – is preclosure time. The preclosural nature of the short form exerts a magnified uncanny influence on the narratives that any writer creates within it, pushing sentence and story into inevitable shapes and designs that cause ending to occur and recur as each preclosural moment reframes what has come before in similar yet modified terms. As a result, the end of a short story is never where you think it is, be you a reader or a writer. Instead, the ending is constantly being anticipated and delayed through the action of preclosure. At best, as preclosure theory and 'Kafka-time' show, the end of the story is wherever you feel it might be, at once about to arrive and yet ever distant, and always, always densely shrouded in the uncanny.

Works Cited

Aristotle (1984), 'Physics', in *The Complete Works of Aristotle: The Revised Oxford Translation*, trans. J. Barnes, Princeton: Princeton University Press, pp. 315–446.

Bennett, A. and Royle, N. (2009), *An Introduction to Literature, Criticism and Theory*, Fourth Edition, London: Routledge.

Carlson, R. (2007), *Ron Carlson Writes a Story*, Minneapolis: Graywolf Press.

Fisher, M. (2016), *The Weird and the Eerie*, London: Repeater Books.

Freud, S. (2003a), 'Beyond the Pleasure Principle', in *Beyond the Pleasure Principle and Other Writings*, trans. J. Reddick, London, New York: Penguin Books, pp. 43–102.

Freud, S. (2003b), 'The Uncanny', in *The Uncanny*, trans. D. McLintock, London: Penguin Books, pp. 121–62.

Hoffman, M. (2007), 'Introduction', in Kafka, F., *Metamorphosis & Other Stories*, trans. M. Hofmann, London: Penguin, pp. vii–xv.

Ingarden, R. (1973), *The Cognition of the Literary Work of Art*, Evanston: Northwestern University Press.

Iser, W. (1972), 'The Reading Process: A Phenomenological Approach', *New Literary History*, 3:2, 279–99.

Lohafer, S. (2003), *Reading for Storyness*, Baltimore and London: The John Hopkins University Press.

Powell, D. (2014), *Looking Out of Broken Windows*, Cromer: Salt Publishing.

Powell, D. (2019), 'Dissolution', unpublished draft.

Powell, D. (2021), *Shaping Storyness: Developing a Preclosural Approach to Writing Short Fiction*, Doctoral Thesis, University of Leicester.

Todorov, T. (1977), *The Poetics of Prose*, Oxford: Blackwell.

Trussler, M. (1996), 'Suspended Narratives: The Short Story and Temporality', *Studies in Short Fiction*, 33:4, 557–77.

9

The Anxiety of Influence in the Age of Authenticity, OR

Salt in the Soup

By Jemma Kennedy

Are all writers by nature cannibals? As a playwright and screenwriter, I know that at times I've consciously and unconsciously seasoned my work with ingredients taken from other people's lives. A pinch of a friend's personality trait; a sprinkle of reconstituted anecdote heard at a dinner party; and a dash of colour seen in a passing stranger that flavours the soup of a fictional character.

Although there are certain ethical questions around this sort of creative borrowing, taking inspiration from what's around us isn't usually seen as cheating. As writers, we're encouraged to use lived experience to create stories that have heft and depth. We praise human credibility in good drama. Real life – our own and that of others – is considered fair game.

I truly cannibalized my own experience in order to write my play *Genesis Inc.*, which ran at London's Hampstead Theatre in 2018. The play is set in a private fertility clinic, Genesis Incorporated, and dramatizes the experiences of two pairs of clients who are trying to conceive. One couple is a husband and wife; the second is a straight single woman and her male gay best friend who has agreed to be her sperm donor. As we watch the financial and emotional costs take their toll on all four characters, the clinic owner prepares to float his business on the stock market and capitalize on the booming private fertility industry.

The play was inspired by my own experiences in the luxurious but sterile environs of the private fertility industry. After several months of being poked, prodded and diagnosed, then prescribed an expensive treatment plan (egg freezing) with no guarantee of success, I knew I had to write about it. This industry was, I decided, not just selling fertility treatments; it was flogging hope to desperate would-be parents, who, like me, were happy to overlook the grim statistics for an outside chance to have a baby. The various experts I saw weren't just trained medics, they were trained salespeople.

In 2015 the play was commissioned by the National Theatre. I'd never leaned so heavily on my own personal life to create a story, but I had no qualms about that. I was more concerned with how to wrestle a dramatic narrative from my big, complex themes. I laid them out in notes to the play's eventual director, Laurie Sansom, before we went into rehearsal:

> In our society women are made to give up control of their bodies, careers, and relationships in pursuit of having a baby. The biological imperative has been commodified and clinics are exploiting it. My point is that the market, and market logic, corrupt things that should ideally not be privatised and turned into competitive consumerism.

Exploring this central idea had sent me on a deep dive, not only into my own lived experience but into extensive research into the industry. I went to medical conferences, I read academic essays and I interviewed fertility specialists, scientists, counsellors, egg and sperm donor agents. I also spoke to financial analysts and former bankers who knew the inner workings of the stock market. My working title for the play was *The Bank of Britain*, as I was thematically mirroring the privately owned banks of frozen eggs and sperm which keep the fertility clinics afloat with the corporate finance companies that increasingly own them. This is referenced in the play's opening monologue, spoken by Dr Marshall, the charismatic, greedy owner of the clinic in which the play is set. Here, at a conference, he sets out his moral crusade (with strong Thatcherist overtones) to help combat the current fertility crisis via the capitalistic baby-making industry.

Dr Marshall As a generation of women struggles to conceive, we must ask ourselves, how do we intend to populate our nation with the brightest and the best? How can we empower women and restore their potency, instead of punishing them for wanting it all? The answer lies not in caution but courage. Innovation. Stimulation. The market may have brought us to our knees but in it lies the seeds of recovery. We must restore the bank of

Britain and its precious stocks of eggs and sperm, take it back into profit, protect our future from a stagnant and unpopulated decline.

(From my first draft, written in 2015)

This monologue was intended to foreshadow the climactic scene of the play, in which Serena, one of the four protagonists, miscarries the embryo implanted by Dr Marshall as traders sell his company shares on the open market. As Serena's blood drains out of her, the stock price soars, turning Dr Marshall into a multimillionaire.

While it was important to me that I grounded the play in reality, anchored in both my experience and my research, I also knew early on that to tell the story in the way I wanted, I would need to move away from my habitual theatrical realism. The notion of the clinic as a place that sold dreams as well as science was central to the play. So as well as creating a believable reality for my characters who were, for various reasons, unable to conceive, I knew that fantasy and projection would also be part of the play's stagecraft, and this would require a more stylized theatrical grammar. Although this pushed me out of my comfort zone, I had great fun writing these scenes. I was experimenting with a new theatrical voice that blended comedy and fantasy and, I hoped, helped the play come alive.

The following excerpt is from the penultimate scene, where all the characters meet up in a fantasied collective Marxist utopia. They have become a blended communal modern family, sharing breastfeeding duties, and watched over by Karl himself.

Marx *enters wearing a pinny, carrying a basket of laundry. He addresses the audience as he folds baby clothes.*

Marx So, utopia. The religious called it Paradise. The Russian peasants saw it was a cow with an infinite supply of milk, as long as everyone took only what they needed. As for you workers of this weary, pixelated century? You call it parenthood.

Jeff *takes the baby from* **Serena** *and begins to breastfeed it*

(Kennedy 2018: 97).

But the collective has already started to fall apart, unable to live up to its utopian ideals about the shared ownership of children:

The baby cries louder. The group tries to soothe it but it doesn't work. They start to fight over it. The baby unravels and turns into a blanket.

(2018)

Marx goes on:

> **Marx** If the product cannot be owned, perhaps its absence can. Every age of revolution comes with great human loss. So, collectivise your loss. Yes. For in this unequal world, inequality might be the only human currency that unites us all.
>
> (2018: 98)

In this scene, and others I wrote with a similar theatrical grammar, I felt I was able to articulate some of my central ideas in a way that I couldn't have done in a 'real' conversation between the characters. Along the same lines, I dramatized another character's biblical fantasy in which she becomes Sarah, the barren wife of Abraham, who was granted the gift of fertility by God.

During the writing process, I had re-read Tony Kushner's seminal (in several senses of the word) masterpiece, *Angels in America*, set during the Reagan era as the AIDS crisis unfolded. I had long admired Kushner's playscript, which managed to deftly weave big political ideas into a sprawling tragicomedy. In particular, I loved the liminal dream spaces he creates in which various characters who haven't yet met in real life are able to connect and communicate. The following excerpt is from Kushner's stage directions to Scene 7 of the play, in which two key characters meet for the first time in such a space.

> *A week later. Mutual dream scene. Prior is at a fantastic makeup table, having a dream, applying the face. Harper is having a pill-induced hallucination. She has these from time to time. For some reason, Prior has appeared in this one. Or Harper has appeared in Prior's dream. It is bewildering.*
>
> (2007: 36)

Long before I knew about the existence of *Angels*, I had been awed by a production of Brecht's *The Caucasian Chalk Circle* that I'd seen in London's Riverside Studios when I was ten. I was gripped by its fluid, dynamic narrative form; its use of music to help tell the story; and the way it invited us audience members to be part of the theatrical experience, including an invitation for us to join the actors in a dance on stage at the end. As I watched it, I felt I was *inside* the play. This was a defining moment in my youthful understanding of what theatre could do.

Brecht is the progenitor of Epic Theatre – broad-brushstrokes storytelling that seeks to remind the audience they're watching a play, rather than convince them they're witnessing reality. His overtly theatrical techniques aim to create what he called *verfremdungseffekt* – an effect of distancing, or alienation. In his 1936 essay 'Alienation Effects in Chinese Acting' (trans. J. Willett 1964), Brecht describes how traditional stylized Chinese acting techniques, often involving masks and familiar symbolic costumes, prevent the audience from having a purely subjective, emotional response to the characters in the play. He believed that by using similar techniques to remind his audience that theatre is made from a box of tricks, his plays could more powerfully communicate his sociopolitical ideas. Ironically, I remember distinctly, even now, how personal, human and real the story felt to me, even though I was aware I was watching a theatrical parable. It's not hard to see the influence of the play and Brecht's epic theatre tropes on *Genesis Inc.*, which contains songs, dreams and semi-skits.

Tony Kushner has spoken extensively about his own debt to Brecht and its direct influence on *Angels in America*:

I was ... very much drawn in Brecht to the epic form, to the chronicle play. It was almost immediately as soon as I read *Mother Courage* that it became my favourite Brecht. I loved the multifocal, the multiple perspective of it. You, know, Brecht talks about it when he writes about Breughel and the lack of a single point of perspective, the complexity of signs, and the physical conflict in a terribly grandiose prism.

(1997: 107)

The echoes of this are clear in Kushner's own 'Playwright's Notes' that he wrote in the published playtext of *Angels in America*:

The play benefits from a pared-down style of presentation, with minimal scenery and scene shifts done rapidly (no blackouts!), employing the cast as well as stage-hands .... The moments of magic – the appearance and disappearance of Mr. Lies and the ghosts, the book hallucination, and the ending – are to be fully realized, as bits of wonderful theatrical illusion – which means it's ok if the wires show, and maybe it's good that they do, but the magic should at the same time be thoroughly amazing.

(2007: 11)

Nonetheless, at the time of writing my play, I wasn't thinking about Brecht, although I did cast my mind to *Angels* when I was thinking about the overall structure of the play. Looking through old files, I can see that at some point I elongated the structure from three acts into five. I'd never used a five-act structure before – it's not common in modern playwriting and I only really knew it in Shakespeare, and in *Angels*. Judging from my notes from the time, this choice helped me create a clearer timeline for the action of the play.

which takes place over about eight months and tracks Serena's preparation for fertility treatment, egg extraction and fertilization, embryo implantation and subsequent miscarriage. This extended structure helped me clarify major turning points and escalations in the drama. Screenwriter and dramaturg John Yorke has usefully described the use of five-act structure like this:

> While not all stories have five acts, you can break all stories into five parts. Why do this? The simple answer is that it gives you so much greater control over the shape of the story .... It creates regular gripping turning points that increase narrative tension. In other words, if structure is about joining dots, then the five-act structure gives you more dots. This makes the final drawing easier to fill in, increases the forces of antagonism and forces you to create a classic story shape.
>
> (2024)

I ended up with a decent first draft and then, after notes, wrote a second and third. The literary manager of the National Theatre said that *The Bank of Britain* reminded him of Joan Littlewood's iconic satirical musical from 1963, *Oh, What a Lovely War!* I knew a little about this musical – or rather, about Joan's radical Theatre Workshop where it was devised – but had never read the script or seen a production. Littlewood's play is a sort of political musical revue with a strong anti-war sentiment, using Brechtian techniques to satirize her serious subject. At the time, I took the compliment, as I think it was intended. I hoped my own play was able to deliver political ideas in an entertaining and surprising way.

Sadly, when the nominally attached director dropped out, the play got passed on by the National Theatre, and I set about trying to find another home for it. A year later it was picked up by the Hampstead Theatre for production, and then the search for a new director began.

One of the early readers of *Genesis Inc.* (at that point still called *The Bank of Britain*) was the late, great theatre and film director Roger Michell. He politely passed on directing it, but in a nice email to my producer at Hampstead, he said this:

> I think this play is terrific fun, very inventive, stuffed full of great things like a great big Christmas pudding ... there's so much to enjoy. It reads like a mash up of those free-for-all agit-prop plays of the seventies with a salty dash of *Angels in America* thrown in.

The producer forwarded me the email as a kind encouragement, but when I read it, I was taken aback by the reference to *Angels*. Salty, Roger? What did it mean? Vulgar? Flavoursome? Mashed up with too much Kushner Seasoning?

It's hard looking back to understand quite why I was so discomfited by this throwaway comment of his. t was a totally fair comparison to make, after all. And I was aware of my nod to Kushner's structural arrangement. But I'd put so much creative blood, sweat end tears into writing my play, and I knew it came from the heart. I'd been in those clinical rooms I was dramatizing, I'd had those crushed dreams experienced by my characters. Had my quest for emotional authenticity blinded me to a lack of *creative* authenticity?

His other remark about the echo of 70s agitprop made me recall the comparison with Joan Littlewood. Suddenly I found myself wondering if somehow I'd also been influenced by a play I'd never seen. Was this even possible? Had that early teenage run-in with Brecht's *Chalk Circle* created some sort of creative stea th osmosis in me, whereby I'd unconsciously absorbed stories by other theatre makers through the collective cultural consciousness? Growing up with a politically radical father, I'd absorbed many adult conversations about socialism, anarchism and activism. It was my Dad who'd taken my siblings and me to see the Brecht show, and we were no strangers to alternative theatre and comedy, which was performed at the demonstrations and political festivals that he regularly took us to. Surely all of this might fall under the umbrella of 'influence' without causing me undue worry?

Things were about to get a lot more salty.

I had by then met Laurie, a wonderful and experienced director. He related to it personally, having beccme a parent with the help of IVF, and he agreed to direct the play. In an odd twist of fate, Laurie knew *Angels in America* far better than me – he had actually written his MA thesis about it. Ear y on in our initial discussions, he ra sed its obvious influence on my own play in a far more analytical way than Rcger had, and my blood ran cold.

Angels opens with a character monologue that lays out the play's themes. As did mine. *Angels* has a five-act structure, with each act given a thematic title. As did mine. *Angels* is characterized by its theatrical use of limina dream spaces, including biblical ones. As did mine.

Oh dear.

Most galling of all: wasn't my working title, *The Bank of Britain*, a clear mirroring of *Angels in America*?

Oh God. How had I naively missed this obvious artistic echo?

I went into a tailspin. Was I borrowing from *Angels*? Paying homage to the point of imitation? Had artistic inspiration become, without any conscicus intent, a form of theft? Had I actually *cannibalized* Kushner's play?

I knew that taken separately (title aside) none of the elements our plays had in common were of Tony Kushner's own invention. Five-act structure has been around for several millennia; it was good enough for Shakespeare anc the Romans before him. The same went for monologue as dramatic prologue

And of course, magical realism techniques appear in swathes of modern drama. If I owed a debt to Kushner, didn't I also owe a debt to Brecht? And if so, why didn't that debt bother me in the same way?

Here's Kushner again on the relationship between reality and fantasy on stage, with reference to the concept of *verfremdungseffekt*:

> As [Brecht] ... wrote in one of his theater poems, let people 'see that this is not magic, but work, my friends.' His most famous, and most misunderstood, idea about staging is what he calls the distanciation effect – he wants theater to enable you to see the familiar as strange and the strange as familiar, so that you greet reality with an appetite to interpret it.
>
> (2012)

It's easy to accept that all playwrights are influenced by the great ones who came before them. The question is, what one *does* with that influence? Kushner may have borrowed Brechtian techniques, but he evolved them into his own art form. *Angels* is a trailblazing, brilliant play because it speaks with Kushner's erudite and original voice. My problem was that now I could see just how much *Angels* had influenced some of my stylistic principles and theatrical techniques, I was doubting my own voice. In trying to create some artistic distance from my lived experience to help me dramatize it in the play, had I merely copied someone else's voice?

David Hare commented on the dangers of literary influence in a National Theatre interview in 2011:

> I think that certain playwrights in my lifetime, by being great, have also been disastrously influential. And Harold Pinter is the obvious example. You know ... when the curtain goes up and we're in a room and two un-named people are vaguely threatening each other with very short rhythmic dialogue – which I'm afraid is a play you see more than any other in the British theatre now – you do go, 'Oh Harold, what is being done in your name?'
>
> (2011)

Would my own play invoke a similar question? 'Oh Tony'?

Thankfully, Laurie was immediately practical. His priority was to start wrangling the play into production; it had to be cast, with a creative team assembled, and there was much work to be done on the script. But before I went off to start rewriting, we jointly agreed that I would change the play's title. It was one thing to lean creatively on a famous play, but another to echo its title quite so overtly, even if it was an unconscious decision. We landed on *Genesis Inc.*, the name of Dr Marshall's clinic.

We also, for various mainly practical reasons to help with staging, reconfigured the action of the play into three acts instead of five and removed the act titles. Now, no member of the audience to my knowledge sits watching a play in order to identify act breaks, which are often invisible in the staging, apart from the very obvious ones signalled by an interval. But somehow, psychologically, Laurie and I also both felt that in restructuring the play we were moving another subtle step out of the shadow of *Angels* and giving *Genesis* a form more germane to its story.

The play continued to evolve in rehearsal, as they invariably do. The rehearsal process for any play is one of intense interrogation – of the text, its ideas, its stagecraft. Dialogue changes, scenes get cut or trimmed, the structure shifts. The minute we were in rehearsal with our talented cast, and I witnessed the actors creating the characters I'd written, they took on a life of their own. It was immensely reassuring to me that despite the liberal salting of *Angels* on to *Genesis Inc.*, Laurie never doubted the originality of my play overall. He reassured me that the voice coming through the play was mine and not a weak emulation.

It's hard to pinpoint exactly what constitutes a playwright's 'voice'. Tone, style, themes, ideas, stagecraft – all these elements contribute to the overall sense of a writer's creative personality. But the dramatist's voice is also created through our primary tool – the dialogue spoken by our characters. As Linda Anderson has said: 'Sometimes giving voice to others can be the most effective way we can find of expressing what we want to say' (2005: 198). To doubt that your own dramatic voice is 'authentic' – as in, your dialogue is a shallow imitation of that of a famous dramatist – is to be shaken to your core.

It's curious looking back that I'd always accepted artistic influence as an inescapable part of any writer's development. As David Hare pointed out, Pinter's influence on theatre dialogue is vast, as is Caryl Churchill's. The In-yer-face theatre movement of the 90s, led by playwrights such as Mark Ravenhill, Anthony Nielson, Philip Ridley and Sarah Kane, influenced an entire generation of writers, to which I belong. Their plays rejected realism and experimented with deliberately provocative and shocking subjects and experimental theatrical forms. I had seen and loved many of these plays – they have all contributed seasoning to my developing playwright's voice.

I was also well acquainted with literary influence in fiction. When I was in my teens, the novel *du jour* was *Less Than Zero* by Bret Easton Ellis, a coming-of-age story which follows a set of disenfranchised rich high school kids along their decadent road to nowhere; the writer's voice was languid, cool, knowing. He was somehow above them all, yet one of them.

> People are afraid to merge on freeways in Los Angeles. This is the first thing I hear when I come back to the city. Blair picks me up from LAX and mutters this under her breath as her car drives up the on-ramp. She says, people are afraid to merge on freeways in Los Angeles. Though that sentence shouldn't bother me it stays in my mind for an uncomfortably long time. Nothing else seems to matter.
>
> (1985: 9)

Years later, I read Joan Didion's peerless essays and immediately recognized her influence on Ellis. This is from her *Los Angeles Notebook*:

> It is three o'clock on a Sunday afternoon and 105 degrees and the air so thick with smog that the dusty palm trees loom with a sudden and rather attractive mystery. I have been playing in the sprinklers with the baby and I get in the car and go to Ralph's Market on the corner of Sunset and Fuller wearing an old bikini bathing suit. This is not a very good thing to wear to the market but neither is it, at Ralph's on the corner of Sunset and Fuller, an unusual costume.
>
> ([1968] 2017: 167)

Interestingly, discovering this strong echo of Didion in Ellis's work didn't make me think any less of him as a writer. The salt is but one ingredient in the soup. Ellis would, of course, go on to influence a whole generation of writers himself and has never been coy about acknowledging his debt to her:

> *Slouching Towards Bethlehem* was a revelation. What is so apparent when you're reading those essays is that it really was in the style that the meaning of everything was located .... I sat and typed up paragraph after paragraph of her work in order to figure out how she did it. A writer only needs one or two influences, and I had mine.
>
> (2022)

Didion has written about her own debt to Hemingway, admitting that she taught herself to write by retyping his stories on her own typewriter, just to see how it felt to have his words beneath her fingertips. And Hemingway is said to have been influenced by the Modernist American novelist Gertrude

Stein, who apparently advised him to use the continuous present tense in his prose, as seen in both Ellis's and Didion's writing here.

I think my anxiety at the time over the relationship between *Angels* and *Genesis Inc.* was because the shadow of this one *particular* play on mine seemed so obvious to others. A novelist might wear their stylistic influences on their coat sleeves or hide them in their pockets, but they are more easily absorbed in the sheer breadth and depth of a long-form novel, the act on of which takes place in the reader's subjective mind. In stark contrast, plays are performance pieces, enacted in 3-D to a collective audience, and creative influences on a playwright are perhaps more obvious when externalized in dialogue and physical stagecraft.

I do wonder if I'd also been blinded to the possible shadow of Kushner's play on mine *because* my own was based so much on my own life. Although I had never consciously worried about cannibalizing my own experience in the play, perhaps I had buried some unconscious concerns about exposing myself. Hanif Kureishi wrote recently in his Substack blog, 'The Kureishi Chronicles', on using autobiography as theatrical material: 'It is one thing to write a novel about your life, and another to see actual actors wearing your clothes, mimicking your expressions and cadence' (2024).

On a fundamental level my story was, to me, both 'true' and experientially 'mine' – but it also needed to become a fully fledged work of fiction. Perhaps by busying myself intellectually with questions of structure and form, I was able to distance myself from my own personal experiences enough to write about them – achieving a sort of Brechtian *verfremdungseffekt* on my own story. had made an intellectual separation between the instinctive 'lived' elements of my story's genesis and my writing craft, where Kushner's influence could be seen by everyone, it seemed, but me.

None of this was clear to me at the time of writing. 'You're so brave to expose your life like that' was a common response from friends and family who eventually saw the play. 'Isn't it terrifying?' Ironically, my lasting terror during the play's development and production came from the idea of having my ignorance of my creative influences exposed.

Creative authenticity is an elusive quality that is found, I think, in the cloudy intersections between experience, feelings, ideas and thoughts, which eventually coagulate into an original work of art. Anyone can research a particular subject matter. And anyone can study classical dramatic structure or copy techniques used by great writers, but we have to be careful not to swallow the work of others whole. Or indigestion will follow.

At the same time, we should not be afraid of nourishing ourselves with rich sources of inspiration. Like Didion typing out Hemingway or Kushner studying Brecht, we might use a great work to light the fire under our own cooking pot.

American writer and essayist Adam Gopnik recently said in an interview with comedian turned screenwriter and novelist Steve Martin:

> Nobody ever finds their voice by shutting off their influences. You find it by imitating other people and then through the process of osmosis, of putting in those people, internalizing their sound. Suddenly, one day you wake up and you say, 'Oh, that doesn't sound like anybody else. That sounds like me'.
>
> (2023)

Now, seven years after the play finished its run, I still believe the interplay of authenticity and imagination in creating a piece of drama is a complex one. But I can see with hindsight that submerging myself in *Angels* spurred me on to try new things and to push my theatrical ambitions. It helped me find a new tone in my creative voice that I've continued to use in subsequent works. Thankfully, I can now acknowledge my play's debt to Kushner's masterwork without feeling reduced or marginalized by it. When I read the play now, instead of fearing I'll bump into Tony, I just see my characters. And in their dialogue and in their stories, I meet myself.

Works Cited

Anderson, L. (ed.) (2005), *Creative Writing: A Workbook with Readings*, London: Routledge.

Brecht, B. ([1936] 1964), 'Alienation Effects in Chinese Acting', in *Brecht on Theatre: The Development of an Aesthetic*, trans. J. Willett, New York: St Martin's Press, pp. 91–9.

Didion, J. ([1968] 2017), 'Los Angeles Notebook', in *Slouching towards Bethlehem*, London: Fourth Estate, pp. 164–9.

Ellis, B. E. (1985), *Less Than Zero*, New York: Simon & Schuster.

Ellis, B. E. (2022), 'Personal History: Bret Easton Ellis', as told to Steffie Nelson, *Alta Magazine*, 5 April. Available online: https://www.altaonline.com/books/nonfiction/a39187806/personal-history-bret-easton-ellis-joan-didion/ (accessed 6 May 2024).

Gopnik, A. (2023), in 'Steve Martin on Finding Your Authentic Voice', *ReThinking with Adam Grant* (series), TED audio collective, 4 May. Available online: https://podcasts.apple.com/us/podcast/steve-martin-on-finding-your-authentic-voice/id1554567118?i=1000611667002 (accessed 8 April 2024).

Hare, D. (2011), 'David Hare on Playwriting', National Theatre Youtube Channel, 11 November. Available online: https://www.youtube.com/watch?v=v8N2WwZFNDo&list=PLtINNPNOafm8Kt07hefK8bbrebYdPmrv2&index=3&t=22s (accessed 18 June 2004).

Kennedy, J. (2018), *Genesis Inc.*, London: Nick Hern Books.

Kureishi, H. (2024), 'Sunny Afternoon/Black Dog', in *The Kureishi Chronicles*, Substack, 8 June. Available online: https://hanifkureishi.substack.com/p/sunny-afternoonblack-dog.

Kushner, T. (1997), *Tony Kushner in Conversation (Triangulations: Lesbian/Gay/ Queer Theater/Drama/Performance)*, R. Vorlicky (ed.), Michigan: University of Michigan Press.

Kushner, T. (2007), *Angels in America: A Gay Fantasia on National Themes*, London: Nick Hern Books.

Kushner, T. (2012), 'The Drama of Belief: Tony Kushner on Theatre', by James K. A. Smith, *Fors Clavigera*, 12 July. Available online: https://forsclavigera.blogspot.com/2012/07/drama-of-belief-tony-kushner-on-theatre.html#:~:text=As%20he%20wrote%20in%20one,familiar%2C%20so%20that%20you%20greet (accessed 18 June 2024).

Littlewood, J. (1967), *Oh, What a Lovely War!*, London: Bloomsbury Modern Classics.

Yorke, J. (2024), 'The Power of Five-Act Structure'. Available online: https://www.johnyorkestory.com/five-act-structure (accessed 21 August 2024).

10

'Go Outside'

Nature and Chance as Poetic Influence

By Shaindel Beers

The 1980s, a wood-paneled bedroom in the humid, Indiana summer. Looking back in my mind's eye, two books existed for me, though I know there were others. *Poems of Byron, Keats and Shelley*, selected and edited by Elliott Coleman and *Poetry of the Victorian Period*, edited by Jerome Hamilton Buckley and George Benjamin Woods. These had been my mother's college textbooks in the 1960s, and just opening them could transport me. I could get lost over and over in George Meredith's 'Modern Love', a sequence of sixteen-line sonnets about a marriage falling apart, and I thrilled each time I read John Davidson's companion poems, 'A Ballad of Heaven' and 'A Ballad of Hell'.

In 'A Ballad of Heaven', a composer is so focused on writing his magnum opus that he hasn't noticed that his wife and child have died of starvation. It is high melodrama:

He thought to copy down his score;
The moonlight was his lamp; he said,
'Listen, my love'; but on the floor
His wife and child were lying dead.

([1894] 1965: 846)

When he discovers that he has neglected his family to the point of allowing them to starve to death, his heart bursts, and he immediately goes to Heaven where he is reunited with his wife and child. In the last line, God comforts him that his composition '[i]s now the music of the spheres' ([1894] 1965: 847).

In 'A Ballad of Hell', a woman is tricked by an untrue lover into a suicide pact. They agree that they will both die by suicide at midnight so they can be together even if it is in Hell, and he won't be forced to marry his cousin in an arranged marriage. When the heroine arrives in Hell after her suicide, Satan greets her, 'Comely, and tall. and black as jet' ([1894] 1965: 848), and tells her that she has been tricked. When she finally realizes that her lover, Malespina, will not be joining her in Hell, she tells the devil, 'I was betrayed; – I will not stay' ([1894] 1965), and walks straight into Heaven:

Seraphs and saints with one great voice
Welcomed that soul that knew not fear;
. Amazed to find it could rejoice,
Hell raised a hoarse half-human cheer.

([1894] 1965)

To my evangelically raised, adolescent mind, this was madness. People could fall in love with other people while they were married? You could die by suicide and still go to Heaven? You could neglect your family to the point of death, yet find forgiveness and love, and be rewarded by God?

I realized even then, as a young teen, that poetry was a world without rules. It existed outside of the strict moral code that I had grown up with, where everything was a sin, and good begot good, and bad begot bad, and because of Eve's original sin, I could never be good enough, especially because I was a girl. Poetry was the outlaw religion my heart desired. When other people sought answers in the Bible or in prayer, I took comfort in poetry. I immediately started writing the most daring, horrible Victorian style poetry my adolescent mind could produce. One poem started out:

I must confess, my dear, sweet Bess,
I have done a most hateful deed,
But the things I have done
With your man each night
Were strictly out of need.
You see, he offered me great riches,
And I have no aversion to greed.

Like many young writers, my influences were long dead, and I wasn't exposed to contemporary writers until much, much later. I went through stages of imitating Donne and Milton as well; I was an amoeba, surrounding and becoming one with whatever I read. As Saul Bellow once said, 'A writer is a reader moved to emulation' (Tartt 2006: 188), and literature moved me in a way that nothing else had. I don't think there was anything wrong with my obsession with these long-dead poets. Milton is amazing. Imagine being the person to coin the word 'pandemonium' by combining the Greek prefix pan-, meaning 'all', with the Late Latin daemonium, meaning 'evil spirit'. Imagine being the person to invent the saying, 'all Hell broke loose' ([1667] 2003: 443). Imagine writing a seduction poem using a flea as your vehicle, daring a 'three-person'd God' to '[b]atter [your] heart' (Donne [1633] 2004: 320). I was doomed to be a poet. There was no way around it. I just didn't know how to be a poet as myself in the correct century because no one had introduced me to any contemporary poets. Even though we were separated by gender, geography and time, these influences were inspirational. These writers were literally *making* language the same way that Shakespeare invented or introduced 1,700 new words into the English language. The word *poet* comes from the Greek word poiētēs, meaning 'maker' or 'creator'. This meant, in a sense, that poets were *gods*. This was everything that I wasn't supposed to be as a girl being raised to be demure, where my parents constantly told me what *nice* girls did and didn't do. In writing, I could do whatever I wanted, and no one had to know about it.

Later in undergrad, I took Literature by Women and discovered Sylvia Plath, Anne Sexton, Margaret Atwood and more. I read Anne Sexton's 'For My Lover, Returning to His Wife' ([1969] 1981: 188) and gasped! The audacity! Just the title admits more than some people are willing to do in their entire lives. That was what I had been trying to do with my 'Bess' poem in my teens, except that my poem had been all imagination and no lived experience at all. These poets, just by virtue of being female and North American and born during the same century I was born in, had more in common with me than any I had read before. I wish as a young writer I had been exposed to a wider variety of poets. I, especially, wish I had been introduced to poets with a lived experience similar to mine so that I could have seen myself, more easily, as a poet. This is why representation matters and why we need young poets to stretch outside of the boundaries of their experience to broaden themselves but also to read poets who resemble them in areas of race, ethnicity, nationality, regionality, gender identity and so on. Young writers need to realize that poetry is a big umbrella, and there is room for all of us underneath.

Years later, in graduate school, I was exposed to world poets, poets in translation. I was told to read whatever interested me and make it a part of my poetry. One of my professors said to our class, 'If you love mountains, read about mountains; if you love philosophy, read philosophy'. That is the freedom that more young writers should be given earlier in their writing careers. Instead of being focused on writers of a certain era or region, they should read widely – poets from the past, contemporary poets, world poets – and they should read about any topics that interest them. But they also need to look up from their books. They need to go outside and experience the natural world. Notice the wildflowers, notice the songs of the birds, and beyond noticing them, *learn* them. Writers need to discover all they can. They should load their phones with apps like PlantSnap, which identifies plants with a picture, and BirdNET, which identifies birds by their song. They need to become citizen scientists of the world around them and let these be the things that inform their poems. They can't be inside, alone with books, and really be a poet. The influence has to come from outside of themselves.

Wallace Stevens once said, 'The poet is the priest of the invisible' (Biespiel 2015: 42). David Biespiel interprets this to mean the poet 'is astonished by all things, including by what is barely known or fleetingly known, by what is all but imperceptible or what is suddenly realized, and even by what is absent entirely. For Stevens, the poet is both a seer and a clarifier of meaning' (Biespiel 2015: 42). In Stevens' poem 'Notes Toward a Supreme Fiction', he writes, 'Perhaps / The truth depends on a walk around the lake' (1954: 397). Stevens, who never learned how to drive, walked nearly two and a half miles each way to work five days a week, and often composed his poems while walking to work.

I also spend a lot of contemplative time outdoors, either walking, running, or hiking, and find much of my inspiration there. One July day in 2014, I was running along the Umatilla River when I saw a flock of American white pelicans, and I almost didn't stop. In fact, I kept running for a bit until curiosity got the better of me. I couldn't recall that I had ever seen so many pelicans in the wild before, so I went back to investigate. What were pelicans doing so far inland? How many of them had there been? I counted them, and much to my delight, there were thirteen. That particular number seemed like an omen, and when I got home, decided that I would write, 'Thirteen Ways of Looking at a Pelican', inspired by Wallace Stevens' 'Thirteen Ways of Looking at a Blackbird'. At the time, I had signed up to write a poem a day for a month and committed to emailing my poem to the publisher at the end of each day as a fundraiser for their press, and I looked forward to taking a deep dive into exploring pelicans. By this time, I had already published two volumes of poetry, and I wrote many of my poems during April poem-a-day challenges or challenges like the one I had signed up for. If this experiment worked, I would have my assignment of writing a poem a day for thirty days nearly half finished! Whereas Stevens' poem was inspired by haiku and had mostly short stanzas, roughly haiku-length, I was going to write a poem a day about the pelicans for thirteen days and see where it took me.

Like Stevens, I had a river, and I had birds who became characters in many of my poems. Some days, I researched pelicans online, and some days I walked to the river to observe them. Even when the pelicans weren't there, I could write about the absence of the pelicans, the way that Stevens did with the blackbirds:

I do not know which to prefer,
The beauty of inflections
Or the beauty of innuendoes,

The blackbird whistling
Or just after.

(1954: 93)

My first pelican poem dealt with a previous experience I had had with the pelicans the month before, when a lone pelican seemed to be injured in the river:

The lone pelican in the reeds
of river's edge seemed odd.
I stopped – watched –
did nothing.

(2018: 65)

At the end of the first poem, I was surprised by what I had written: 'Forgive me, pelican. I also, am always alone, / also fly too recklessly for my own good' (2018). Somehow, the story of the pelican had become *my* story as well. What I learned quickly in writing this series of poems was that I needed the pelicans, something outside of myself to write hard truths. I couldn't have faced my truths directly. I needed the pelicans in the same way John Donne needed the flea.

In Donne's case, 'The Flea' is a seduction poem:

Mark but this flea, and mark in this,
How little that which thou deniest me is;
It sucked me first, and now sucks thee,
And in this flea our two bloods mingled be.

(2004: 309)

In the beginning of Donne's poem, the lover tells his beloved that a flea has bitten him and has bitten her, so their blood is already combined. They are already married, so having sex wouldn't be a sin. Even though this is a cheeky poem, especially for the time in which it was written, the speaker still uses a vehicle (the flea) to justify their actions (premarital sex). There was no way for Donne to just say this in a poem; he had to find a coy way of doing so. I felt this way about my pelicans.

They were going to be my vehicle of self-discovery and my way of discovering so much more outside of myself. Through this one chance encounter, I learned the science behind *dynamic soaring*. I learned about the orphaned pelican, Bigbird, in Africa, who was taught to fly by humans. My son was three years old at the time, and I took him to see the pelicans and wrote about his language acquisition as he tried to talk about them. I wrote about the history and taxonomy of pelicans and their place in myth and religion. I wrote about pelicans and climate change, the possible ruination of our environment. And without realizing it, I wrote about my impending breakup with my son's father. In my mind, then, in 2014, I didn't know it was happening, but reading those poems ten years later, all the signs were there.

In the first pelican poem that I wrote, I looked back to the first time I had seen a pelican on the river. It was alone, which seemed strange to me, and that lone pelican had been a sign. A wildlife expert was quoted in our local newspaper as saying, 'When you see / a pelican alone, it usually / means something is wrong', and I borrowed that line for use in my first pelican poem (2018: 65).

When I read in the newspaper that the pelican had been eutharized, I didn't know if it would have been better for me to have called the local wildlife rescue sooner. I expressed my doubt in the first poem:

Did I cause that pelican
more hours of suffering
or gift it a few more hours
of floating in the reeds,
a little while longer to bob
in the gentle current,
the coolness of water over webbed feet?

(2018)

In my second pelican poem, I wrote about trying to communicate this event and the emotional heaviness of it to my son's father:

When I told you about the pelican –
That I thought I should have called someone.
You said, *That's your problem. You always*
doubt your instincts.

(2018: 66)

The accusatory *That's your problem* was the way he always spoke to me. Everything about me was wrong. There was always something about me that needed to be fixed. Even now, I wince when I read these words, even though I am the author of the poem. I reflected on how I had known in the first pelican poem that I also was always alone, 'Forgive me, pelican. I also, am always alone, / also fly too recklessly for my own good' (2018: 65). In these poems, I had done what poets before me had done for centuries, taken the world in and used it to learn about myself. The pelican poems had a life of their own, and I was merely along for the ride, the same way Milton never intended for Satan to be the hero of *Paradise Lost*. Something in the poem, in the writing of it, takes over, and we are at its mercy. The only way into the poem is by giving up control. This is where inspiration comes in. The poet can't be a control freak. The very word *inspiration* comes from *inspirare* (Latin 'to breathe or blow into'). To be inspired is to be a vessel, to literally have an idea 'breathed' or 'blown into' you. To give up control and let the poem batter and break you the same way that John Donne's Holy Sonnet says that one should surrender to God ([1633] 2004: 320).

Every time I let the poem take me somewhere, I am better for it. Even though writing poems might seem narcissistic or egotistical (who wants to know that much about *me*?), it seems that it is something outside of myself guiding me, and when I give up that control, I write the best poems. It is whatever comes to me when I look at the world with childlike curiosity, when I stop to count the pelicans, when I think about how I can transpose language in new and playful ways, when I realize the world is endless and will give me endless topics to write about. I just have to go outside and look outside of myself and go where the poems take me.

Works Cited

Beers, S. (2018), *Secure Your Own Mask*, Buffalo: White Pine Press.

Biespiel, D. (2015), *A Long High Whistle: Selected Columns on Poetry*, Champaign: Antilever Press.

Coleman, E. (ed.) (1967), *Poems of Byron, Keats and Shelley*, Elliott Coleman (ed.), New York: Doubleday.

Davidson, J. ([1894] 1965), '"A Ballad of Heaven," "A Ballad of Hell"', in J. Hamilton Buckley and G. Benjamin Woods (eds), *Poetry of the Victorian Period*, Chicago: Scott, Foresman, pp. 846–7, 847–8.

Donne, J. ([1633] 2004), '"The Flea," "Batter My Heart, Three-Person'd God"', in M. Ferguson, M. J. Salter and J. Stallworthy (eds), *The Norton Anthology of Poetry*, Fifth Edition, New York: W. W. Norton, pp. 309, 320.

Milton, J. ([1667] 2003), *Paradise Lost*, in S. Orgel and J. Goldberg (eds), *The Major Works*, Oxford: Oxford University Press, pp. 355–618.

Sexton, A. ([1969] 1981), *The Complete Poems*, Boston: Houghton Mifflin.

Stevens, W. (1954), *The Collected Poems of Wallace Stevens*, New York: Alfred A. Knopf.

Tartt, D. (2006), 'Character Is the Very Life Blood of Fiction', in S. A. Johnson (ed.), *The Very Telling: Conversations with American Writers*, Lebanon: University Press of New England, pp. 187–92.

11

Jesus, Fairy Tales and Flash Fiction

By Kit de Waal

I first heard of flash fiction in 2011 when I discovered The Fish One-Page Prize. Until then I thought of short stories as a piece of writing with an average word count of three thousand words. Flash fiction, by contrast, is a short-short story, slimmed down to under a thousand words, with many flash fiction competitions imposing a maximum word count of 250 words.[1] Flash fiction is also called 'micro fiction', 'sudden fiction' and 'smokelong' (a story lasting only as long as the time it takes to smoke a cigarette). The term 'flash fiction' was popularized and came into general use after the publication of the influential anthology Sudden Fiction: American Short-Short Stories in 1986.

The appeal of flash fiction is the absence of information, an economy of language to achieve maximum effect, or, as Hemingway said:

If a writer of prose knows enough of what he is writing about, he may omit things that he knows and the reader, if the writer is writing truly enough, will have a feeling of those things as strongly as though the writer had stated them. The dignity of movement of an iceberg is due to only one-eighth of it being above water.

(1958: 183)

I became aware that every single word has to work hard, harder than in a novel, where you have pages and pages to get your point across. Each word and

---

[1] Bath Flash Fiction Award, Bridport Prize, Reflex Fiction, Mslexia, Flash 500, Fish Prize.

each sentence have to allude to something beyond the story, something that started before the story began and continues after the story is over. Hence, flash fiction 'should be read like a poem. That is, slowly', says Grace Paley (Faulkner 2023: 99), but unlike a poem, flash fiction must be a proper story with a narrative arc, with characters that develop or change, with a beginning, a middle and an end, even if that ending is only implied.

Furthermore, it is not simply a case of compressing all the elements of a standard short story into an even shorter form. Tara L. Masih, in her introduction to *The Rose Metal Press Field Guide to Writing Flash Fiction*, describes it as 'a story in miniature, a work of art carved on a grain of rice' (2009: xi), but this suggests that it is somehow the same as a short story, with all the same elements simply shrunk down. But it is so much more than that. It's a collection of words, yes, but it also has something unique, and that is the forced absence of words. Flash fiction is 'not a diminutive version of anything. It's its own self' (Shapard and Thomas 1986: 244).

The craft of the author involves a process of distillation, achieved through meticulous editing and an acute awareness of the story's essence. This refinement requires not only a deep understanding of the narrative but also a confidence in the reader's ability to engage with and interpret the work beyond what is explicitly stated. By exercising precision in language and structure, the writer shapes a text that is both succinct and resonant, allowing meaning to emerge organically from what is present and, perhaps even more significantly, from what is left unsaid.

This trust in the reader is perhaps best explained by George Saunders who characterizes the reader as

> humane, bright, witty, experienced and as well intentioned as you, and that, to communicate intimately with her, you have to maintain the state, through revision, of generously imagining her. You revise your reader up, in your imagination, with every pass. You keep saying to yourself: 'No, she's smarter than that. Don't dishonour her with that lazy prose or that easy notion'.

> (2017)

I entered The Fish Flash Fiction Prize the following year with a piece entitled 'The Taste of Death' (2012) about a dying chef passing on a recipe to his wife. It didn't make the shortlist or the longlist, but it was highly commended – the first competition I had ever entered – and with that modest success I realized I'd found a form of fiction that intrigued and challenged me, and I thought perhaps I might be good at it. I spent the next few years reading and writing flash fiction, trying to decipher what made it work: what was the best structure and form and the precise ingredients that could render a whole world – a past, a future and a turn – in so few words; how to have a satisfying ending – surprising yet inevitable – and how, in short, flash fiction could condense a novel's worth of information into a much smaller container.

'Proof Positive' (1947) by Graham Greene and 'The Three Fat Women of Antibes' (1940) by Somerset Maugham demonstrate concise, detail-rich storytelling, full of allusion and absence, as do the works of contemporary writers such as Nuala Ni Chonchúir in *Mother America* (2010) and Tania Hershman in 'My Mother Was an Upright Piano': 'My mother was an upright piano, spine erect, lid tightly closed, unplayable except by the maestro. My father was not the maestro (2012). In *Papa* (de Groot 1984), a one-man play about Ernest Hemingway, the following six-word story is attributed to Hemingway. Although the authorship has never been verified, this illustrates how brevity can intensify emotional depth: 'For sale: baby shoes, never worn (1984: 25).

Flash fiction as a literary form offers another parallel: the Gospels – the books of Matthew, Mark, Luke and John of the New Testament of the Holy Bible. These stories, told by Jesus to illustrate a moral lesson, were designed to be more than the words, a tale with a deeper meaning, a story with another story lurking beneath. Jesus conveyed narratives that were immediately comprehensible to his audience, as they were rooted in everyday life yet also encapsulated profound and occasionally disconcerting truths.

As a child I had spent hours and hours in draughty meeting rooms listening to these stories and the way in which Jesus (or the writers) used characterization and structure, dialogue and description to lure the reader to the end where the moral or lesson lay. 'Jesus was not a theologian. He was a God who told stories' (L'Engle 2000: 58). Indeed, listening to the minister tell these stories and hearing him dissect Jesus' parables was often the only interesting part of a long sermon, so I paid attention. I discovered that although I was a very reluctant reader as a child and never read for pleasure, the grounding I received in storytelling would serve me well as later I began to grapple with this very short form of prose. So, despite my rejection of this severe Christian cult and its teachings, I realized these stories had gone in, and on a deep level, they had done their work, not in a moral sense but in a literary one.

I found a Bible and began to read. As a starting point, I read the story of 'The Good Samaritan', the parable that speaks to the notion of neighbourliness and the difference between following the letter of the law and being godly. In the book of Luke, Jesus is speaking with a lawyer, who asks what he must do to ensure eternal life. Jesus answers with a question, asking the lawyer what is written in the law. The lawyer correctly summarizes the passage, which includes the famous commandment to 'Love thy neighbour as thyself'. Jesus affirms his answer, saying, 'Do this, and you will live'.

However, seeking to justify himself, the lawyer then asks: 'And who is my neighbour?' (Luke 10. 30–7).

It is this question that prompts Jesus to tell the Parable of the Good Samaritan, illustrating that a neighbour is not defined by social or ethnic boundaries but by acts of compassion and mercy:

> And Jesus answering said, 'A certain man went down from Jerusalem to Jericho, and fell among thieves, which stripped him of his raiment, and wounded him, and departed, leaving him half dead. And by chance there came down a certain priest that way: and when he saw him, he passed by on the other side. And likewise a Levite, when he was at the place, came and looked on him, and passed by on the other side. But a certain Samaritan, as he journeyed, came where he was: and when he saw him, he had compassion on him. And went to him, and bound up his wounds, pouring in oil and wine, and set him on his own beast, and brought him to an inn, and took care of him. And on the morrow when he departed, he took out two pence, and gave them to the host, and said unto him, Take care of him; and whatsoever thou spendest more, when I come again, I will repay thee. Which now of these three, thinkest thou, was neighbour unto him that fell among the thieves?' And he said, 'He that shewed mercy on him.' Then said Jesus unto him, 'Go, and do thou likewise'.
>
> (Luke 10)

This parable has all the ingredients of a good short story: a protagonist, antagonists, three acts, peril, a crisis point and a resolution.

Rereading the Bible, I was reminded of other New Testament parables that I had been taught as a child brought up in a strict evangelical Christian household. In the Gospel of Matthew, the parable of the mustard seed encapsulates profound theological significance in just a few lines: 'The kingdom of heaven is like to a grain of mustard seed, which a man took, and sowed in his field: which indeed is the least of all seeds, but when it is grown, it is the greatest among herbs, and becometh a tree' (Mt. 13.31–2).

Much like a well-crafted flash fiction piece, both forms invite readers to engage deeply with the subtext, relying on suggestion and resonance rather than explicit explanation. Defined by its brevity and impact, flash fiction demands economy of language while still delivering profound meaning. Like Jesus' parables, flash fiction relies on implication rather than exposition.

Once I began examining the parables, however, I moved on further into the New Testament and re-read other much shorter scriptures that I learnt as a child, experiencing disturbing insights into the all-knowing, all-seeing God who could discern the deepest desires of the heart. I thought about the book of Romans Chapter 1 verse 29, written by St Paul, which speaks of sin being an attitude nestled deep within and that even the desire to do wrong – even without a sinful act – was enough to earn God's displeasure:

> And they were filled with all unrighteousness, wickedness, greed and badness, being full of envy, murder, strife, deceit and malice, being whisperers, backbiters, haters of God, insolent, haughty, boastful, schemers of what is harmful, disobedient to parents, without understanding, false to agreements, having no natural affection and merciless.
>
> (Rom. 1.29)

The phrase 'schemers of what is harmful' made me recall an incident in my childhood relating to my very upright mother's infidelity, something that I somehow knew and yet did not know, or at least could not have articulated, as a child. It was the very lack of certainty and the absence of knowledge that made me think of the absences and hidden information alluded to by Hemingway's iceberg principle – only one-eighth of it being above the water. What I knew about my mother's emotional affair was hidden even from my consciousness, and only much later, as an adult, could I bring it to life. I recalled her unhappiness and distractedness around this time and imagined the agonies of her deceit and scheming when she heard this scripture from the minister. I wondered how I could bring all of this – her yearning, her excuses, her cover ups, my childhood, my innocence, the sense of danger and wrongness – all together into one short piece of fiction. In essence, I wanted to write a parable. I knew I had the bones and all the ingredients, and I knew that the story would lie in the absences, in the unsaid.

'Romans Chapter 1 Verse 29, The Sins of the Heart' became the title of the piece of flash fiction which won the Bridport Prize in 2013:

Romans Chapter 1 Verse 29

The Sins of the Heart

She needs bread.

'I'll be five minutes,' she sings and her heartbeat drums her across the road, around the corner, down the hill. She wears slippers and carries a tea towel, clean, unused. She has neighbours, her journey needs the proof of innocence.

But he is not there tending his front garden. His neat and slender house is shadowy and locked.

'We need milk,' she chimes. and fastens her baby in the pushchair as restraint. She sees him waiting and his smile is worth her shame.

One Sunday the minister points to close print on rice paper and speaks of sins imagined, words unsaid. He traces footsteps from her husband's bed all the way across the road, around the corner, down the hill and she has weeks to wait before God looks away.

She has a list and calls us inside.

'Do we have to?'

'Yes, you have to,' she mutters and foists cold coins in my sister's hand. We cross the road, around the corner, down the hill. A man as tall as my father leans on an open gate like he knows us. Dark soil escapes from his trowel.

We carry her bag home one handle each, potatoes, flour, unnecessary things and, as we pass, he tips his hat and says hello. He has sweets, dusty, pink and everlasting.

'Did you see anyone?' she asks.

We spill her change and our adventure on the kitchen table, and she slips away.

'Forgot the sugar,' she whispers, 'forgot the eggs.'

I wrote this piece quickly, over the course of a day. I wrote over 500 words and edited it down to 250 because I wanted it to meet the criteria of the flash fiction competition. I used the repetition of 'around the corner, down the hill' to denote both the passage of time and proximity of danger. As a literary device, repetition can evoke strong emotions while mimicking the forced or overwhelming nature of the character's thoughts or experiences. The use of repetition in this piece also references the poetic repetitions in scripture, particularly the use of *begat* in the Old Testament, for example: 'And unto Enoch was born Irad; and Irad begat Mehujael and Mehujael begat Methusael and Methusael begat Lamech' (Gen. 4.18). I wrote that the man was 'as tall as my father' to denote that on some level, I likened him to my father because he was in danger of taking my father's place, and I used the cover story of trips to the shop to denote both the innocence of the child and the cleverness and deceit of the adult.

But all this seems to suggest that there is methodical, step-by-step process to writing flash fiction or to creative writing in general. This is not my experience. Writers absorb a lifetime of influences – music, art, family, language, literature, overheard snatches of conversation, the view from the top of the bus – and when we come to write, it's all there inside and we access it not so much as we would look for something particular in a filing cabinet but more fluidly, drawing on anything and everything in service of the story, as Christopher Isherwood wrote: 'I am a camera, with its shutter open, quite passive, recording, not thinking' (1939: 1). The 'thinking' part of the creative process that renders up the story continues to fascinate and elude our attempts to explain it. It is inherently difficult to observe oneself actively engaged in a creative process. Creativity does not simply involve generating an idea and then directly translating it into words – or sound (music), images and shapes (photography, painting, sculpture), movement (dance) – rather, it unfolds in a more complex and elusive manner.

I never expected to discover a route into writing flash fiction to come from the excessively limited confines of the fundamentalist Christian cult that had blighted my childhood. As an adult I considered the Bible as nothing but fairy tales, misogyny and condemnation, and that the many hours I'd spent reading it were wasted time. But as Tolkien wrote, 'Why should a man be scorned if, finding himself in prison, he tries to get out and go home? Or if, when he cannot do so, he thinks and talks about other topics than jailers and prison-walls?' (1947: 76). Tolkien further emphasizes that the world beyond our immediate perception endures, even if we cannot see it, underscoring the legitimacy of imaginative exploration. So, it was perhaps the very restrictive nature of the religion, coupled with snippets of story and parables, as well as the structure of the biblical writings and the very proper use of language in the church's publications (and indeed language analysis and critical analysis of scripture, in five crushing hours of Bible study every week), that were the incubator for my imagination. That I can use all those stories learned, during those years of discomfort, as the inspiration for flash fiction, for stories that would win prizes and for many other stories that came afterwards, is surprising and gratifying.

Works Cited

Chonchuir, N. Ni (2012), *Mother America*, Dublin: New Island Books.

de Groot, J. (1984), *Papa: The Legendary Lives of Ernest Hemingway, a Play in Two Acts*, Fort Lauderdale: S.i.

de Waal, K. (2013), 'Romans Chapter 1 Verse 29, The Sins of the Heart', Bridport Prize International Creative Writing Competition. Available online: https://bridportprize.org.uk/writers-room/kit-de-waals-winning-flash-fiction/?srsltid=AfmBOorZTrsu6vZ0aLmbWqEsme8voGY3dAcoKHka6USWSPyKBZnt_yFe (accessed 31 January 2025)

Faulkner, G. (2023), *The Art of Brevity: Crafting the Very Short Story*, Albuquerque: University of New Mexico Press.

Greene, G. (1947), *Nineteen Stories*, London: William Heinemann.

Hemingway, E. (1958), *Death in the Afternoon*, London: Jonathan Cape.

Hershman, T. (2012), 'My Mother Was an Upright Piano', *Fictionaut*. Availble online: http://fictionaut.com/stories/tania-hershman/my-mother-was-an-upright-piano (accessed 1 April 2025).

The Holy Bible, New King James Version (1975), Nashville: HarperCollins Christian Publishing.

Isherwood, C. (1939), *Goodbye to Berlin*, London: Hogarth Press.

L'Engle, M. (2000), *Walking on Water: Reflections on Faith and Art*, US: Harold Shaw Publishers.

Masih, T. L. (ed.) (2009), 'In Pursuit of the Short Short Story: An Introduction', in *Field Guide to Writing Flash Fiction*, Brookline: Rose Metal Press, pp. xi–xxxviii.

Maugham, W. S. (1940), *The Mixture as Before*, London: William Heinemann.

Saunders, G. (2017), 'What Writers Really Do When They Write', *The Guardian*, 4 March. Available online: https://www.theguardian.com/books/2017/mar/04/what-writers-really-do-when-they-write (accessed 30 July 2024).

Thomas, J. and Shapard, R. (eds) (1986), *Sudden Fiction: American Short-Short Stories*, Salt Lake: Gibbs-Smith.

Tolkien, J. R. R. (1947), 'On Fairy-Stories', in C. S. Lewis (ed.), *Essays Presented to Charles Williams*, Oxford: Oxford University Press, pp. 38–89.

12

Alternate Truths and Fake News

By Anietie Isong

Introduction

In 2017, my debut novel, *Radio Sunrise*, was published in the UK. The novel, set in Nigeria, tackles corruption, environmental justice, insecurity and other socio-economic issues in that country. It also illustrates the various ways in which journalists in the country negotiate and represent facts in their work, as well as the ways in which they abide by their professional ethics. I intended to use the novel to explore how journalism can highlight Nigeria's challenges. Satire, in my opinion, was the ideal genre to do so. Indeed, humour was among the few ways Nigerians had left to express their discontent with the state of affairs in their country.

Satire in African culture

Satire aims 'to highlight and ridicule an act of folly to effect change in an individual, group, or society behind the act' (Falola 2022: 151). According to Falola, in Africa, many satirists employ figurative techniques including humour, hyperbole, irony and sarcasm. Satire also features 'in songs of abuses, which are very prominent among the Yoruba. These songs are often sung or performed when people are deemed to have fallen short of societal set standards' (Falola 2022).

Orji (2018) contends that stand-up comedy has successfully adopted satire within the Nigerian performance space. Comedians in the country have cleverly explored topics that are real and are of interest to the citizens. A common theme is politics, where jokes on corruption are performed live on stage. Orji notes that, in several instances, comedians have made humorous remarks about Nigerian leaders regarding their poor handling of the economy. More interestingly and daringly, 'most of the time, the stand-up acts generate ideas while on stage using the audience as fill ups. This enhances the intimacy enjoyed by the comedians and the audience alike' (2018: 34).

Satire's popularity in African novels is intricately linked to the sociopolitical issues in many countries before and after their independence from Europe (Nwezeh 1982). Ayi Kwei Armah uses satire to convey his fury at the politics of his nation in *The Beautyful Ones Are Not Yet Born*. Armah presents a rather bleak picture of Ghanaian society during the time of Kwame Nkrumah, the first president of Ghana. Corruption was rife in the country at that time. One of the characters in the novel 'is a public official who embezzles government funds to enrich himself .... He has a new Mercedes, a well-stocked liquor cabinet, a large house, a closet full of suits and a wife who smells sweetly of perfumes' (Nyamekye 2021: 70). Similarly, in the novel *A Man of the People*, Chinua Achebe satirizes the political class who took over power from the British in Nigeria. A Nigerian minister is described as the 'uncultured minister of culture', who has been appointed a minister for 'notoriously leading the pack of back-bench hounds against the prime minister's opponents during a parliamentary crisis' (Nwezeh 1982: 163). This Nigerian minister 'is anything but a man of the people. His primary concern is to safeguard his seat in the government rather than the welfare of people. He can adopt any corrupt means to come to power and retain his seat' (Bhat 2014: 15).

Satire in *Radio Sunrise*

Radio Sunrise was published over fifty years after Nigeria's independence. Yet the issues Chinua Achebe decried in his novel still persist in the country. Government officials and politicians caught stealing are rarely subjected to significant penalties for their involvement in such acts. Allegations, where they are investigated, often lead to punishment that may be no more than a slap on the wrist. But it appears everyone in the country is guilty of stealing:

We were a nation of thieves. I stole news stories from the CNN. The fat accountant in my station stole millions of naira with his pen. The politicians stole people's votes and declared themselves winners of elections. The rich stole from the poor. The cycle never stopped.

(Isong 2017: 42)

I also chose to satirize the belief in supernatural powers because of its prevalence in Nigeria. In 2015, a Nigerian governor was reported to have vacated his official residence after unknown people allegedly made traditional sacrifices at the house to harm him. As a child, I remember the hysterical rumours circulating in Lagos, that some people could turn into an animal or a stone to get out of tricky situations. Interestingly, the police often took these matters seriously, as depicted below:

The Police Public Relations Officer came out to address us journalists and gasps filled the room when he announced that his men were holding a goat on suspicion of attempted armed robbery in addition to claims that it used juju to change from a human being to escape justice. 'Vigilantes brought the animal to us, claiming it had been a person trying to steal a car,' the policeman said.

(2017: 62)

Journalists in many societies are expected to shape public opinion and expose corruption as well as other wrongdoings. Yet in Nigeria, this is often not the case. According to Reporters Without Borders, a media advocacy group, reporters and news editors are frequently arrested and questioned by authorities. Although freedom of expression and opinion is guaranteed by the country's constitution, there are numerous laws whose provisions allow for the obstruction of journalists' work. These include, for example, legislation pertaining to cybercrime, counterterrorism and state secrets. Furthermore, defamation is considered a felony under the penal law. In *Radio Sunrise*, I acknowledged how journalists in Nigeria can often be rendered powerless in this context: 'The truth is that you cannot fight a corrupt system. I cannot. None of us in the radio station can' (2017: 186).

The attack on press freedom is, of course, not limited to Nigeria. Moene and Søreide suggest that: 'As various forms of authoritarian government take hold around the globe and curtail freedom of the press, promoting and protecting journalists' ability to investigate corruption and publish their findings becomes ever more important and in need of support' (2019: 113). Today, journalists continue to face harassment, even in some so-called democratic societies – simply for witnessing events of public interest and providing objective accounts to the people. Unfortunately, such continual threats could undermine the institutions of democracy around the world.

Although *Radio Sunrise* is fiction, I presented some basic 'facts' on journalism in the book: in the newsroom, investigative journalists often spend time researching a story because accuracy is an essential part of their work. And the newsroom team – including producers, editors and reporters – all have a role to play in preparing and presenting news bulletins on air. Fact-checking for me also meant ensuring the technical details in the book – such as the National Theatre and the Niger Delta – are correct. I followed the example set by journalists, who usually verify all information before publication or broadcast, to avoid fake news. In the excerpt below, the description of Nigeria's National Theatre is true:

The National Theatre was an architectural masterpiece, a cultural landmark and a melting pot of actors, musicians and other artistes. The building always reminded me of a sailor's cap. It was said that the design was taken from the Palace of Culture and Sports in Varna, Bulgaria.

(Isong 2017: 110)

Similarly, in describing the Niger Delta, I included real events regarding militancy in the area, which had plagued Nigeria for many years. In *Radio Sunrise*, just like in real life, 'militants claimed to be fighting for a more even distribution of Nigerian oil-generated wealth on behalf of the local inhabitants, who felt they were being exploited' (2017: 27). To put it in perspective, the oil and gas sector in Nigeria contributes more than 50 per cent of government revenue and over 85 per cent of total exports. This high dependence on fossil fuel has unfortunately put the oil industry at odds with environmental management and conservation. I detailed other oil-related facts in the book: how the Niger Delta's abundant natural wealth stands in stark contrast to its underdevelopment; the government's amnesty programme for militants in the region, and the Nigerian president who proposed it:

Here is the news. The Nigerian President, Umaru Yaradua has proposed an amnesty and unconditional pardon for militants in the Niger Delta in an effort to end years of attacks on Africa's biggest oil and gas industry. The government estimates that up to 20,000 militants could take part in the scheme.

(2017: 90)

Radio Sunrise was influenced by my own experiences and beliefs because I only write about what I know. Nevertheless, scholars continue to question what the book industry considers 'authentic' and the burden it places on certain authors:

The idea of being true to oneself now extends into identity poltics. It pigeonholes writers to produce a certain type of narrative. It's not write what you know; it is write what only you know. Deviation renders the work (or worse, the writer) inauthentic – one of the last taboos of postmodern culture.

(Iyer 2024)

Furthermore:

Marginalized writers are still often expected to only write about their own identity, in their own voice, while being scolded for writing things that are not 'universal' .... In parallel, marginalized writers are held up as spokespeople for their community.

(Afferez 2019)

I set out to write a satirical novel that highlights the deep issues in Nigeria. I have seen how governance and corruption have become intertwined and feed off each other, destroying the foundations of prosperity. I started my writing career in journalism, and was privileged to write satirical pieces (criticism of the government could not be freely expressed) that were broadcast on air, and helped listeners laugh their troubles away. *Radio Sunrise* is my portrayal of the situation in Nigeria as I know it.

I wrote the novel long after I had left journalism. Therefore, upon completion of my first draft, I wondered if my efforts were adequate. Were my characters fully developed? Were they funny enough? Was I being 'authentic'? Fortunately, I knew practising journalists who were happy to critique the draft. These objective eyes helped uncover ways to strengthen the storytelling, including finding satirical angles on some of the most challenging issues. Based on their feedback, I was able to strengthen the plot, develop believable characters and enhance the satire. Collectively, the early readers of the manuscript helped me come up with many of the realistic scenarios in *Radio Sunrise*.

I believe that writers need to be cautious about how they market themselves and their writing. We do not need to make undue claims. *Radio Sunrise* is a fictional representation of life in Nigeria. It is not life in Nigeria. As Leigh argues:

For a work of literature must not be mistaken for a mere copy of human experience, much less of human experience of ultimacy; rather, literature embodies through its symbolic form some analogue with human experience of ultimacy.

(1995: 223)

Conclusion

Literature often takes us beyond what is reported in the news, to show how issues can affect ordinary citizens. In Africa, there is no shortage of literary works dealing with corruption and other pressing issues. These books are intended to assist readers in navigating challenging periods, serving as a reminder that even in the most trying times, the human spirit always triumphs.

Works Cited

Achebe, C. (1966). *A Man of the People*, London: Heinemann.

Afferez, A. K. (2019), 'Authority, Authenticity, and Representation Critical Essays', *Ploughshares*, 22 May. Available online: https://pshares.org/blog/authority-authenticity-and-representation/ (accessed 13 September 2024).

Armah, A. K. (1988), *The Beautyful Ones Are Not Yet Born*, Oxford: Heineman.

Bhat, M. A. (2014), 'Satire in Post-Independence African Novel: A Study of Chinua Achebi's *A Man of the People* and Ngugi Wa Thiango's *Wizard of the Crow*', *International Journal on Studies in English Language and Literature*, 2:6, 17–21.

Falola, T. (2022), *Decolonizing African Knowledge: Autoethnography and African Epistemologies. African Identities: Past and Present*, Cambridge: Cambridge University Press.

Isong, A. (2017), *Radio Sunrise*, London: Jacaranda Books.

Iyer, S. (2024), 'Why Are Authors Expected to Be "Authentic"?', *The Conversation*, 26 August. Available online: https://theconversation.com/why-are-authors-expected-to-be-authentic-228104 (accessed 12 September 2024).

Leigh, D. J. (1995), 'Literature, Imagination, and the Study of Ultimate Reality', *Ultimate Reality and Meaning*, 18:3, 222–45.

Moene, K. and Søreide, T. (2019), 'Combating Corruption: Investigative Journalists on the Frontlines', in R. Krøvel and M. Thowsen (eds), *Making Transparency Possible: An Interdisciplinary Dialogue*, Oslo: Cappelen Damm Akademisk, pp. 109–35.

Nwezeh, E. (1982), 'Satire in Post-Independence West African Fiction', *Ufahamu: A Journal of African Studies*, 11:2, 162–71.

Nyamekye, P. A. (2021), 'Corruption in Postcolonial Africa: A Study of Ayi Kwei Armah's *The Beautiful Ones Are Not Yet Born*', *IOSR Journal of Humanities and Social Science*, 26:12, 68–72.

Orji, B. E. (2018), 'Humour, Satire and the Emergent Stand-Up Comedy: A Diachronic Appraisal of the Contributions of the Masking Tradition', *The European Journal of Humour Research*, 6:4, 24–38.

Reporters Without Borders (n.d.), 'Nigeria'. Available online: https://rsf.org/en/country/nigeria (accessed 13 September 2024)

13

Memoir and Main Character Syndrome

A Reflection

By Jenn Ashworth

In an early draft of a memoir I've been working on this year and last, I wrote:

A while ago, I was at a university open day with my daughter. We decided we needed something to eat and left the atrium where we'd been browsing subject stands and went outside. A week or so before I had been diagnosed with a brain tumour; the tumour had already taken away some of my hearing, and though I felt well enough that day, there was a period ahead when I knew I wouldn't. Of illness, surgery, and a long recovery. Outside, we found a truck selling hot-dogs and burgers and joined the queue. The truck was parked up on a pedestrianized square outside the main campus building we'd just come from, and there were other trucks there giving away free donuts and keyrings and cups of coffee. It was crowded and there was music playing. We got to the front of the queue. We ordered. While I was paying, the woman serving us said something to me that I couldn't hear. I leaned forward and asked her to repeat herself. She did. It was the music and perhaps it was the softness of her accent that caused me the trouble. And it was the brain tumour too; the way it was growing through my ear canal and into my skull and pressing against my brain stem. My daughter noticed what was happening and stepped forward.

She wants to know if you want red sauce on it, she said, bending her head slightly, because she's taller than me, and mouthing the words carefully. I nodded, and she held out her hand for my cash card and used it to pay. Hers was an instinctive sort of kindness; unshowy and practical. A stepping in to do what I suddenly could not. I'd seen this sort of thing happen before: children who were carers or who spoke the language more confidently than their mothers taking charge, translating, easing the path of the one who cared for them. Once it was done, my daughter took the hotdogs and led the way to a bench.

Memoir is not really about what happened. What actually happened is the slippery, contestable truth we chase and never get to. As Micaela Maftei writes in *The Fiction of Autobiography*, the memoirist must both engage herself in a wholehearted attempt to represent 'an honest version of events' while also refusing 'a belief in a single true version, either the author's or anyone else's' (2013: 10). This is a tall order. I tend to make peace with it by telling myself that while I will attempt to render 'an honest version' of what happened, more importantly, I will commit to understanding why what happened *mattered* to me. When memoir owns its subjectivity like this, it gains a different kind of authority, one based not on the chasing of externally verifiable fact but on its fidelity to the performance of the complex process of meaning-making. Because 'mattering' always happens variously and is always a work in process, I can layer the way events mattered to me at the time they occurred with the way they mattered later, in the remembering and once again in the writing.

The commentary, too, even in its most critically informed and technically focused incarnations, is a species of writerly memoir that seeks to narrate and expose the mysterious privacy of the writing process. In universities, the act of reflection is taught and graded and is one of the distinctions between studying writing or researching in the field of Creative Writing and just – being a writer. In the commentary, the writer seeks to narrate what happened when they wrote and make it matter. The recollections of the writer about their own writing process are subject to much of the same slipperiness around truthfulness and evasion as more obvious forms of memoir are. Still, the commentary is written in the hope that what the writer thinks she has come to know about the process of composition might matter not only to herself, but to some other writer, some other time. Or, to put it in the terms of the academy, one of the contentions of practice-based research is that any insight gleaned from it offers some utility to other researchers (Candy 2006). This is where memoir and reflective writing on practice come together again: reflectiveness is not merely self-development, just as memoir must be something other than personally cathartic or healing if it is to be art.

Yet to reflect about memoir writing entangles these two similarly elusive kinds of mattering. There is a risk here. In an essay about her own journey into memoir – the writing and the teaching of it – Tara DaPra remembers her own teacher 'wrestling to separate reflection, that fundamental element of creative nonfiction, from the task of general psychological introspection' (2013: 62). The connectedness between these forms – the memoir and the commentary – s fertile and strange, not least because in both the personal – the *person* of the writer – 'matters' in a way that is both fundamental and embarrassing. Jonathan Taylor's remarks on the unseemliness of the confessional mode in memoir – the 'here I am' display of emotion, of meaning-making (which he characterizes as 'judgement') – that is so prevalent in the genre of memoir (he links this unseemliness to Englishness – to reticence, the stiff-upper lip of demonstration rather than frank explication) (2021) also apply to the writing of commentaries, which, unlike the literary texts they comment upon, are required to delineate their meanings and state what matters rather than perform it. Taylor describes this divided work of memoir in terms of two literary modes – the *showing* (the dramatization of what happened) and the *telling* (the narration of the process of making meaning or drawing conclusions about it) that are sometimes divided by a more or less obvious time-lapse – the before and after and change in mood, or an alteration in mood and tone. What felt frightening or tragic at the time can sometimes become entertaining in the telling, and, more horrifyingly, our best-hearted decisions can, as the process of writing memoir unfolds, reveal themselves to be self-serving misjudgements. These two voices (Taylor uses Phillip Lopate's formulation of the 'double perspective' (Lopate 2005: 143)) are present in the reflective commentary too: it is not only enough for the writer to describe what she did as she wrote (to 'show' her workings out, as I sometimes describe it to my students, nearer to their last math exams than I am) but also to develop some kind of conclusion or interpretation about writing and language itself. Taylor argues that while there are exceptions, for example, memoirs written in the present tense, the presence of the other voice that comments on what is dramatized and draws some conclusions about it is one of the most significant formal differences between the memoir and the novel. Without this other voice, memoir isn't quite memoir, and reflective commentaries aren't quite reflective commentaries either.

*

I'll start with what I thought I understood about my own intentions when I wrote the scene about my daughter helping me out at the hot dog truck. The point of me writing about this moment was never to demonstrate some unexpected kindness or empathy from my daughter. I thought the reason it mattered was because it helped me articulate a question I had about what it had felt like to notice mothering was flowing in the wrong direction – from my nearly adult daughter to me. Memoir often starts like this: powered by questions rather than expertise, curiosity rather than authority, even as we start with what we think we know most intimately: what happened to us. My question was to do with mothering, and let's say I define mothering as *the work of imagining someone else's experience and using the fruits of that imagining to gently adjust your shared conditions to care for the other, often at your own expense.* This moment of mothering from my daughter was new, and I was curious about how it mattered. But when I showed the paragraph to my daughter, she only said, *that's not how I remember it.*

My daughter and I had gone outside to get hot dogs after attending a talk given by the vice chancellor of the university about the value of higher education. He'd finished his remarks by showing us a video of last year's students at their graduation. They'd thrown their caps, then walked off the stage together and into a future we in the audience were invited to imagine. I'd felt tears coming as I watched the video in the packed lecture theatre and held them back so I wouldn't be embarrassing.

Their mothers would have been there, is what I wanted to say.

I attend graduations every year and the campus is loaded with parents in their Sunday dresses, fussing, weeping, clutching, preening, awkward or loud; the full range of variations on motherhood is in evidence. Not in this film, though: we'd all been edited out.

Shh, I told myself, then and now. *This isn't about you.*

Memoir's bias, its inevitable partiality, its inability to reliably do what fiction does and inhabit the minds of others, is the first thing we talk about when we start writing it in the workshops I teach at the campus I've been part of for over a decade now. I don't have to teach the students this or to direct them to the shelves of critical and reflective writings by memoirists clotted with essays about this fact. My students already know that memoir is not documentary. It is not journalism. It is not even history. We *remember*, then we write, only ever creating a cover version of the facts, and in our first attempts we discover every time how self-serving memoir can be. Nobody knows this better than the memoirist herself, faced with the inevitable embarrassment of her own unruly presence on the page.

The way we address this crisis of mattering in the writing workshop, these nineteen-year-olds I am writing with and I, is through a return to the first attempt, through editing, through technique. My definition of motherhood, when I retrace my steps and return to it, opens the door to technique. The phrase, applicable to both mothering and writing – 'imagining someone else's experience' – invited me to consider the way I'd used narrative focalization to narrate an event my daughter didn't remember the way I did. It felt both ethical and writerly in that moment to consider the ways in which my daughter might remember this moment and acknowledge her in the scene. That is why I had asked my daughter what she thought and how she remembered the moment at the hot dog truck. I wanted to understand how this event had mattered differently to her. I also wanted to improve the work. This was relationship maintenance and writerly research all in one. But my daughter would not be drawn. (Would not be set down on paper, would not be drawn *from*, like a well). While there are examples of memoirs that take a more collaborative approach – Michele Hanson's *Living with Mother* includes an epilogue by the daughter (2006: 253–66) – my technical problem was not with handling a competing or contradictory account of what happened. These conflicting accounts are to be expected and are an absolutely inevitable feature of memoir. The real problem was my daughter's insistence that this event mattered to her too (she *remembered* it, after all, and remembering is something that we do with and to an experience that means something), and she was not going to tell me *how*. Still, I went back to the draft to try to open up some space for her. Perhaps this secondary character I had made her into, performing her role-reversed action of nurturing and care, was actually bored and embarrassed by my deafness and resented the way it brought her mother centre stage into a scene that should have been about her. Could I work that in somehow?

If I am going to 'adjust our shared conditions' in the text – or in other words, edit the piece to give the character of my daughter an inner life as prominent and meaningful as my own – perhaps I could, I thought, insert some sentences into the paragraph where I'd imagine her fear. She could have wondered if I was telling the truth about my illness. I'd tried to convince her that I wasn't in pain, not really, and that yes, things would get worse, and there would be surgery, but I would be okay, and she should concentrate entirely on her exams and think only about her own future. Perhaps my daughter wanted to think solely of herself, hoped she could do it, felt guilty about the possibility of having to shut out what was happening to me and devote herself to her books. Perhaps she did not quite trust it was all right to do that, or maybe she worried that if she did what I asked I would end up resenting it and somewhere down the line I would punish her for being all the things I had been: undutiful, selfish and too ambitious.

Shh. It isn't about you.

It's just as possible that the point of it mattering was that it didn't matter to her at all. Not even a little bit. That she actually hadn't spent a moment remembering this scene – not until I'd given her my draft to read, that is. Any scene's dimensions can be endlessly elastic, depending on where we choose to bestow our attention. So instead, I give the reader some sentences that would allow them to imagine that someone my daughter knew had caught her eye. Or that she'd changed her mind and was wishing she'd ordered a burger instead. Or that she was worried we'd be late for our next appointment: a lecture about writing personal statements. Perhaps she was having second thoughts about university or she was wondering if the charge on her phone would last the day. Maybe she was wishing she was there with her father and not me, or she'd remembered, for no reason, that time over a decade earlier when we'd taken her to see a pig at a farm outside Liverpool and she'd become enraged and lost a shoe because the pig had her name.

As I larded up the scene and wrote my new versions, inhabiting my daughter's point of view by deploying a close third person while making it clear I was only imagining what she might have thought, the memoir became speculative and my daughter became a fictional creation, her body merely a hollow container for me to pour more of myself into. The problem is partly ordinary human narcissism and partly one of memoir's built-in fissures. My tinkering taught me that in memoir, all attempts to inhabit the point of view of someone else inevitably lead back to you, the attempt revealing nothing but your own assumptions.

*

Claire Lynch, a memoirist experienced in writing about her own children, is keenly aware of the problem of the single point of view in memoir and, in a commentary about her own process, suggests that a practical solution to the ethical problem of narrating a relationship is 'to redistribute power by offering a right of reply, or even the right to veto, to those written about in the memoir' (2019: 15). I'm thinking now of my daughter, who didn't want to tell me how she remembered this moment. If she had taken her 'right to reply' and told me how that moment mattered to her, should I have incorporated that into a later draft? I imagine what this might look like: 'I didn't know this at the time, but later my daughter told me that' and wondered about the endless timeframes of memoir and the way this careful, literary reflectiveness could turn into an ouroboros – the snake that eats its own tail, the story that lingers anxiously in one spot forever. Should I have asked my daughter for her permission to write about this moment at all – one that might not have mattered that much to her, but mattered a lot to me? And what would it feel like for her to read my attempts to imagine what she thought? Empathy – if that is what it is – can so easily be intrusive. The mothering question had become a technical question about point of view, about narrative focalization and about style. Then the technical question slipped and became a mothering question again.

My attempt to inhabit my daughter's perspective may only have provided more of my own and meant I'd put myself where I had no business being: into her head. I think about the missing mothers in the graduation day video again. Of course, they should not have been there: their bodies had become intrusive and extraneous in the construction of a neat narrative about the end of childhood and the beginning of adulthood. How does a mother matter in a story like that? Sally Cline, in her opening 'reflections' included in the *Arvon Book of Life Writing*, invokes these same metaphors of space when considering memoir's relationship to other literary genres. For Cline, the life writer is an invasive species, an unwanted immigrant, an intruder in the house, uninvited: her body is in a place it should not be.

The embarrassment of memoir becomes clearer to me. It comes not only from its adolescent insistence that what happened to me matters. Not only because it insists that what happened to me matters even as I acknowledge the corrupt and sneaky ways we all learn who is interesting or important enough to listen to. Not only because it insists that what happened to me matters in spite of all the other impossibilities to do with ethical narration and reliable remembering. But most of all because at the heart of memoir's intrusiveness is the persistent, invasive, embarrassing insistence that what matters to me should start to matter to you, too.

I don't know why my daughter wouldn't tell me how she remembered it. Perhaps she was afraid I wouldn't like her answer. Maybe she preferred not to provide me with anything more in the way of material. Maybe me knowing that she remembered it differently from me – that she had a mind of her own that was none of my business – was the thing she most wanted to communicate. There's something about my daughter's silence, her resistance, that I admire. It provides a purpose I didn't choose for the work of reflection that I am attempting now.

Gloriously thwarted by my daughter, I go to other memoirs written by mothers for guidance and notice how often these mother memoirists write about pregnancy and babyhood. These accounts are about the work of pregnancy and breastfeeding, the shattering of a life when a baby arrives, what being at home with a child teaches you about your body, about sleep, about the world of work, about men and about what is invisible to them. The baby itself is never a point-of-view character and hardly exists because mother memoirists have enough on their hands as they acknowledge the legal personhood of the baby and the sheer amount of labour this new person generates without mucking about with representing the interiority of a preverbal being. In *A Life's Work: On Becoming a Mother*, Rachel Cusk outlines her frame of reference with a characteristic precision of focus: 'I have merely written down what I think of the experience of having a child' (2002: 10). Anne Enright, in an introduction to *Making Babies: Stumbling into Motherhood*, lets us know that the two children – a boy and a girl – have been amalgamated throughout: 'though the baby is a "she" both babies are in there somewhere' (2005: 3). When the point of view of the child of the mother memoirist is missing or sidelined, as Enright did with a general 'baby' and Cusk did with the clear focus on her own experience, there is a relief and a freedom inherent in this. These mothers might do in memoir what they don't often get the chance to do in real life and foreground how the scene mattered to *her*, how she remembered it. Perhaps for the first time in a long time – in this relationship at least – she's permitted to become the main character in one of the shared scenes of her own life.

I go back to Claire Lynch, who, when writing about her own children, suggested the memoirist should ideally give the right of reply or even veto to others involved in the text. The 'babyness' of babies, their preverbal state, their inability to, as far as we know, make much of anything matter (these are my formulations, not hers) lets her off the hook of being able to realistically do this: 'I am writing about them when they are too young to read and (mercifully) too young to offer me a detailed critique of their representation' (2019: 15). This freedom has a time limit on it, however. At some point during the murky years of adolescence, the mother memoirist becomes matter out of place, an intruder, Cline's unwelcome invader. As the memoirist Melanie Gideon said in an interview with *The New York Times* about the task of writing about her son, 'I told myself I had until he was 10 to write about him. Any appearance after 10 (anything bigger than a walk-on role) would be an invasion of his privacy' (Editors 2009). Ten years old had whistled past a long time ago for my daughter and her mother. We are where we are, there outside the atrium, her nineteenth birthday a couple of weeks in the past, and the Universities and Colleges Admissions Service (UCAS) application lying in wait. And there I am, trying to tell something that mattered about my own life but invading hers.

Mothers who write about their teenagers, well, we know what happens to them. I came of age as a writer in the aftermath of the publication of Julia Myerson's memoir, *The Lost Child: A True Story* – a memoir of parenting a son through drug addiction. In Myerson's text, she has it both ways – both acknowledging the possibility of a competing point of view and insisting on the validity and perhaps even the supremacy of her own. 'I don't actually throw him out. This is important, because later he will say I did – he will insist this is what happened. But I don't' (2009: 15). This self-assertion is what we want from a memoir and it is also the reason, more than the delicate and private subject matter that Myerson chose to narrate, that some critics objected so powerfully to her work.

Kate Kellaway, in a review of Myerson's book for *The Observer*, understood why other memoirists could write about their children and face less censure:

> Perhaps it is no accident that memoirs about children by their parents often focus on those unable to answer back. Mothers (Rachel Cusk, Anne Enright, Kate Figes) write about their struggles with babies. Autistic children are given voice (*George and Sam* by Charlotte Moore) and mental illness is beyond the reach of retaliatory comment (Michael Greenberg's *Hurry Down Sunshine* being the most recent example).
>
> (2009)

'Is It Ever Okay to Tar Your Kid in Print?' Amy Benfer asked in *The Salon*. In a few hundred words, using a faulty question, she examines Myerson's violation of what she determined is one of 'the most serious prohibitions facing any writer: You Do Not Write About Your Children' (2009). The merits of the book were overwhelmed by the verdict: Myerson's memoiring was a crime against motherhood itself. A memoirist may insist on the validity of her own remembering unless that remembering conflicts with the view of her child. This says something more, I think, about what our culture expects from mothers than it does about any particular piece of writing. I think of the mothers in the Victorian photographs, hidden from the camera by a sheet while she holds up her baby towards the eye of the baby and the world to be photographed. In many of these photographs, the mother is visible, her hands protruding uncannily from beneath a bolt of patterned cloth, a curtain (I want to say: *a shroud*). Her visibility is an ostentatious mistake: her presence and her unwantedness are alarmingly obvious. Once the children are old enough to sit still and upright, the mother disappears: that's why there were no mothers in the graduation film my daughter and I had watched that day. Yet Kellaway, although she responded positively to Myerson's work, still looked at it in terms of her mothering. For her, Myerson's memoiring was itself a maternal act, a way of bringing a lost child back into the home where he belonged, or at least, the room in the home where the writing happened.

These are old arguments now: what was, in 2009, the talk of all the literary pages on both sides of the Atlantic has largely faded away. But still, I was influenced by it. I learned that memoiring and mothering could be both mutually exclusive and indistinguishable.

*

In my memoir workshops, with other people's sons and daughters, I've become a delinquent reader. As I read the stories of injustices they've experienced at the hands of their parents, I wonder what the other story might be. I find myself empathizing with the characters off-stage, the parents who in these tales are sometimes abusive but more often just incompetently present when they should have withdrawn or absent when they should have been present, in the way humans tend to be when they blunderingly share space with each other. Sometimes I try offering this part of the truth of my reading:

I wonder how the other people in this scene would remember this? Would tell this story?

But what's the point of a question like that? Those under-the-cloth mothers could write their own memoirs if they wanted to. There's no shortage of courses; anyone can open a Substack. Maybe all I am doing with a question like that is pushing myself into the work as an unwanted foreign body, attending to nothing more than my own desires, being the child devouring all that is there and still asking for *more more more*, and in this case, asking for something that memoir can't give.

These students have taught me a new phrase: *main character syndrome*, which is what the TikTokers call it when someone behaves as if they are in a story about their own life, with everything and everyone only mattering – only existing – as if they are at best secondary characters and, at worst, mere props – cardboard cutouts of people, extras on set. I catch myself inhabiting the wrong end of the see-saw, wanting to do the work of late adolescence and shoving away anyone's point of view other than my own.

You exist. You matter.

I have always wanted my daughter to hear this from me.

Teaching is a kind of mothering and requires me to remember that I have to both turn up fully and to always know it is *not about what I want*. That is how I want to influence another writer: to be there, but gently, unobtrusively. Less invasively than this.

But now something else, something new makes its cry for attention.
This is *my* story, it says. This is about how it felt for *me*.
Just one bloody paragraph.

At the end of her memoir, Myerson offers a curious afterword where she dramatizes the moment when her son, having read a draft of the book we now hold in our hands, meets with his mother to tell her what he thinks of it. The pages are in the scene, 'the marked-up manuscript on the table between us', signalling to us that this afterword is as much of a reflective commentary – a consideration of the work the writer has made earlier – as it is a memoir of a relationship. I always invite my students to explicitly consider the feedback they have received in the workshop in their own reflective commentaries and, in this afterword, Myerson records her son's response to the scenes which dramatize parts of his life: 'don't you go thinking I approve of what you've done,' he says (2009: 320).

The meeting between mother and son becomes a bit of a creative writing workshop: the young man admires the book his mother has written and comments on the sentences to praise his mother's ability as a writer while speculating about her intentions. Then he proceeds to correct the factual record and suggests additions to several key scenes of the book. The specific details of this are carefully delineated, and the mother in the scene promises edits, 'I can easily adjust it,' she says, though these details are so specific that we already know Julia the memoirist has not kept her promise because we've read the scenes in question and realize, as we read, that she has allowed her original version to stand. The afterword reminds us that the version of this shared life we have read will not be the single true version of the facts, but it remains faithful to the way the memoirist remembered it. There is a multiplicity to this approach. First, a kindness, a motherliness, in allowing her child to reply and in dramatizing and not excusing her own broken promises (aimed at repairing their relationship, if not improving the book?). Then a writerly fierceness too: a mother may also become a memoirist, but in the maternal and writerly tussle for space, a child may always be welcomed home, but he may never become an editor.

*

I go back to my draft and elide my attempts to either inhabit or hint at or acknowledge my daughter's point of view. I am taking the fiction out of the scene but taking my own smother-mother attempts at empathy out of it too. The place where I should not have been – where I intrude the most, in Sally Cline's terms – is into my daughter's perspective. I am not the only one of us with something in my head that should not be there. The irony pleases me as I highlight whole swathes of text and send them to the recycle bin, precise as a surgeon. There's a second irony here too: I am not eliding my daughter, only myself.

A friend told me once, when we were talking about writing novels and what the commentary was for, that a finished work always kept some of the flavour of anything you'd deleted from it. We'd been arguing about whether we should ask our students to do more or less reflective writing. I'd said the commentary allowed you to narrate the making-of the piece, to expose your workings-out, to report on or even dramatize the process; that the process of making even a piece of 'bad' writing was worthwhile, was worthy of interest and could matter. He didn't agree. A fully formed piece of art, he said, should stand alone. No need to narrate the handwringing about what you put in and what you took out. And that's when he said what has stuck with me: the work itself will retain the flavour of anything you cut out of it anyway. I think the metaphor he'd used was about the soup still tasting of the bay leaf even once you fished it out of the pot. I had thought instead about haunting. Something unwanted, hanging around?

So I am still tempted, as I fiddle with the sentences and try to extract all traces of myself from my daughter's perspective, to make some excuses for excising what I imagined my daughter might have seen and thought and felt. It isn't, I want the reader to know, that I don't think her point of view is important. I want to write this in such a way that the reader knows what I think I know, that (in the words of the late Queen herself on the memoiring of her delinquent grandson) *recollections may vary*. I want my reader to know (I want my daughter to know) that my daughter is a human being, that she *matters*. I don't want you to think (her to think) that I've forgotten about her, or that I think I am more important than she is.

How to get the sentences to do that? My excuses for my deficiencies are ready: *all* writing is selection – especially memoir, which doesn't even pretend to tell a life story, as autobiography does, but takes a theme, an angle, a slantwise glimpse. I look at the places where I have tried to explain myself to my reader, and the craft question morphs into a life question again. Is this how controlling I am? Do I really want to smother the reader so completely in sentences that she can't bring a thought of her own to the work but must respond with precisely the thoughts and impressions I wish to extract? Is that how I am? I highlight more of the text; *perhaps she was embarrassed by me and felt guilty about it,* and delete. Outside a university my daughter wants to go to, standing there buying fast food, is not the time or the place for my protestations: it is a matter out of place, uncontrolled growth, a tumour in the text, causing deafness.

Allowing yourself to be influenced involves a certain softness: it goes beyond reproducing what you admire, or cribbing technique from an elder and better (though that too). It requires the writer to trust – to be open to being changed by what she reads, to letting go of what she thinks she knows or what has always worked before. In the end I find influence, not in another writer, but in a writer's mother.

The American memoirist Terry Tempest Williams, in *When Women Were Birds*, tells the story of inheriting three whole shelves of her mother's journals. She'd anticipated receiving not only a life's work but also the story of a partially shared life written from the point of view of her mother and a perspective, surely, on the years of her childhood she did not remember. On the death of her mother, she received the journals and discovered all the pages were blank (2012: 2). There are lots of ways of reading this elision, but today someone else's mother shows me the way to be – as a writer, as a teacher, as a mother. My anxious attempts to hold these parts of myself separate for inspection relax a little: the murkiness can be fertile. This space making – not an absence, but a bounded space packaged and gifted and bestowed – is something akin to Kate Kellaway's reading of Myerson's writing about her lost son. For Kellaway, this literary choice was not a sin against motherhood but motherhood itself, a literary means of bringing him back to the house, of making space for the lost child inside the maternal home. And also, I think, in Myerson's insistence on remaining faithful to her own point of view, a way of coming out from under the cloth, of making herself available to be seen. We play peekaboo with our babies, and the game relies on making yourself visible and taking up room, then withdrawing. We do it, apparently, to teach them about separateness and to show them we will always come back. Similarly, Tempest Williams' mother gifts her daughter what every writer needs: the spacious home of blank page, and invites her into the space that it creates. Tempest Williams, welcomed into the absence her mother left and designed for her, writes her own book, a book containing and making meaning out of her mother's absence but never obliterating it. Eventually I too find what *matters* in the various silences I allow into the text. The point is not to fill the space my daughter left for me, but to say what it meant to me to encounter it.

She wants to know if you want red sauce on that, my daughter said and held her hand out for my card. In the end I am left with the two of us. I am nodding and pretending to hear what I can't, watching her talk to the woman serving us and not being able to hear that either. That is how I remember it. How terrible and lovely it felt. The truth is, I don't know how my daughter remembers it. That's terrible and lovely too. Main character syndrome abounds: my daughter is hardly a person in this version of the paragraph – only a line or two of dialogue, some brief choreography of action, the way she (she's been taller than me for some years now) bent towards me and didn't raise her voice but mouthed the words slowly in a slightly exaggerated fashion. The facts in the scene vanish. I saw my daughter caring for me. I felt frustrated, sickly, feeble, proud, tender, surprised, not knowing how to receive what was being given, worried it would harm her not to receive it, or harm her differently to accept it, and yes, it was only a hot dog, but something terrible was coming, and there we were, practising how to handle me being sick, and her being an adult, and having her own life in her hands. I can tell you how tall she is, but you don't need a number in feet and inches; all you need to know is that she's taller than me. You know her in relation to me, my shortness, my tilted-up chin as I strained to listen. Even the size of my nearly grown-up daughter surrenders to the built-in problem of memoir and the lonely relentlessness of its main character syndrome. Her height is only worth mentioning because of how it made me feel.

We find somewhere to sit and eat our hot dogs while flipping through the prospectus. She tells me we're going to an interactive lecture about how to write a good personal statement for the UCAS form. They're going to tell her how to frame her extracurricular interests and the difficulties of lockdown into a piece of writing – another species of memoir, I suppose – that manifests a version of self that is suitable for admission into the university. We go back inside and find the lecture theatre. I need to sit at the front so I can hear, but she doesn't, so I follow her to the back and watch as she takes out her notebook and pen. I've given talks like this before. I have advised students and offered comments on countless applications and proposals. In this version of the paragraph and in my life, I keep my mouth shut and sit beside her as she takes notes. I watch her, this strange adult whose mind I do not know, put up her hand to ask her questions. I can't hear what advice the lecturer gives my daughter as she prepares for the task of writing about herself.

Works Cited

Ashworth, J. (2025), *The Parallel Path: Love, Grit and Walking the North*, London: Sceptre.

Benfer, A. (2009), 'Is It Ever Okay to Tar Your Kid in Print?', *Salon*, 2 September. Available online: https://www.salon.com/2009/09/02/julie_myerson/ (accessed 9 April 2025).

Candy, L. (2006), 'Practice Based Research: A Guide', *Sydney: Creativity and Cognition Studios*, November 2006. Available online: https://www.researchgate.net/publication/257944497_Practice_Based_Research_A_Guide (accessed 9 April 2025).

Cline, S. and Angier, C. (2010), *The Arvon Book of Life Writing: Writing Biography, Autobiography and Memoir*, London: Bloomsbury.

Cusk, R. (2002), *A Life's Work: On Becoming a Mother*, London: Fourth Estate.

DaPra, T. (2013), 'Writing Memoir and Writing for Therapy: An Inquiry on the Functions of Reflection', *Creative Non-Fiction*, 48, 60–4.

The Editors (2009), 'The Memoir and Children's Privacy', *The New York Times*, 31 August. Available online: https://archive.nytimes.com/roomfordebate.blogs.nytimes.com/2009/08/31/the-memoir-and-childrens-privacy/ (accessed 9 April 2025).

Enright, A. (2005), *Making Babies: Stumbling into Motherhood*, London: Vintage.

Hanson, A. (2006), 'Grandma Clarice by Amy', in M. Hanson, *Living with Mother: Right to the Very End*, London: Virago, pp. 253–66.

Kellaway, K. (2009), 'A Potent Dose of Mother Courage', *The Observer*, 15 March. Available online: https://www.theguardian.com/books/2009/mar/15/lost-child-julie-myerson (accessed 9 April 2025).

Lopate, P. (2005), 'Reflection and Retrospection: A Pedagogic Mystery Story', *Fourth Genre*, 7:1, 143–56.

Lynch, C. (2019), 'Writing Memoir', in K. Douglas and A. Barnwell (eds), *Research Methodologies for Auto/biography Studies*, London: Routledge, pp. 13–8.

Maftei, M. (2013), *The Fiction of Autobiography: Reading and Writing Identity*, New York: Bloomsbury.

Myerson, J. (2009), *The Lost Child: A True Story*, London: Bloomsbury.

Taylor, J. (2021), 'Scenes of Judgment: Genre and Narrative Form in Literary Memoir', in M. Moore and S. Meekings (eds), *The Place and The Writer: International Intersections of Teacher Lore and Creative Writing Pedagogy*, London: Bloomsbury, pp. 75–92.

Tempest Williams, T. (2012), *When Women Were Birds: Fifty-Four Variations on Voice*, London: Picador.

14

Experimental Poetic Autography

Writing the Languaged Self

By Lila Matsumoto

When I was twelve years old, I wrote a spate of letters to authors I admired. I wanted the authors to share something of themselves with me, so that I might gather clues to becoming a writer. But I worried that these questions were nosy. My solution was to nest my inquiry within a request for an autograph, a licensed form of encounter between writer and reader I'd seen at author book signings at the local bookstore. Alongside a piece of paper for their signature and a self-addressed stamped envelope for mailing it back, I sent a letter which asked the authors about their writing lives: what books they enjoyed, what they were inspired by. I was surprised when most of the authors wrote back, thoughtfully and generously. Unexpectedly, the autographs too proved interesting to examine. Dashed and looped, cramped, childish, elegant, abstracted. What was the relation between these artful signatures and the person who had penned them? I put the autographs away in a folder, confirming both the reality and mystery of authorship; my mother inadvertently put them in the recycling bin a few years later.

I tell this story as a way into discussing my poem 'Wieners' as autography: writing about a self that foregrounds the act of writing in the presentation of that self. The autograph, with its idiosyncratic and impersonal flourishes of the pen's ink, is a synecdoche of the authors' letters to a young me: it offers a graphic performance of personhood conveyed by the author's hand and style of writing. Performance is the operative word here: if it is the contention of conventional autobiography to reliably and transparently give an account of the writer's life (though of course, that too is debatable), then autography loosens that pact, presenting a self that is evidently fabricated – and fabulated – through language's forms and textures. This commentary will think about the ways 'Wieners', as an autographic text, channels the impulses of life writing (to share stories of the self) through the performative gestures and procedures of poetry. Throughout, I use the term life writing to refer to work that uses material from the writer's life, while acknowledging the multifarious ways in which this can be done. I agree with Lauren Fournier's characterization of life writing as text 'where attention might be placed on literary form and the knotty problematics of memory' (2021: 15).

Jeanne Perreault, who was instrumental in aligning autography to feminist life writing, defines autography as 'texts that explicitly make the process of being a self contiguous with the inscription of selfhood' (1995: 2). For Perreault, the term allows her to mark out a genre that mixes autobiography with feminist theory and identify a kind of writing that is essential to the feminist project of claiming self-definition. Writers of autography invent their own forms, enabling them to enact their subjectivity in multiple ways and modes (including prose, poetry, and 'non-literary' writing). For feminists, then, these imaginative tactics of writing affirm the unstable category of 'woman', and as Perreault asserts, 'make "I" and "we" signify both continuity with an ongoing life in the body and a community, and disassociation within that life – gaps, amputations, silences' (1995: 4). Autographic texts can widen, complicate, make public, and communalize the political and aesthetic cultures we live in and hope to live in. An example of such a project is *Raving*, McKenzie Wark's exploration of queer rave culture in which she positions herself as protagonist and theorist, declaring: 'I'm in the writing. Hi! This is me. The stories here are fictions dancing around the facts. These things did not happen. The person to whom they did not happen is me' (2023: 4).

Autography is a fruitful framework for my poem because it allows me to freely draw on, embellish and comment on material from my life to work out ideas and problems about the formations of the (writing) self. It lets me move away from the *genre* of autobiography, with its attendant expectations and interpretation of the work as revealing, instructive or confessional. Lyn Hejinian's 'poetic autobiography' *My Life* and Lisa Robertson's autofictional novel *The Baudelaire Fractal* are foundational reference points for 'Wieners'.[1]

---

[1]The term 'poetic autobiography' describes Lyn Heinian's *My Life* on the back cover of the 2002 edition of the book published by Green Integer Press. I understand the use of 'poetic' here not as a descriptor of the work's lyricism, but as a description of the work's mode and genre. Autofiction is a term to describe work that combines fiction with autobiographical materials. The term was first coined by Serge Dubrovsky in 1977, and like any critical label has been debated, contested and expanded.

Both works draw on and ornament their authors' lived experiences, presenting selves through strategies which Hejinian calls 'permeable constructedness' (2013: 81) and Robertson, the 'infinitely unfolding generosity of artifice' (2020a: 142). These supple and imaginative strategies I identify as poetry, what Audre Lorde called 'the revelatory distillation of experience' (2019: 26).

In this commentary, I discuss the ways in which 'Wieners' is a life-writing experiment in inscribing subjectivity as a response to language's cultural politics. I consider the ways in which 'Wieners', alongside Robertson's and Hejinian's works, positions encountered texts as constitutive and transformational to writerly subjectivity and the ways the poem uses fictionalization as a strategy of self-inscription. I will consider how live performances of autographic writing afford further possibilities of enacting a self, through a commentary on performances by Emilia Weber and Jordan/Martin Hell, and conclude with a discussion of 'Wieners' as a feminist project.

This commentary names Robertson, Hejinian, Weber and Hell as key influences on my poem; I could equally say that other works played significant roles in my thinking, writing and editing, but that would be for another commentary. On the surface, naming the influences of a piece of work seems to suggest that there is a one-to-one, explicit relation between two things. For me, determining the influence for my work is like peering into the nebulous soup that is the creative process. Temporal distance is necessary for me to critically attempt the question of influence; only hindsight lets me understand how an idea or something I read alchemized with other ingredients to have propelled me to begin writing and what additional ingredients then sustained the text-in-becoming. I believe that influence is often dormant: that after having read or experienced something, it sits for months and even years before that curiosity or compulsion is carried out. Rather than ask how A and B influenced C (C being the creative work in discussion), a more useful approach for me, which I have attempted to take in this commentary, is to ask: How does C enter into a conversation with A and B? In what ways does C pick up on the questions and provocations raised by A and B?

Autographic Experiment

'Wieners' is a poem sequence which addresses the question, 'How did I become myself?' The poem is set in the United States, where I emigrated to with my family when I was six years old and left when I was twenty-three. The titled sections present scenes and images from my childhood and early adulthood in non-chronological order as I learned English, went to school and then university, became an American citizen and aspired to become a writer.

In thinking about those years, I found myself remembering texts from that time – not the epiphanic texts of literature, but the texts of the everyday: names of shops, phrases overheard, brands of foods, stuff printed on signs on the side of the road. As a child in a new country with its unfamiliar culture and customs, I often experienced America as a bewildering place. The new language reflected the attitudes I saw around me, and I often had the sensation that I was an alien observer on the football field during marching band practice or behind the window of the family car on our annual car trip across the country. Sometimes autobiography is (rightfully) charged with accusations of self-aggrandisement, with the writer recalling the unique recipe of their formation. My experience of recollecting my life in America seemed to generate the opposite effect of self-diminishment: what jostled to view – texts and phrases that promised, cajoled and sometimes disenfranchised – did not seem to make up the materials of a singular life, but told the common experience of a person watering the weedy garden of writerly ambition in late capitalist suburban settings.

I began to wonder about the connection between these daily encounters with unremarkable language and the sense I had that I was a person who wrote. 'Wieners' became a space to test out – to experiment with – the articulation of this writerly subjectivity. I began by writing down those remembered texts and the feelings, sensations, and scenarios I associated with them. Within the self-imposed constraint that each section of the poem address a particular textual memory, I allowed myself a lot of creative freedom, compressing timelines, creating composites of characters and inventing images. Handling memories in this way, reminiscence, nostalgia and chagrin fell away so that the person who experienced the events and thoughts in the poem was not me but a fictionalized version of me, the autographic subject. The exploration of autographical materials provided me with the raw materials which I could manipulate to examine constitutive elements of selfhood, such as gender and geography, without pinning me, the author, as the focus of the examination.

For instance, the section Filibuster began as a textual memory of the meat manufacturer and distributor Omaha Steaks, where my parents ordered products from when I was a child. Everything about the Omaha Steaks experience beguiled me, from the fact that our meats came from so far away (Nebraska, shipped to our home in South Florida), to the arrival of the meats in a polystyrene box (with a packet of dry ice and a free gift of a frozen calculator), to the names of the meats ('jumbo franks') printed on the shrink-wrapped hunks. I allowed the metaphors to grow from the descriptions of the meats as they took on meanings of extravagance, bombast, and environmental damage. These ideas then linked to the hurricanes which arrived in Florida from June to November, which Filibuster takes as the main event. Hurricanes, too, have their own language of extravagance, bombast and environmental damage.

Each section of the poem uses the procedure of taking a personal textual memory and regenerating it through found materials and figurative language. The focal point of the poem is not me as the author, but my experiences of language that shaped my subjectivity, the sense of myself in the world. 'I' is always already languaged, but the story doesn't have to end there: in the present moment, we can use language to critically reflect on our languaged selves and the cultures and environments that formed us.

From childhood I kept a diary, and I understand the quotidian transcriptions in it (predictably embarrassing to read now) as central to the act of self-inscription. To write 'Wieners' I purloined memories and phrases from the diary, which makes a cameo in the poem:

Walnut, North Carolina This town has a liquor store, an Arby's and a Chinese restaurant. There is a suburban rural mix feel. I have to keep my memory knife sharp, even if that means throwing logic to the wind. My diary is double locked, combination and key, and is written in a gnomic script to deter brothers. I crochet furiously in the backseat. Anyone can take time off to play sports, but the lush world of interiority admits only a few. Yes, my secret projects make me feel secure, and my heart stronger for trusting the sweet pain of adolescence. *Sway of the sash! Oncoming supple roses!*

The diary was instrumental in allowing me to not only remember feelings and events long forgotten but in giving me insight into my psychology at that time. The contrast between the romantic ambition of the adolescent writer and the banality of their actual surroundings (strip malls, the backseat of a family car) is narrated with irony but also, I think, tenderness. For the aspiring young writer, place names, fast-food restaurants and scribbles in the diary, however ordinary, have use: they are materials to be recorded and reflected upon for potential artistic production. The language of the subject's immediate surroundings, despite being at odds with language signalling the extraordinary and literary ('Sway of the sash!', 'lush world of interiority'), has significance because it provides a backdrop for the development of a writerly self who refuses to be incorporated unthinkingly into the 'suburban rural mix feel'.

In Robertson's *The Baudelaire Fractal*, the protagonist Hazel Brown remembers a kiss that 'transcribed' her, only remembered because the event was written about in her diary:

In black ink on blank cream-coloured laid paper, I had found a few phrases for the boy's kiss, for his silver necklace, for the soft light that afternoon, which was caught glinting in the necklace, in the midst of pages of lists and awkward drawings of coffee cups, park benches, and sculptures at the Louvre. The diary was a character in the drama I was constructing, the drama of my life, or at least my imagination of a possible and necessary life. It was my dirty and smudged receiver. Obediently it harboured the augmented kiss of the green afternoon.

(2020a: 143)

The kiss is a seed for the generative event of remembrance and description that follows. The textual response of joyous embellishment elongates the kiss into the future and catapults it into our hungering imagination. Hazel aligns authorship to 'augmentation' (2020a: 142), asserting writing as a powerful self-agential act: I have chosen this detail; I have decided to nurture it into import. Robertson's text imparts the vital idea that it is not so much the 'real' events or even the 'real' person that matters in the (life)story, but the style and manner in which those events and personal thoughts are recalled. As Robertson stated about *The Baudelaire Fractal* in an interview, 'For me subjectivity is linguistic, therefore stylistic' (2022).

In another interview, Robertson explained a motivation behind *The Baudelaire Fractal*: 'I was interested in referring to autobiographical material in order to create a pathway and a point of return in the novel, which itself is a fictional structure, formally related to poems' (2020b). Robertson's alignment of the novel to the form of the poem is compelling to me, calling attention to the linguistic and imaginative embroidery that takes place in both kinds of writing, at the level of information and stylistically at the level of the sentence and phrase. The 'fictional structure' of a work that uses autobiographic material is also seen operating, for example, in Gwendolyn Brooks's novel *Maud Martha*. As Margo Jefferson notes, Brooks described *Maud Martha* as stories taken out of her life, 'twisted, highlighted, or dulled, dressed up or down' (2022: x). Each of the thirty-four chapters reads as prose poems that detail the protagonist's lifeworld with sensory precision: 'But dandelions were what she chiefly saw. Yellow jewels for the everyday, studding the patched green dress of her back yard' (2022: 1).

In 'Wieners', the ornamenting impulse of life writing is both a strategy and a recurring theme. In the section <u>Remember the Alamo</u>, the speaker states:

I saw where the pen had pierced the page with the full force of annotation. Be-sassed page, covered entirely in jotty rocaille, denouncing the sentence as tomb and mausoleum. Lascivious, curlicued jets of ink nest the phrase: *In the long gone but never dead days.*

Isn't writing with the materials of one's life always an act of annotating, editing, revising and selecting? Here, the information conveyed on the page and the ornamental artistry of annotation complement each other: the 'jotty rocaille' and 'curlicued jets of ink' are intersemiotic translations of the idea of 'the long gone but never dead days'.[2] The annotation and marginalia, like scribbles in the diary, are attempts to keep an idea – and sentence – from decaying into lost thought, as well as visual receipts of the annotator's preoccupations. Far from sombre reflection, writing about and with one's past becomes an act of efflorescent flamboyance.

Language and Me: Personal Experience as Linguistic Encounters

Lisa Samuels characterizes Hejinian's poetics in *My Life* as a 'verbal memory' that presents 'personal experiences as linguistic encounters' (1997: 1, 16). In *My Life*, these linguistic encounters often take the form of quoted words, suggesting that the term or phrase had been overheard or has an idiomatic function: 'I had "hit upon" an idea'; 'My grandmother was in the kitchen, her hands on her hips, wearing what she called a "wash dress"'; 'You cannot linger "on the lamb"'; 'As for we who "love to be astonished"' (Hejinian 2013: 15, 8, 6, 18). In one section, the person speaks about their grandmother:

> She had come upon a set of expressions ('peachy' being one of them and 'nuts to you' another) which exactly suited her, and so, though the expressions went out of everyone else's vocabulary, even years later, when everyone was saying 'far out' or 'that's nowhere', she continued to have a 'perfectly peachy time' on her vacations.
>
> (2013: 12)

Allegiance to particular expressions says volumes about someone, suggesting a flavour of their attitudes to life; in the case of the grandmother's 'perfectly peachy time', we sense her cheery groundedness within her experiences, in contrast to another generation's attitude of abstracted carelessness ('far out'). The acute focus on how others phrase experiences in *My Life* indicates the nascent development of the speaker's writerly disposition, and their recognition of the tremendous power words have in shaping our sense of the world, and ourselves in it.

Following Hejinian, 'Wieners' probes remembered language to ask: How did particular linguistic encounters shape me? One preoccupation in the poem is the names of American commodity objects, which both amused and puzzled

---

2 The phrase is from Janet Malcolm's book *Psychoanalysis: An Impossible Profession* ([1995] 2018). Rocaille is a style of furniture and interior decoration popular in France in the eighteenth century.

me as a child, and still do as an adult. U-Haul, Fighting Conchs, Food Lion and La-Z-Boy shaped my perception of America as a country of no half measures: self-made, enterprising, mightily proffering foods, grandiosely lazying. Like the remembered idioms of Hejinian's *My Life,* brand names play a central role in the formation of subjectivity in 'Wieners'. Positioned at different moments in the poem, the names of products communicate the ideals, motivations and goals of a country as perceived by the subject, whose attitude to them, and to their new cultural landscape, is estranged and disoriented.

Names of meat products and descriptions of them are everywhere in the poem: jumbo franks, bacon bits, Vienna sausages and teriyaki-flavoured dog treats. The meat motif is a way of thinking about the language of products, processed and packaged, and its constitutive role in the formation of an American subject. (On a related note, the word 'wiener' refers both to a frankfurter sausage and to American slang for someone who is weak). Alienation in the face of aggressive product naming is compounded when the subject encounters, in the section Arizona, signs on the side of the road announcing 'Delicious – Strawberries – Friendly Indians'. In a bid to sell their products, the merchants reassure their potential customers that they are harmless; indeed, they are even friendly. The racialized landscape which has prompted this tactic of code-switching is echoed in the section Paul Bunyan, where the subject remembers how her father 'pretended not to speak English to evade a traffic ticket'.

Another theme in 'Wieners' is the language around acts of performance, from the compulsory talent show, Friday night marching band rallies, youth orchestra concerts, ontological theatre pieces, charity saxophone serenades, synchronized swimming and piping college reels. America is the country of 'showy cheer' and 'not apologizing', where personal worth is demonstrated through abilities to 'ingratiate myself to my customers'. I include these details to think about the murky line between entertainment and selling stuff, boldness and solipsism, sincerity and falsehood. The poem is a critique of America and the cultural expectation to constantly express yourself and strive for success. Performance – whether in a show or in social interactions – is the embodiment of these values, and in making performance a motif in 'Wieners', I poke fun at American culture, and at the same time address my own complicity within the 'complex' of performance, as I write and perform myself into being through the poem.

For the non-native speaker, language holds out potential for self-fashioning, but the path can be fraught and hostile, and the self-making not necessarily liberating. In revisiting and 'augmenting' (qua Robertson) my American childhood, I recognized a theme of detachment and subservience in my position to the new language, English. I recollected instances where my inability to correctly adhere to the rules of English grammar led me to believe that there was a fundamental mismatch between my thoughts and expression, as well as being somehow inferior to the native speakers of the language. This idea of the deferential position to language (that one must serve it but can't have meaningful access to it) is dramatized in the section Jennifer Fisher:

> A game we played: me as your servant fetching you glasses of full fat milk as you read your paperback on the La-Z-Boy, the thumb of your right hand crossed over the forefinger in a fleshy cipher.

The 'fleshy cipher' here is the sign of privilege and gatekeeping, denying the subject access to the (mysterious) riches that the book contains.

Building on the theme of subordination to language, the section Walt Whitman recounts the citizenship procedure I went through when I was twenty-one. Under a picture of George W. Bush, I was sworn in as an American subject, having learnt to the government's satisfaction the country's grammar, history, culture and codes of behaviour:

> The naturalisation test was to be administered orally. Like foie gras or a vaccine, citizenship is a privilege wrought from studied pain. In my grammar book I learn: 'Henry is always getting into accidents'. Who is Henry, in this country of ubiquitous accident. Sounds in my mouth are gawky big marbles or too many sticks of bubblegum. Parsed into language. Now that I had renounced prostitution, communism, and genocide, I was, at last, an American.

The function of language is to allow us to communicate – but in this case, there is a suspicion that we are communicated by language. Through grammar, we are verbalized as institutionalized subjects. I am interested in Robertson's statement, 'The kinds of subjects we become, the kinds of subjectivity we can experience, are limited by the normalizing of a political economy as aesthetics. By means of stylistic norms, we internalize censorship' (2020b). 'Wieners' is an attempt to think through the impasse of linguistic/stylistic censorship by treating formative linguistic encounters as integral, yet not irrevocable, constituents of the self. I can 'twist' (qua Brooks) those linguistic encounters to claim authorial agency.

Performing 'Wieners'

I have shared 'Wieners' in a number of different contexts: in a literary journal as poetic text, at a gig as a musical act, and in a gallery space as an 'art writing' performance. The poem alters depending on the platform, for example, the visual formatting afforded by the page and the use of sonic elements and props at a live performance. Here, I want to make some notes about the influence of the theory and practice of performative writing on 'Wieners', and the possibilities created by live performance in enhancing the poem's self-inscriptive quality.

My understanding of performative writing is drawn from Anna Poletti's discussion of life narrative. She writes:

> The performative construction of the subject changes the understanding of the role of the author of life narrative by shifting our understanding of life narration from an act that 'expresses' and 'documents' a subject and a life to one that creates that self and life through narration.

> (2016: 359)

For Poletti, a life that is narrated is a life that is wrought, or conceived, through art. The word 'performance' articulates the difference between writing that documents a subject and one that intentionally creates it. Performative writing, therefore, shares many qualities of autographic writing but isn't necessarily limited to writing about the self. Lauren Fournier, in discussing Maggie Nelson's autotheoretical work *The Argonauts,* writes, 'Memory is associated with the genre of memoir, while performative writing approaches memory with a reflexive sense of instability and play' (2021: 16).[3]

These qualities of instability and play characterize two performances of autographic texts that I attended: Emilia Weber's poem 'the dictionary of my tongue' at a reading for the 'Front Horse' poetry series in Nottingham in 2017, and Jordan/Martin Hell's essay *AUTOLINGUA DIDACTICA* for the 'Feature' performance event at Café Oto in London in 2023. Weber's 'the dictionary of my tongue' began:

> 'i'd like to read this out loud'
> i say to you – you, the person in the kitchen
> your face grimaces, involuntarily

> (Weber forthcoming)

---

[3]Fournier defines autotheory as 'a self-conscious way of engaging with theory – as a discourse, frame, or mode of thinking and practice – alongside lived experience and subjective embodiment' (2021: 7).

The opening lines placed a curious pressure on the 'I' and the 'you' at the reading: Weber the poet's desire to read the poem out loud to the gathered listeners was immediately reframed as a statement that was spoken to a person in the context of the past or in fiction. This tension between direct address (that Weber was speaking 'honestly' to us, offering us a document of thoughts) and performance (where statements are made in the realm of fiction or something else) was maintained throughout the reading. Alongside a slideshow projection of family photographs, Weber told stories of growing up thinking and living between two languages and cultures. A recurring character was the Russian mother who insists on reading out loud in English despite the mortification of her British daughter that she is 'butchering' it. What stood out about the reading was how the anecdotal mode, associated commonly with orality and memoir, was continually undermined by rhetorical moves of intertextuality (the poem cited research on, among other topics, linguistic speech acts, Russian idioms, and Batyr the Soviet elephant), parataxis and repetition. In the performance, the 'condition' of the poem was constantly toggled back and forth from memoir to something odder and more theatrical. A repeated phrase stated:

no mother tongue for you
no thank you mothers
all patriarch you

(Weber forthcoming)

Like a refrain of a song, the repetition 'catches', provoking an immersive engagement with how a particular subjectivity is wrapped up in gender, nationality, tricky familial relations, stories about elephants, jokes, embarrassment, outmodedness, mastery and obedience (or lack thereof).

In Jordan/Martin Hell's performance of the essay *AUTOLINGO DIDACTIA*, which also marked its launch, Hell gave an extensive, laughter-filled 'preamble'. They described the haphazard assemblage of the text, repeatedly announced that they were nervous, cited literary and theoretical heroes (many cited or quoted in the text), and sketched plans for the reading (2023a). This introduction both charmed and disarmed: had the 'performance' started? Was Hell being sincere, ironic or both? In between reading from the text, described on the publisher's website as 'an essay on falling in love with your teachers, following them home from school, and the emancipatory potential of DIY culture' (Monitor Books 2024), Hell gave commentaries and played punk pop songs on guitar, abandoning the pieces halfway. The performance, with its improvisatory form that bordered on the chaotic, was a complete aberration from the mannered predictability and humblebrag tone we expect of the conventional book launch reading. It seemed to embody an enduring idea about punk ideology as described in the text:

> The fact remains that whatever way I took the lesson, punk was disciplining me in the epic trade of survival by any means necessary. It was teaching me that bars, basements, the street, & anywhere I could jam myself into was a place I could use to essentially go berserk so long as I had some element of art in it & I gave everything. As a hardcore absurdist (& schizophrenic antisocialite) I was easy with the public performance of rage (via lament) & wreckage because girls (or fidgety people who looked like girls) were *supposed* to be sad, were supposed to marry melancholia to their makeup, cake it on even.
>
> (2023b: 17)

'I could jam myself' and 'I had some element of art in it' speak directly to the 'do it yourself' autographic impulse to write and perform oneself into being, despite the material and psychosocial challenges thrown one's way. Like Weber's performance, Hell's reading was characterized by its dynamic, tricksy and critical approach to self-presentation.

In performing 'Wieners' live, I want to bring an element of 'serious entertainment' that I found in Weber's and Hell's performances in playfully provoking questions of the 'self'. In the live performances I use violin, pan pipes, tape player, party blowers and various effect pedals to enhance the sound and tone of my voice and instruments. The sections of the poem, read live or played on a tape player, are interspersed with music and sounds, either pre-recorded on my loop pedal or performed live. For instance, the section U.S.A. is played on a tape player, repeated multiple times with intonation placed on different words and phrases to create an eerie incantation (in reference to the chants of 'U.S.A.!' heard at international sporting events and patriotic rallies). The reading is then gradually slowed down via manipulation of playback speed. The entire text reads as follows:

Country Creek Acres Crunchy Texture Imitation Bacon Bits Shaker Jar.

In performing 'Wieners' I experiment with pacing, repetition and pitch shift to call attention to the stultifying effect that the diction of American brands can produce, as well as to the ubiquitous and threatening trumpeting of national zeal. Through these strategies, which I have changed and sometimes improvised with each iteration of the performance, I want to unsettle the projection of the self as unified and transparent while conveying a particular story of growing up in America. Live performance can highlight the fabricated nature of the 'life story' by making fun play out of linguistic encounters.

Conclusion: Autography as Feminist Project

In my research around 'Wieners' (that is to say, the incubation period, writing, editing, and now critical assessment of the poem), I engage with the legacy and contemporary praxis of feminist life writing that address questions of identity, agency, and authoriality in multivalent, experimental and often unclassifiable modes.[4] For me, autographic works reconfigure and politicize autobiography by putting something at stake in the inscription of a life. Rosi Braidotti states, 'Axes of differentiation such as class, race, ethnicity, gender, age, and others intersect and interact with each other in the constitution of subjectivity' (1994: 4). Autography pays attention to the articulation of particular subjective experiences, placing difference in the same purview as identification. In that important way, it is a provocation against phallogocentrism (embodied in the line from Weber's poem, 'all patriarchy you'), creating space for theorizing the personal as political aesthetic and linguistic.

During my early adulthood, the writers and artists who offered cultural and literary alternatives to the more mainstream offerings were predominantly male. Some of these figures are referenced in 'Wieners': Richard Foreman, Matthew Barney, Albert Camus and Walt Whitman. I include these figures to dramatize the disparity between visible, bombastically important male work and the invisible, doubt-filled writing of the girl who scribbles in her diary in the backseat of a car: 'Yes, my secret projects make me feel secure'. In the poem, literary achievements are (ironically) couched in macho language and women are lovers, ex-lovers or aide-de-camps to male authors, not authors themselves:

Meaty minute The train doors open to admit your ex's mother and her triangular lips. The last time you saw her was on the rooftop of her coldwater apartment: drunk, she had eaten the taramasalata with the serving spoon, and tearfully remembered her ex-husband who had *philandered* and

---

[4] I have close-read some chosen texts in this commentary, though there were many other autographic texts which were influential to my thinking around 'Wieners' which I could have discussed, such as *Index Cards* (2020) by Moyra Davey, *Manual for Cleaning Women* (2015) by Lucia Berlin, *I Love Dick* ([1997] 2006) by Chris Kraus, *A Ghost in the Throat* (2020) by Doireann Ní Ghríofa and *Monstrous Motherhood* (forthcoming) by Stephanie Limb. Lauren Fournier's *Autotheory as Feminist Practice in Art, Writing, and Criticism* (2021), which I reference in this chapter, was integral in widening my understanding of feminist autography to theory and visual/multisensory art practices.

gallivanted with the editor of his academic book on empire. *I am an ecstatic loser!,* she said.

The story within the story condenses the tragedy of the ex's mother, whose situation we are only given a small stage (a train car, a rooftop) to know. But she takes that stage extravagantly, wielding a large spoon to eat dip and emphasizing the severity of her compromised state through italics and exclamation. Although she has been cast aside by her husband who wears all the hallmarks of historical success (man, academia, empire), she refuses to be unseen, casting herself as the main player, the 'ecstatic loser'.

Faced with the Medea-like dramatics of the romantically and artistically spurned mother of the ex, the subject considers another option, of quietness and obscurity:

> Pellet You suspect you turned to poetry because it took up less space on the page. If writing is subjecthood sashaying on the runway, you are a dumpy owl hooting in a dank and bygone hollow.

If authorship is a space occupied and defined by male figures, characterized by mastery, verbosity and eloquence, then an alternative for the girl writer is to create another space where the writing self may be fashioned through strategies of ironic detachment. In this 'hollow', poems indiscernible to the general public will be written, carrying features of a pellet: small, discreet, wadded and undigested. By bluntly turning away from the model of glamorous self-proclamation, the subject of the poem stakes out new forms of authorship.

Nicky Marsh writes, 'Hejinian's aim in writing is to discover the "agency" that exists in the articulation of everyday existence: to exploit the point at which the subject's own self-evident knowledge of experientiality and the subject's discursive constructedness collide' (2003: 73). Likewise, my poem thinks about the particular ways that subjectivity is shaped by linguistic experiences and by the ways we choose to construct, order, and edit those experiences. The epigraph of 'Wieners' is 'Everything has an end, except for a wiener, which has two'. The path of a life story is indeterminate because the story is always at least partially made up and reimagined. In autography, the question of 'How did I become myself?' is approached upon a fictive stage, where materials from one's life are fashioned through appropriation, embroidery and irony.

This passage in Hejinian's *My Life* is poignantly attuned to the feminist autographic project:

She wanted to stand aside, keep to herself, remain quiet, but too frequently something in her nature presented a conflict, a confusion, a sound. Wanting to 'explain' is like having a memory – the person posits itself elsewhere, adolescent-like, as a figure in the distance escaping, while awaiting the advent of its more glorious self but modestly, even piously.

(2013: 33)

Writing about, and with, one's own life is a profoundly personal affair, but the 'personal' can be a trap if it doesn't allow for a measure of critical and imaginative engagement with one's past – to recognize that one's path to becoming oneself is not irrefutable. Hejinian's 'adolescent-like' female speaker who is 'awaiting the advent of its more glorious self' is the girl who is too close to her experiences ('a conflict, a confusion, a sound') to formalize them into a retelling but who waits for a future self to do so.

Speaking about *The Baudelaire Fractal* in an interview, Robertson stated: 'I still think girls' intellectual experience is not represented and honored and respected in literary or popular culture .... I felt I could contribute some data towards the broader project of making room for girls' intellectual life' (2020b). I have hopes that 'Wieners' participates in the feminist project that Robertson names, of adding to the varied archive of female-identified experience, and more specifically to an archive of how a girl became a writer. Perhaps with this poem, many years later, I am writing the letter to the young me that describes (and inscribes) myself as a writer.

Works Cited

Berlin, L. (2015), *A Manual for Cleaning Women*, London: Picador.
Braidotti, R. (1994), *Nomadic Subjects: Embodiment and Sexual Difference in Contemporary Feminist Theory*, New York: Columbia University Press.
Brooks, G. (2022), *Maud Martha*, London: Faber.
Davey, M. (2020), *Index Cards*, London: Fitzcarraldo Editions.
Fournier, L. (2021), *Autotheory as Feminist Practice in Art, Writing, and Criticism*, Cambridge: The M.I.T. Press.
Hejinian, L. ([1980] 2013), *My Life and My Life in the Nineties*, Middletown: Wesleyan University Press.
Hell, J/M. (2023a), Performance at 'Feature', Café Oto, 17 September.
Hell, J/M. (2023b), *AUTOLINGO DIDACTICA*, London: Monitor Books.
Jefferson, M. (2022), Forward in *Maud Martha*, London: Faber.
Kraus, C. ([1997] 2006), *I Love Dick*, Cambridge: Semiotext(e).
Limb, S. (forthcoming), *Monstrous Mothers*.
Lorde, A. (2019), *Sister Outsider*, London: Penguin.
Malcolm, J. (2018), *Psychoanalysis: An Impossible Profession*, London: Granta.

Marsh, N. (2003), 'Infidelity to an Impossible Task: Postmodernism, Feminism and Lyn Hejinian's *My Life*', *Feminist Review*, 74:1, 70–80.

Matsumoto, L. (2023) 'Wieners', *Happy Birthday?* 1, np.

Monitor Books (2024), 'AUTOLINGUA DIDACTICA'. Available online: https://www.monitorbooks.co.uk/books/autolingodidactica/ (accessed 19 May 2024).

Ní Ghríofa, D. (2020), *A Ghost in the Throat*, Dublin: Tramp Press.

Perreault, J. (1995), *Writing Selves: Contemporary Feminist Autography*, Minneapolis: University of Minnesota Press.

Poletti, A. (2016), 'Periperformative Life Narrative: Queer Collages', *GLQ: A Journal of Lesbian and Gay Studies*, 22:3, 359–79.

Robertson, L. (2020a), *The Baudelaire Fractal*, Toronto: Coach House Books.

Robertson, L. (2020b), 'Textures of Personhood: Lisa Robertson Interviewed', interviewed by Allison Grimaldi Donahue, *BOMB Magazine*, 17 January. Available online: https://bombmagazine.org/articles/2020/01/17/lisa-robertson-interviewed/ (accessed 19 May 2024).

Robertson, L. (2022), '"Reading Is Like Dreaming": An Interview with Lisa Robertson', Interviewed by Louis Klee, *Sydney Review of Books*, 21 March. Available online: https://sydneyreviewofbooks.com/interview/lisa-robertson/ (accessed 19 May 2024).

Samuels, L. (1997), 'Eight justifications for Canonizing Lyn Hejinian's *My Life*', *Modern Language Studies*, 27:2, 103–19.

Wark, M. (2023), *Raving*, Durham: Duke University Press.

Weber, E. (2017), Performance at 'Front Horse', Sneinton Hermitage Community Centre, Nottingham, 9 December.

Weber, E. (forthcoming), 'The Dictionary of My Tongue'.

15

Digital Narratives, Technology and the Domestic Gothic

By Kate Pullinger

In 2001, I began to teach short story writing courses online at Nottingham Trent University's trAce Online Writing Centre. I'd been writing and publishing for more than a dozen years by this stage; my first book came out in 1988, a collection of short stories called *Tiny Lies*. Like many people, I was accustomed to firing up the modem – I can hear it still – to book flights and send emails; I was surprised to find that the internet was also a useful forum for teaching Creative Writing. The fact that an international cohort of students could log in and work together asynchronously had advantages over the live creative writing workshop, especially for people who aren't comfortable speaking in groups, who need time to digest and consider, or simply prefer writing to talking.

Once I found that I was comfortable working online, a year-long research fellowship at trAce in 2002 gave me the opportunity to think about the potential of the internet for narrative experimentation. I discovered a world of hyperlinked poetry, branching game-like narratives, and online discussion forums. Given my background as a novelist, I could see the potential for a more story-led or narrative-focussed approach. From that point onwards, I embarked on a parallel writing practice in the digital realm, creating works of fiction that rely on digital networks and devices. Perhaps my best-known work from this period is the multimedia story-in-episodes for young readers (Pullinger & Joseph, *Inanimate Alice*), which, despite being internet ancient (the first episode was published in 2006), is still finding its way to new audiences.

My new novel, my ninth, builds on a theme that has persisted and developed in my writing across both fiction and digital fiction over the past several decades, a theme I think of as the domestic gothic, or the gothic in everyday life. I'm interested in the way that in fiction the ordinary can slip quickly into the extraordinary and how the supernatural can heighten reality, rendering our quotidian lives uncanny. For me, this has resulted in literary novels and digital fictions that play with classic tropes of the genre and its offshoots, horror and the psychological thriller. This includes the house as a character or agent of influence and characters who may or may not be witches and vampires. And while the idea of haunted technology has been with us for as long as we've created and used machinery, I'm interested in the technologies that are embedded in our lives today, exploring, for example, the way ghosts might use digital technology to communicate with both the characters in a story and, as is the case in my smartphone ghost story, *Breathe*, the readers of that story.

If I were to pin down an original source or influence for this theme, it would be Bram Stoker's unhinged and gripping masterpiece, *Dracula*. As Joseph O'Connor explains in an author's note to his wonderful novel about Stoker, *Shadowplay*, *Dracula* failed to ignite readers when first published in 1897 and was 'like Stoker's other books ... almost forgotten' (2019: 289). First resurrected in popular culture a decade after Stoker's death by 1922's silent film *Nosferatu*, the story has since spawned entire subcultures across books, film and television. The novel contains multiple scenes that are familiar from countless adaptations, from Jonathan Harker first spotting the Count crawling along the outside of the castle wall, 'face down, with his cloak spreading out around him like great wings' (Stoker [1897] 2003: 41) to Harker's horrifying encounter with three young female vampires, one of whom 'bent over me, fairly gloating. There was a deliberate voluptuousness which was both thrilling and repulsive, and as she arched her neck she actually licked her lips like an animal' (Stoker [1897] 2003: 45).

I first read the novel when I was twenty-one, living in a squatted house in Vauxhall across the Thames from what was then the only Tate: Tate Britain. I had a room of my own with a single bed, an electric typewriter on which I had begun to write short stories, and a paraffin heater – a truly frightening contraption my young Canadian self could never have imagined but was absolutely ordinary in 1980s Britain, where central heating was a luxury. I remember the reading experience vividly, which in and of itself is unusual for me – at night I'd lie in my narrow bed reading *Dracula*, which so terrified and enthralled me I'd have to hide the book under a pile of clothes and blankets to somehow prevent myself from falling prey to whatever might crawl out from its pages.

The novel gripped me when I was a young adult, when I was thinking about how and what I might want to write myself, and it has haunted my subconscious ever since. In *Dracula*, the dead make demands of the living, taking what they need in order to continue to exist, forcing a response. While my own writing style tends towards restraint and understatement, there is something about the melodrama of *Dracula* that I find beguiling and enlivening, like the movies of 1950s Hollywood director Douglas Sirk and Mary Elizabeth Braddon's 'sensation' novel, *Lady Audley's Secret*. While Sirk and Braddon are often positioned as proto-feminist, it's clear Stoker was profoundly uneasy about the role of women in late Victorian society. The novel makes frequent reference to the baffling figure of the New Woman – and of the two main female characters, one dies because she's simply too attractive, while the other survives because 'She has a man's brain' (Stoker [1897] 2003: 250).

My own feminism emboldened me to write a version of the story in my 1993 novel, *Where Does Kissing End?* While we, perhaps, live in more sexually enlightened times than Stoker, we still carry enough of our own taboos and fears to relate to what his characters' experience, from the allure and terror of submission to a horror of disease and contagion. While in the 1980s we were stalked and menaced and killed by AIDS, in the brilliantly gender-fluid 2020s we argue over what a woman is while maintaining our usual double standards over how boys, girls, men, women – people – are allowed to behave. And of course, Dracula himself is the ultimate bad immigrant – he arrives in England at night, on a small boat, to suck our blood from our veins.

Dracula is an epistolary novel, constructed from letters, diaries, newspaper articles, a ship's log. It is also a novel with contemporary technology at its heart. In it, an international team of vampire hunters is forced to harness all manner of technologies in order to defeat the vampire, including shorthand transcription, a phonograph, telegrams, blood transfusions and that most newfangled of contraptions, the typewriter.[1]

The idea that the dead might make demands, or might have something to tell us – about the past, about ourselves in the present day – remains compelling to me. There's a particular story I find myself telling and retelling about the ways in which the dead might attempt to communicate with the living, the ways in which the dead might attempt to influence or manipulate the living. I've returned to this theme in my new novel, *The Recent Dead*, as well as my most recent digital fiction project, *Breathe*.

Back in the early 2000s, when I first began creating works of digital fiction, exploring what my friend Professor Sue Thomas[2] liked to call 'whole new worlds', I thought these two realms – mainstream book publishing and digital

---

[1] For an interesting discussion of these two novels, their film adaptations, and genre, read *Frankenstein, Dracula, and the Workings of Genre,* by Eric S. Rabkin. Available here: https://websites. umich.edu/~esrabkin/FrankensteinDracula.pdf

[2] Sue Thomas set up the trAce Online Writing Centre at Nottingham Trent University, which for a decade from 1997 provided funding and advocated for creative writers who were interested in experimenting with the then new and emerging technologies.

experimentation – would eventually come together and that the idea of the book itself would expand to include newer screen-based forms of reading. I was wrong. These two streams have remained separate, with book publishers getting burnt first through unsuccessful investments in CD-ROMs in the 1990s, then in the 2000s and 2010s yet more unsuccessful investments in apps for phones and tablets.[3] While some apps hit the market at the right time, like Touch Press and Faber's collaboration on a multimedia version of T. S. Eliot's *The Waste Land*, these products, unlike books, required ongoing maintenance or risked breaking down after every browser and operating system update. During this period e-books arrived and almost immediately failed to live up to their early promise, rapidly becoming simply another format for delivery, serving up often inferior digital copies of print books instead of new sites for experimentation with more networked and interactive reading experiences.

Despite this failure and its accompanying lack of viable business models, I persisted in working in this parallel realm, beguiled by the potential for new forms of storytelling and new ways to reach readers. Examples of works that I felt both challenged and expanded our notions of what reading might be include *Welcome to Pine Point*, produced by the National Film Board of Canada, created by The Goggles.[4] This 2011 interactive work blends the high school yearbook with archival material to tell a story about a town that no longer exists. Christine Wilks' 2010 work, *Underbelly*, maps a story about young female miners, prized for their small size, in the coal mines of Yorkshire in the nineteenth century.[5] Inkle Studios' *80 Days* reworks Jules Verne's novel *Around the World in Eighty Days* into a vast interactive storytelling landscape, available across many platforms and devices.[6] In 2023 the British Library exhibition *Digital Storytelling* showcased *80 Days* alongside a selection of other works from the last two decades, including my 2018 work for the smartphone, *Breathe*.

Breathe is a ghost story. The main character, a young woman called Flo, can communicate with the dead through her phone. She longs to make contact with her mother who died when she was a small child; instead, multiple other ghost voices keep interfering. *Breathe* grew up out of another project I had worked on with a digital content start-up, who created a commercial platform

---

[3] I've thought a lot about what puts publishers off, as have my students; it's at least partly down to the fact that the book is an easily mass-produced product with a workflow established over a couple of centuries: author, editor, copy editor, designer, printer, distributor, bookseller, whereas app and web development not only adds a developer into that workflow for an app to continue to function, it needs to be constantly maintained, or it will break every time an operating system or browser is updated.
[4] https://pinepoint.nfb.ca/ – the work has been updated and continues to function admirably well.
[5] https://crissxross.net/archive/underbelly – this site no longer works.
[6] https://www.inklestudios.com/80days/ – this project remains actively updated.

for smartphone stories. When they went bust less than two months after launching, I was determined to salvage the work I'd done on developing my character Flo and her storyworld. Both the smartphone story *Breathe* and my new novel, *The Recent Dead*, are supernatural thrillers that centre on Flo and her miscommunications with dead people.

One key factor for me with everything I write is the marriage between form and content, and this is particularly important when it comes to creating works that are built using digital networks and read via digital devices. For me, form and content are inextricably linked. A work that exists in one format, for example, a smartphone web app, cannot simply be ported from one platform – a phone – to another – the novel – but must be adapted to the new format, much like a film adaptation and its source novel are two entirely different versions of a story. *Breathe* is a work for the smartphone and is notable for its bookishness – it has a digital version of pages which the reader turns, and the story is told primarily through text, so there is no soundtrack accompanying the story, no video. Initially, I was keen to use audio but one of *Breathe's* great advantages as a work for the smartphone is that it resides on the web and is accessed via a URL, without requiring the reader to download an app, which for many people is an inconvenient barrier to access.[7] At the time, integrating sound files into a web app was difficult, so we took the decision not to use audio and this, in turn, makes the experience feel more like reading a book.

However, this bookishness is, in fact, a skeuomorphic illusion, as both the form of the story and the content of the story make use of the affordances of the smartphone in a way that makes it as unlike a book as a calculator is unlike an abacus. For example, the story personalizes itself to readers by using three different APIs – application processing interfaces – a software intermediary that allows two or more computer components or programmes to talk to each other. The APIs built into *Breathe* are time, weather and location, and for every reader the text of the story alters according to these variables, placing the story in, for example, the reader's location – the current weather outside, and the time of day or month they happen to be reading.

Sometimes this is obvious, and the effect is uncanny and, hopefully, a little frightening. For example, the ghosts in the story know where you are. A few pages in, the ghost deletes the text you've just read and inserts their own, saying, 'Stupid stories. Stupid girl. I'm close by. I'm on X already': the API replaces 'X' with the name of a street close to your – the reader's – location. But often the algorithms are much less obvious – if it is spring when you are reading the story, the story takes place in spring. If it is unseasonably warm where you are, it will be unseasonably warm in the story.

---

[7]https://breathe-story.com/

Breathe was developed as part of the Ambient Literature Research project,[8] a two-year academic project funded by the UK's Arts and Humanities Research Council, where we were looking at the idea of situated storytelling – digital stories that work with or rely on the physical location of the reader. In a world where we are surrounded by data flows, we were interested in exploring the statement that forms part of the famous liner note from Brian Eno's album *Music for Airports*: the ambient should create 'a space to think'.[9] What would a digital book look like if it was able to acknowledge the reader's whereabouts, if it was able to layer a story on top of the reader's data, to become part of that data flow instead of requiring the reader to step away from the world and into the text?

In part, *Breathe* was my reaction against the long tradition of works that use geolocation, requiring readers to move from location to location in order to find the next piece of the story. Many people aren't comfortable with the idea of wandering the city alone, headphones on, absorbed in locating a story. *Breathe* is best experienced alone in bed at night. A bit like when I first read *Dracula*.

Breathe uses other smartphone tools: with the reader's permission, the story takes a single photograph with the phone's camera and then uses and re-uses that photo in the visual background of the story. Parts of the story rely on haptics – at certain points the reader is required to tilt or rub the screen in order to reveal yet another playful or sinister message from a ghost. But, despite these elements, *Breathe* remains persistently bookish – like I said, the story is conveyed mainly through text. And this is part of why this particular work of digital fiction has pleased readers – it's interactive but that interactivity is largely hidden; it relies on a vast network of algorithms (my collaborators on it included Google Creative Lab) but is more like a book than any other form of media you might access via your phone; and it's short, each page only a paragraph long, the pages themselves counting down quickly, 2/105, 3/105, 4/105, etc., requiring only fifteen minutes or so of the reader's time. Form and content work together seamlessly, as they do in a print book, which is, after all, a content delivery technology so familiar we don't think of it in that way and haven't for many generations.

Of course, a ghost story for your phone that takes a picture of your room and in which the ghost knows where you are is also a story about the surveillance technology we carry around in our pockets. In *The Age of Surveillance Capitalism*, Shoshana Zuboff explores

---

[8]https://research.ambientlit.com/

[9]From the liner notes from the initial American release of Brian Eno's *Music for Airports / Ambient 1*, PVC 7908 (AMB 001) http://music.hyperreal.org/artists/brian_eno/MFA-txt.html

the widespread collection and monetization of personal data by corporations. This data is often collected without the user's explicit knowledge and can include search histories, social media posts, physical locations, and product keywords. The data is then used to create new commodities and monetized through targeted advertising or other means.[10]

This was a theme I hoped readers of *Breathe* would think about as they interacted with the story, despite the fact that a disclaimer makes it clear that the story will not save any of your data.

When it comes to marrying form to content in the digital realm, technology itself has been a form of influence in my writing. I carry my novelist's instincts through to all my digital work, asking questions about what kinds of stories will work on a screen and what level of interactivity will interest readers who don't think of themselves as gamers. And perhaps most importantly, at least in the first instance, what would I like to read myself?

Lately, however, I've found myself stepping back from working in digital. I've grown weary of those 'whole new worlds', dismayed by the corporate takeover of the internet that has accelerated since Facebook first arrived on our screens.[11] The more recent arrival of accessible artificial intelligence (AI) and machine learning content-creation tools is equally problematic; these tools are built using vast databases that rely on the massive land grab of copyright materials, requiring unimaginably huge energy consumption. It's easy to forget the military origins of the internet when the US Department of Defence created ARPAnet, which begat the internet and, in turn, the World Wide Web; it should surprise none of us to see these tools being militarized with the use of AI weapons in the Israel–Hamas war and elsewhere. My smartphone story, *Breathe*, with its playful take on the way we allow ourselves to be surveilled and tracked by technology, is sharpened into focus in ways I didn't quite anticipate. Where are the data farms that service the story located?

I see this weariness with digital mirrored in colleagues and friends: the digital dance pioneer who has taken up stained-glass making; the tech-theatre artist who has helped create a children's book in collaboration with her local community; and the games designer who has written a bestselling debut novel. This isn't to say I think the era – my era – of digital experimentation

---

[10]This description of *The Age of Surveillance Capitalism* (Zuboff 2019) was generated by Google's AI Overview in response to my search for the book. Of course, Google's AI Overview is itself generated by the widespread collection and monetization of personal data by Google, often without the user's explicit knowledge, which is itself the subject of Zuboff's critique.

[11]Read Naomi Klein's *Doppelganger: A Trip into the Mirror World* for a horrifying analysis of the effect of the internet on political polarization and conspiracy thinking.

is over; things change, things will continue to change, digital is part of the everyday fabric of our lives, today's new technology becomes yesterday's typewriter. But, for now, I'll draw the lid of my coffin shut and lie back to wait and see how things develop, before flinging it open and rushing out to seek fresh blood and inspiration once again. I'll work on my latest novel while tinkering around the edges of where the literary meets the gothic and will reread my favourite bits of *Dracula* yet again.

Works Cited

Braddon, M. E. ([1862] 1987), *Lady Audley's Secret*, Oxford: Oxford University Press.

Eighty Days (on-going), [Interactive story], Inkle Studios. Available online: https://www.inklestudios.com/80days/ (accessed 1 April 2025).

Eliot, T. S. ([1922] 2011) [iPad application], *The Waste Land*, London: Touch Press / Faber.

Eno, B. (1978), *Music for Airports* (album liner notes).

Klein, N. (2024), *Doppelganger: A Trip into the Mirror World*, London: Penguin.

Nosferatu: A Symphony of Horror (1922), [Film] Dir. F. W. Murnau, Germany: Prana Film.

O'Connor, J. (2019), *Shadowplay*, London: Harvill Secker.

Pullinger, K. (1989), *Tiny Lies*, London: Jonathan Cape.

Pullinger, K. (1993), *Where Does Kissing End?*, London: Serpent's Tail.

Pullinger, K. (2018), *Breathe*. Available online: https://breathe-story.com/ (accessed 1 April 2025).

Pullinger, K. (forthcoming), *The Recent Dead*.

Pullinger, K. and Joseph, C. (2006), *Inanimate Alice*. Available online: https://inanimatealice.com/ (accessed 1 April 2025).

Rabkin, E. S. (2008), 'Frankenstein, Dracula, and the Workings of Genre', *Projections*, 2:2, 43–65. Also available online: https://websites.umich.edu/~esrabkin/FrankensteinDracula.pdf (accessed 1 April 2025).

Stoker, B. ([1897] 2003), *Dracula*, London: Penguin Classics.

Welcome to Pine Point (2011), [Interactive film] Dir. The Goggles, Canada: National Film Board. Available online: https://pinepoint.nfb.ca/ (accessed 1 April 2025).

Wilks, C. (2010), *Underbelly*. Available online: https://crissxross.net/archive/underbelly (accessed 1 April 2025).

Zuboff, S. (2019), *The Age of Surveillance Capitalism*, London: Profile.

PART THREE

Postscript

16

Further Reading: Selected Bibliography

While there seem to be no other books like this one, which present a series of critical commentaries as they are understood in universities, there are many other anthologies of authors reflecting on their writing practice in relation to various genres and contexts. What follows is a sample list of some of these anthologies for further reference.

Adsit, J. (ed.) (2018), *Critical Creative Writing: Essential Readings on the Writer's Craft*, London: Bloomsbury.

Baker, B. (ed.) (2006), *The Way We Write: Interviews with Award-Winning Writers*, London: Continuum.

Bigsby, C. (ed.) (2017), *Writers in Conversation with Christopher Bigsby: Volume Six*, Boiler House Press. (*Volumes 1–5 also available through different publishers)

Blythe, W. (ed.) (1998), *Why I Write: Thoughts on the Craft of Fiction*, Boston: Little Brown.

Boylan, C. (ed.) (1993), *The Agony and the Ego: The Art and Strategy of Fiction Writing Explored*, London: Penguin.

Brayfield, C. and Sprott, D. (eds) (2014), *Writing Historical Fiction: A Writers' and Artists' Companion*, London: Bloomsbury.

Brown, C. and Paterson, D. (eds) (2003), *Don't Ask Me What I Mean: Poets in Their Own Words*, London: Picador, 2003.

Chatterjee, A. (ed.) (2013), *Creative Writing: Writers on Writing*, London: Creative Writing Studies.

Conaghan, T. (ed.) (2022a), *Reverse Engineering*, London: Scratch Books.

Conaghan, T. (ed.) (2022b), *Reverse Engineering II*, London: Scratch Books.

Crowe, D. (ed.) (2007), *How I Write: The Secret Lives of Authors*, New York: Rizzoli.

Curtis, T. (ed.) (1996), *How Poets Work*, London: Seren.

Dastidar, R. (ed.) (2019), *The Craft: A Guide to Making Poetry Happen in the Twenty-First Century*, Rugby: Nine Arches Press.

Dooley, M. (ed.) (2000), *How Novelists Work*, London: Seren.

Gebbie, V. (ed.) (2009), *Short Circuit: A Guide to the Art of the Short Story*, London: Salt Publishing.

Gillet, V. and LeMonde (eds) (2009), *The Novelist's Lexicon: Writers on the Words That Define Their Work*, New York: Columbia University Press.

Herbert, W. N. and Hollis, M. (eds) (2000), *Strong Words: Modern Poets on Modern Poetry*, Tarset: Bloodaxe.

Ivory, H. and Szirtes, G. (eds) (2012), *In Their Own Words: Contemporary Poets on Their Poetry*, Cromer: Salt.

Johnson, S. A. (ed.) (2006), *The Very Telling: Conversations with American Writers*, Lebanon: University Press of New England.

Loydell, R. M. (ed.) (2009), *Troubles Swapped for Something Fresh: Manifestos and Unmanifestos*, Cromer: Salt.

Lyons, B. and Oliver, B. (eds) (1998), *Passion and Craft: Conversations with Notable Writers*, Champaign: University of Illinois Press.

Neale, D. (ed.) (2020), *Writing Talk: Interviews with Writers about the Writing Process*, London: Routledge.

Owen, A. (ed.) (2021), *Writers on Writing: A Book of Quotations*, London: Bloomsbury.

Roberts, T. (ed.) (2014), *Poetry in the Blood: Essays on Poetry by Shoestring Poets*, Nottingham: Shoestring Press.

Stevens, K. (ed.) (2014), *Writing a First Novel: Reflections on the Journey*, Basingstoke: Palgrave.

Vida, V. (ed.) (2005), *The Believer Book of Writers Talking to Writers*, New York: McSweeney's.

Websites

There are thousands of websites on which writers reflect on aspects of their creative practice. A simple online search will bring up a host of useful sites in this respect. Here are just a few examples as starting points:

- *Author Interviews*: https://authorinterviews.co.uk/

- *Literary Hub*, Craft and Criticism: https://lithub.com/category/craftandcriticism/

- *Necessary Fiction*, Research Notes: https://necessaryfiction.com/category/researchnotes/

- *The Paris Review*, Interviews with authors: https://www.theparisreview.org/interviews

- *Writers & Artists*, Interviews with authors: https://www.writersandartists.co.uk/advice/interviews-authors

Index

Achebe, Chinua 144
advertising 24, 45, 50, 185
Aristotle 46, 92–3
Ashworth, Jenn 9, 11, 149–62
autobiography 24, 66–7, 125, 160. 164, 166, 175
autography 15, 163–4, 175–6

Barrington, Judith 67
Barthes, Roland 6, 27–9
Bauman, Zygmunt 36, 39
Beers, Shaindel 10, 16, 24, 128–34
Benjamin, Walter 89
Bible 129, 137–9, 141
Blair, Tony 33, 48–9
Bloom, Harold 22, 27, 64, 68
Brande, Dorothea 9–10
Brecht, Bertholt 55, 118–19, 121–2, 125
Burroughs, William S. 75

Cameron, Julia 27
Campbell, Joseph 47n
Carlson, Ron 80, 104
Carver, Raymond 87
character 10, 12, 22, 34–5, 37, 39, 42, 46–8, 54, 56, 86–94, 96, 111, 115, 117–19, 121, 123, 126, 136, 144, 147, 153, 155–8, 161, 166–7, 173, 180–3
Chekhov, Anton 9, 85
class, see social class
closure, see endings
Coco Pops 48
commentaries 3–6, 8–18, 23–9, 79, 82, 110, 150–1, 154, 158–9, 165, 173, 189

conflict 10, 36, 89, 93–4, 96, 119, 176–7
Couser, G. Thomas 67
Cowan, Andrew 9, 14
craft 6, 8–9, 15, 21, 23–4, 101–2, 125, 136, 160
creative non-fiction 6, 16, 24, 62, 151
critical commentaries, see commentaries

Darwin, Emma 13, 15, 17–18
Davidson, John 128
de Waal, Kit 9, 12, 135–42
dialogue 5, 18, 22, 39, 122–3, 125–6, 137, 161
Didion, Joan 82, 124–5
digital narratives, see new media
direct speech, see dialogue
drafting 5, 8, 10, 12, 14, 17, 26, 47, 62–3, 95, 102, 103–8, 117, 120, 147, 149, 153–4, 158–9
drama, see scriptwriting

editing 5, 14, 17, 81, 106, 136, 152–3, 158, 165, 168, 175–6
education 3–4, 6, 10, 15, 21, 33–4, 38, 48–50, 58–60, 70–1, 152
Eliot, George 9
Eliot, T. S. 21–3, 29, 182
Ellis, Bret Easton 123–5
endings 55, 84–5, 91, 101–6, 108–14, 136–7, 158, 176
Enright, Anne 155–6
essays 16, 21–2, 27, 119, 124–5, 151–2, 172–3
experimental, see experimentation
experimentation 6, 10, 24, 28, 123, 163–77, 179, 182, 185

feedback 5, 12, 14, 17, 41, 147, 158
fiction 6, 9, 15, 22, 24, 29, 34, 38,
    41–2, 45, 50, 52–4, 67, 79–80, 83,
    85–6, 92, 94, 100–2, 109, 111, 113,
    123, 125, 135–41, 146, 152, 159,
    164, 164n, 173, 179–81, 184
flash fiction 9, 15, 79–83, 85–7, 89–91,
    94, 135–41
Ford, Richard 8
Forster, E. M. 9, 37, 40
Freud, Sigmund 26, 69, 109, 113
Frost, Robert 85

Gardner, John 93
Gass, William 66, 74, 82
genre 6, 11, 13, 15, 17, 23–7, 62, 66,
    68, 71–3, 101, 109, 143, 151, 155,
    164, 172, 180, 181n, 189
Gopnik, Adam 28, 126
Gosse, Edmund 68–70, 72, 74
Graham, Robert and Leach, Heather
    6, 10, 14, 18

Hanson, Amy 153
Hegel, G. W. F. 61–3, 67, 69, 71
Hejinian, Lyn 164–5, 169–70, 176–7
Hell, Jordan/Martin 165, 173
Hemingway, Ernest 14, 124–5, 135, 137
higher education, see university
history 6, 12, 21, 16–17, 24, 26, 34–5,
    42, 51, 63, 72–3, 94, 133, 152, 171
Hubbard, Sam 78, 87, 89

influence 4–6, 18, 21–9, 34–5, 38, 56,
    62–4, 68, 72–4, 88–9, 100, 107–8,
    110, 112, 114, 119, 121–6, 129–31,
    140, 158, 160, 165, 172, 175n,
    180–1, 185
interviews 89, 122, 126, 156, 168, 177
Isong, Anietie 12, 143–8

Jacobs, Harriet 71, 74
Jansson, Tove 89
journalism 6, 12, 143, 145–7
journals 14

Kafka, Franz 110–14
Kennedy, Jemma 11, 26–8, 115–27
King, Martin Luther 52, 55
King, Stephen 15, 21, 28

Kinnock, Neil 47, 51–2, 55
Kureishi, Hanif 9, 34, 125
Kushner, Tony 119–22, 125

Lacan, Jacques 69, 73
Lancaster, Simon 46–7, 49–50,
    54–6
life writing 67, 164–5, 168, 175
Littlewood, Joan 120–1
Lohafer, Susan 17, 101–2, 104, 106,
    108, 113
Loveday, Michael 81
Lynch, Claire 154, 156

Matsumoto, Lila 163–78
May, Steve 4, 10, 12, 15
memoir 9–11, 14–15, 29, 58–75,
    149–61, 172–3
Michael, Livi 34, 38
Milton, John 129–30, 134
Mokhtari, Tara 18, 23
Morley, David 12, 16, 18, 23
Morrison, Blake 58, 73
multimedia 179, 182
Myerson, Julia 156–60

Nadin, Joanna 12, 24, 45–57
narration 38, 42, 86, 151, 155, 172
narrative 17, 37, 46–7, 47n, 49, 53, 55n,
    62–4, 67–9, 71–4, 81, 85–6, 89–90,
    94–5, 101–11, 113, 116, 118, 120,
    136, 147, 152, 154, 172, 179
nature 24, 130–3
neurology 46–7, 54–5
new media 6, 15, 179–86
Nietzsche, Friedrich 60–5, 69–75
non-fiction, see creative non-fiction
novellas-in-flash 78–82, 89–97
novels 12, 15, 22, 24, 38, 42, 45–57,
    80, 82, 88, 91, 123, 125, 135,
    143–8, 151, 159, 164, 168, 179–83,
    185–6

Oates, Joyce Carol 9, 34, 38
Obama, Barack 50–1
O'Connor, Flannery 41
oulipo 103, 103n

parables 119, 137–9
Perreault, Jeanne 164

personal essays, *see* essays
philosophy 6, 16, 29, 36, 58, 62–5, 72, 92–3, 111, 130
playwriting, *see* scriptwriting
poetry 6, 10, 13, 15–16, 24, 28–9, 128–34, 163–77, 179
Pokrass, Meg 81
politics 6, 16, 42, 53, 55, 144, 147, 165
Pope, Rob 25, 62
Powell, Dan 14, 100–14
practice-based research, *see* research
preclosure 17, 100–11, 113–14
process 4–6, 8–10, 12–14, 16–18, 22, 24–8, 37, 41, 78, 80, 97, 100, 103–7, 109, 118, 123, 126, 136, 140–1, 150–1, 154, 159, 164–5
Prose, Francine 22–3, 25, 27
prose poetry 168
Pullinger, Kate 15, 179–86
pumpkins 83–4, 86

QAA Subject Benchmark Statement 10–12, 15

readers 4, 12, 14, 17–18, 21, 29, 37, 42, 46–9, 52, 55–7, 68, 83, 100–4, 106, 109, 111, 114, 120, 129, 135–8, 147–8, 153, 157, 159–60, 163, 179–80, 182–5
reading 3–5, 11–12, 14–18, 21–4, 27, 35, 91, 101–4, 106, 108, 110, 124, 128–9, 133, 136, 141, 157, 160, 173–4, 180, 182–3
reading as a writer 11–12, 14
redrafting, *see* drafting
reflection 3–6, 8–18, 23, 25–6, 34, 104, 150–2, 155, 158–9
reflective commentaries, *see* commentaries
research 4–6, 13–17, 39, 101–2, 109, 116–17, 125, 146, 150, 153, 173, 175, 179, 184
revising, *see* editing
rhetoric 6, 12, 40, 45, 48, 51–3, 56, 67, 173
Robertson, Lisa 164–5, 167–8, 171, 177
Robison, Mary 15, 79, 81, 83–6
Rosen, Michael 47–8

satire 12, 143–4, 147
Saunders, George 136
scriptwriting 6, 24, 29, 90, 115–26
Sexton, Anne 130
Shakespeare, William 119, 121, 130
short fiction 15, 85, 87, 89, 33–42, 100–14, 135, 179–80
short stories, *see* short fiction *and* flash fiction
slave narratives 15, 71–4
social class 33–6, 38–9, 42, 63, 81, 144, 175
speeches 24, 29, 46–8, 50–3, 55–6
Stevens, Karen 14, 24, 28, 33–42
Stevens, Wallace 131
Stoker, Bram 15, 180–1
Strout, Elizabeth 34, 38
Swann, David 15, 27, 78–99

Taylor, Jonathan 10, 15, 25–6, 58–75, 151
Taylor, Maria 3–5
Thomas, Sue 181
Todd, Selina 34, 42
Todorov, Tzvetan 108, 110, 113
Tolkien, J. R. R. 141
trickster tales 71–4
Trussler, Michael 42, 105

uncanny 107–10, 113–14, 180, 183
unconscious 9–10, 14, 16, 25–6, 41, 66, 72, 109, 123, 125
university 4, 13, 38, 63, 81–2, 149–50, 152, 154, 156, 160–1, 165–6, 179, 181n

Vonnegut, Kurt 82, 85, 92

Wain, John 27, 89
Weber, Emilia 165, 172–3
Williams, Terry Tempest 160–1
workshops 11–12, 14, 17, 41, 103n, 152, 157–8, 179

Yorke, John 90–1, 95, 120

Zeno 111–13
Zuboff, Shoshana 184–5, 185n